THE WRITER'S DIGEST

Guide TO Good Writing

THE WRITER'S DIGEST

Guide TO Good Writing

Edited by

Thomas Clark
Bruce Woods
Peter Blocksom
Angela Terez

WRITER'S DIGEST BOOKS
Cincinnati, Ohio

This hardcover edition of *The Writer's Digest Guide to Good Writing* features a "self-jacket" that eliminates the need for a separate dust jacket. It provides sturdy protection for your book while it saves paper, trees and energy.

98 97 96 95   5 4 3 2

Library of Congress Cataloging in Publication Data

The Writer's digest guide to good writing / by editors of Writer's digest.
  p.   cm.
Includes index.
ISBN 0-89879-640-7
1. Authorship. I. Writer's digest (Cincinnati, Ohio)
PN151.W73   1994
808'.02 — dc20   93-43554
                                                          CIP

Edited by Thomas Clark
Interior design by Brian Roeth
Cover design by Brian Roeth

The following page constitutes an extension of this copyright page.

Permissions

About the Authors

While this collection celebrates the endurance of the writing advice offered by *Writer's Digest* during the past seventy-five years, we don't always consider time an ally. Unfortunately, all that we know of a few contributors represented in this book is that they once wrote for *WD*. While that was enough to earn a spot in this collection, it's not enough for a biographical note. Which is why not all of this book's authors are profiled below. If you can fill in any of our gaps, please drop the editors a note at 1507 Dana Avenue, Cincinnati, Ohio 45207, and we'll include the information in future editions.

Isaac Asimov published more than three hundred books in his lifetime, including the *Foundation* series of novels and the influential *I, Robot*. Along with Arthur C. Clarke and Robert A. Heinlein, he was considered among the top three sf writers in the world.

Lawrence Block is a mystery novelist best known for his hard-boiled series featuring detective Matthew Scudder (*Eight Million Ways to Die*). For many years he wrote the Fiction column in *Writer's Digest*.

Pauline Bloom is a widely published writer whose work has appeared in major national magazines. She has taught and lectured at Columbia University, Rutgers University, Town Hall and Brooklyn College. She also conducts a correspondence course in fiction writing, and lectures at writers' conferences all over the country.

Ben Bova is the author of *Millennium* and other novels. He is best known for his work as editor of the science fiction magazines *Analog* and *Omni*.

Hallie Burnett co-edited *Story* magazine for nearly thirty years, served as fiction editor for *Yankee* magazine, and wrote the book, *On Writing the Short Story*.

Taylor Caldwell wrote a succession of bestselling novels, beginning with *Dynasty of Death* and continuing through *The Captain and the Kings* and *Answer as a Man*.

Orson Scott Card was the first author to win consecutive "best novel" honors in both the Nebula and Hugo award competitions for his science fiction books *Ender's Game* and *Speaker for the Dead*.

Marc Connelly was the author of such plays as *The Farmer Takes a Wife* and *The Green Pastures*, which won the Pulitzer Prize. His frequent collaboration with George S. Kaufman produced *Merton of the Movies* and *Beggar on Horseback*.

J. Everet Courtney

Richard Deming wrote five novels: *The Gallows In My Garden, Tweak the Devil's Nose, Whistle Past the Graveyard, Hell Street*, and *Justice Has No Sword*. He was also a regular contributor to *Bluebook, Manhunt, Ellery Queen's* and *Accused* magazines.

Jude Deveraux is the author of a string of bestselling romance novels, including *The Duchess, Mountain Laurel*, and *A Knight in Shining Armor*.

Louis Dodge was the author of various novels including *Children of the Desert*.

Laurence D'Orsay was the author of *Writing Novels to Sell* and *Landing the Editors' Checks*.

Helen Doss

Gardner Dozois is an award-winning writer of science fiction short stories. He also edited several annual anthologies of sf stories and is the editor of *Isaac Asimov's Science Fiction Magazine*.

Allan W. Eckert is the author of thirty-six books of history, natural history, novels and other works, as well as over one hundred fifty published articles. He has been nominated six times for the Pulitzer Prize. His books include *The Frontiersmen, A Sorrow In Our Heart, Incident at Hawk's Hill* and many others.

Harlan Ellison is a writer, film and TV scenarist, editor and critic whose published works include sixty-two books, the most recent of which are *Mind Fields*, the illustrated screenplay, *I, Robot* and the award-winning *Mefisto in Onyx*. He can be found in *The Best American Short Stories: 1993*.

Eugene M. Fisher

John D. Fitzgerald was part of a writing team with Robert C. Meredith that wrote *The Professional Story Writer and His Art*, a book used in several creative writing classes at college level and at writer's conferences in Indiana and Arkansas. He and Fitzgerald published short stories in a variety of national magazines.

Erle Stanley Gardner was one of the most successful writers of crime fiction. His novels frequently featured detective Douglas Selby and lawyer Perry Mason.

Brian Garfield is best known for his novel *Death Wish*. His other novels include *Hopscotch* and *The Paladin*.

Allen Ginsberg gained notoriety through the publication of his poem

"Howl" and as a leader of the Beat Generation. His later collections include *Kaddish and Other Poems, 1958-1960* and *Collected Poems 1957-1980*.

Arthur Gordon has served as managing editor of *Good Housekeeping*, editor-in-chief of *Cosmopolitan*, editorial director for *Air Force*, staff writer for *Reader's Digest*, and editorial director for *Guideposts*.

James Hilton was a novelist whose books included *Lost Horizons*, *Goodbye Mr. Chips*, and *So Well Remembered*.

Morry Hull

Don James published more than three hundred short stories and nineteen books. He was a freelance writer and advertising consultant in Portland, where he also taught classes in creative writing.

Judson Jerome wrote the *Writer's Digest* Poetry column for nearly thirty years and wrote several books on the craft of poetry writing. His poems appeared in *The Atlantic, Harpers, The Saturday Review*, and hundreds of small press journals.

Carl E. Johnson taught writing at the University of Wisconsin. He also published stories, poetry and articles in fifty periodicals and one book, *How in the World* with Fleming Revell.

Thomas Kennedy

Stephen King is perhaps the best selling horror novelist ever. His novels include *Carrie, The Shining* and *Christine*.

Louis L'Amour was one of the best-known western novelists. He wrote more than one hundred books, including *Hondo, How the West Was Won* and *Jubal Sacket*.

David X. Manners has served as a fiction and nonfiction editor, and has published thirteen books, several hundred stories and articles, and written for radio, TV and motion pictures. He is currently chairman of the David X. Manners Company, a public relations firm in Stamford, Connecticut.

Evan Marshall is a literary agent specializing in genre fiction.

Patricia McGerr

Allis McKay

Don McKinney edited *True Magazine* and *The Saturday Evening Post*, and later served as managing editor of *McCall's* for seventeen years. He now teaches journalism at the University of South Carolina/ Beaufort.

Robert C. Meredith was part of a writing team with John D. Fitzgerald that wrote *The Professional Story Writer and His Art*, a book used in several creative writing classes at college level and at writer's conferences in Indiana and Arkansas. He and Fitzgerald published short stories in a variety of national magazines.

Gary Provost has written more than twenty nonfiction books and novels, including *Make Your Words Work*, *Perfect Husband* and *High Stakes*.

John Nanovic edited fiction for Street and Smith, worked for an advertising agency, and was a freelance fiction writer.

Mildred I. Reid in a long career has published seven textbooks on writing, two colonial-era novels, and many articles and short stories. For over forty years, she conducted a writer's colony in New Hampshire and has traveled widely giving lectures and classes on writing.

W. Adolphe Roberts was formerly the editor of *Ainslee's Magazine* and president of the Writers' Club of New York.

Hugh C. Sherwood is a business and investment writer and author of several books, including *The Journalistic Interview* and *How to Invest in Bonds*. His articles have appeared in *Industry Week*, *Nation's Business*, *Town & Country* and many other publications.

M.L. Stein, a journalism professor, wrote *How to Write Plain English* and other books. His articles appeared in *Better Homes & Gardens*, *The New York Times* and elsewhere.

Albert Payson Terhune made his reputation as a writer of *Lad: A Dog* and other novels about dogs, usually collies.

Thomas Uzzell was fiction editor of *Colliers* magazine, the author of *Narrative Technique*, a literary agent and — quite possibly — the most-often-published contributor in *Writer's Digest*.

S.S. Van Dine was the penname of Willard Huntington Wright, a critic, editor and novelist whose Philo Vance detective novels broke crime fiction sales records in the 1920s and established the genteel "eastern style" (as opposed to the hard-boiled "western" style) of American detective novels.

Irving Wallace wrote more than a dozen bestselling novels, including *The Chapman Report*, *The Miracle*, *The Prize* and *The Seventh Secret*.

Linton Weeks is a freelance article writer and managing editor of *The Washington Post Magazine*.

Phyllis A. Whitney made her reputation both as a writer of juvenile mystery novels (including *The Quicksilver Pool*) and adult romantic suspense novels and gothics (*Dream of Orchids* and *Silversword*).

Introduction

"It contains timely hints and suggestions that we believe will be helpful to you in your literary career."

The words are seventy-five years old, taken from an editorial on page 22 of Volume 1, Number 1 of *Successful Writing*. That magazine's title is long dead—changed after just four issues. *Successful Writing*'s promise, however, is as current as this month's issue of *Writer's Digest*—and as timeless as the book you hold in your hand.

That December 1920 issue spoke of a writing world that had only recently accepted the typewriter and was hot for "photoplays"—scenarios for the then-silent movies. References to the recently completed world war didn't carry a Roman numeral, and annual subscriptions sold for just $3 (just a nickel more than today's single-copy price). But nudge aside these curiosities of time, and the modern reader discovers that good writing—and good advice on writing—knows no era.

That's the logic behind this collection. We chose to mark the magazine's upcoming seventy-fifth anniversary by celebrating within these covers an essential element of the *Writer's Digest* tradition: fine writing about the art and craft of writing. Among the anniversary gifts inside, you'll find advice on selecting and applying viewpoint, creating dramatic plots, handling poetic details, drawing realistic characters, crafting compelling nonfiction, conceiving attention-holding dialogue, mastering the ingredients of the most popular fiction genres—and more. Much more.

You'll recognize many of the names on these articles: Erle Stanley Gardner, Louis L'Amour, Stephen King, Taylor Caldwell, Irving Wallace, Harlan Ellison. And in the center of this collection, you'll find a treasury of short tips offered by some of the best-known writers of this century, including comments from John Steinbeck, H.G. Wells, Thornton Wilder and many more. All drawn from the pages of *Writer's Digest* and its annual offspring, *Writer's Yearbook*.

But you won't recognize the name of every author we've chosen to include in this book. In fact, most of the writers who contributed to the *Digest* during the past seventy-five years didn't etch their names in the enduring literary landscape. They were craftsmen, obviously, but they were also entertainers who wrote for their times and businessmen who were satisfied to earn a living wage. We may not remember their names, but their anonymity in no way reduces the value of their hard-won and freely given wisdom.

As with any collection, *The Writer's Digest Guide to Good Writing* is not complete. Drawing off only a bookful of pieces from a pool of some 5,200 articles means that much good writing, even great writing, was passed over—enough surely to fill several more volumes. And where do the other essential elements of *Writer's Digest*—such as marketing tips and inspiration and reports from freelancing's trenches—fit into *Guide to Good Writing*? They must wait for another time.

Which will come. This collection is not the final word. Even as I write these lines, my desk overflows with articles and submissions and galley proofs for upcoming issues of the magazine—all potential candidates for *The Writer's Digest Guide to Good Writing II*. It should be ready for you about seventy-five years from now. (Heck, if this one sells, we might only wait twenty-five years!) I offer no predictions on what will have replaced the PC by then, or what innovations will have revolutionized scriptwriting, or how much a *WD* subscription will cost (though I do pray that no more Roman numerals will have been added to the list of wars). But I will venture this guess: Future storytellers will still be seeking tips on how to plot, fashion dialogue, deal with viewpoint and much, much more. And they'll likely still be finding these tips in the pages (disk files?) of *Writer's Digest*.

As the first-issue editorialist put it, "Our success is your success."

Thomas Clark
Senior Editor
Writer's Digest

1920s

Why I Rejected
Ten Thousand Manuscripts

W. Adolphe Roberts

March 1921

T he editor worthy of the name realizes that he has a triple responsibility. In selecting manuscripts, he must please the public first of all. But he must also please the owners of his magazine and he must please himself. He cannot make a success of his job unless all three demands are satisfied in every issue.

The first responsibility is obvious. The magazine public reads to be entertained. The editor is under an unwritten contract not to bore his following. If he does, he will lose its support as surely as would the manager of a vaudeville theater who insisted on showing wearisome, dull acts. Of course, there are publics and publics. The readers of the *Atlantic Monthly* undoubtedly chuckle over essays that would cause the readers of the *Smart Set* to groan with ennui, and vice versa. Each magazine must provide the kind of entertainment wanted.

It is regrettable in a good many cases that the editor must please his publisher. The latter is apt to be a businessman with poor judgment where writing is concerned. He wants commercial results from a commodity that cannot be appraised in the terms of, say, Bessemer steel. He hires an expert to get them for him, yet does not hesitate to criticize and offer inept suggestions. So be it. After all, the publisher pays salaries and signs the checks to authors.

But, whomever else he may please, the editor must please himself. A successful magazine always has a personality, an intangible something that sets it apart from its rivals and induces buyers to select it from among hosts of others, probably equally good. This personality is shaped by the editor, who can only go by what he likes and does not like. He cannot afford to publish stories which he regards as trashy, even though other magazines may be printing fiction of the same order. He cannot, at the risk of producing a meaningless hodgepodge, give a hearing to every type of popular story. He cannot, and must not, surrender his individual critical faculty. So it is really his own personality that he puts into his magazine. If it proves to be attractive to the public, well and good. If it does not, he will soon be looking for another job.

The above explains, broadly, why I rejected ten thousand manuscripts in the two and a half years that I was editor of *Ainslee's Magazine*. I rejected them because I did not like them, or because I thought my readers would not like them, or because I knew that the owners of *Ainslee's* would disapprove. Inevitably, I turned down some that appealed to me, in deference to the tastes of the other judges concerned. But every manuscript that I bought and printed, I liked, though I by no means always regarded it as literature.

Far from exhausting the subject, however, this merely clears the way for details that should be instructive to writers.

Ainslee's, under my editorship, was primarily a fiction magazine. Each number contained a complete novelette, running to about 35,000 words, an installment of a serial and from seven to nine short stories. A series of articles about the great enchantresses of history, by Anice Terhune, had been running for many years, and I retained the feature. There were dramatic and book departments. I published an unusually large amount of verses, sometimes as many as twelve or thirteen poems in a single issue.

Manuscripts poured in on me through the mails and from the offices of literary agents. A few were sent because I had asked the authors to let me see examples of their work. The unsolicited manuscripts fell into two natural groups, the amateur and the professional. The former comprised 90 percent of the total, the latter 10 percent.

The large army of untrained and, for the most part, talentless persons in the United States who seem to be determined to become writers is a constant source of astonishment to the editor. The aspirants are well educated and generally earn their livings in semi-literary callings, such as the church, teaching, library work, etc. But they have nothing original to say, and their technique consists of a stilted imitation of classical models. I do not deny that a very few may have it in them to learn and to emerge as craftsmen. But the manuscripts which they have the poor judgment to circulate before they have acquired even rudimentary facility, have no chance of being accepted. Such offerings are weeded out by the editor's reader and returned as a matter of course, though I may say that in well-conducted offices, they are given the benefit of every doubt and are conscientiously examined.

The 10 percent of workmanlike stories and articles by professionals constitutes the raw material which the editor tests and weighs, from which he selects and builds his magazine. I estimate that I hopefully examined for *Ainslee's* one thousand prose manuscripts. The number was not enormous, and the fact that I bought one for every three I rejected indicates that competition among writers is not quite so keen as it is supposed to be.

I had a system, by means of which it was pretty certain that I would not miss important manuscripts. In the morning the mail was placed on my desk, and my first task was to run through it. All stories by former contributors, by writers known to me by reputation or accompanied by letters addressed to me instead of to the magazine, as well as stories which for any reason seemed promising, I marked with a special sign in blue pencil. This meant that, after having been entered on the books, they were to come back to me. The others, the nondescript majority, went to my reader, who had instructions to let me see every effort which showed the least glimmer of promise.

The manuscripts I had marked were read first by me, later by the reader, only in cases where I felt that I needed to reinforce my own judgment. This system is not used in all offices, but I regard it as a good one. It eliminates a favorite complaint of writers—that the editor allows his reader too great a veto power. It proved sound as far as I was concerned, because I found practically all the available stories myself. Of the hundreds passed up to me by the reader, I accepted less than five.

Getting down to the final test of why I rejected three out of four of the manuscripts which were seriously considered, I list a number of reasons which applied in one case or another:

1. Although readable, they were not precisely in the vein characteristic of the magazine. My objective for *Ainslee's* was to please women and the type of man who is sympathetic to the modern woman. I was seeking to entertain rather than to instruct. Many a story that might have been snapped up by the *Ladies' Home Journal* was rejected by me.

2. They resembled in theme, plot or situation some story that I had printed recently, or was about to print. This does not imply plagiarism. More than one writer may be moved to write about a woman going on the stage to escape the ennui of married life, but a magazine that has published a story of this variety is not likely to want another for a year or so.

3. They were too long or too short for the theme handled, too wordy or too nakedly condensed. Both extremes are bad. The former offense,

however, is by far the more common. Countless stories are spoiled by being spun out to 10,000 words when they should have been kept down to 5,000.

4. They were weak in one or more of the three essentials: characterization, plot, atmosphere. From my point of view, the most important factor in a story is characterization. If its people are real people, the things they do are pretty sure to be interesting. Next comes plot—the adroit staging of situations leading up to a denouement. Third, the color and atmosphere of place—the mise-en-scène.

5. They expounded some theory, in which the author doubtless took great stock, but which would be likely to bore the majority of readers. Propaganda has no place in magazine fiction. Religion and partisan politics are the most dangerous topics, but all "isms" are bad. If you must have a socialist in your story, let him keep his place as an actor in the human comedy. Do not permit him to occupy the limelight for the purpose of delivering lectures on socialism.

6. They were sloppily written. I am aware that some editors care only for the narrative quality in a story. My own tastes and those, I am sure, of my public demanded that the English language be not manhandled. I did not insist on every magazine writer being a stylist, but I required something more than grammatical accuracy. I wanted the public to exclaim: "What well-written stories!" in addition to: "What rattling good yarns!"

The best tip I can give to authors is, that they read carefully the magazines for which they propose to write. I do not mean that they should slavishly adapt themselves to the whims of editors. They will not get very far if they do. Fiction, to be effective, must be a form of self-expression, untrammeled by the fear that some critic would prefer to have it differently presented. But if the author is familiar with the idiosyncracies of a number of magazines, he will be able to avoid many a disappointment by sending his story first to the office where it is mostly likely to be welcomed.

A study of *Ainslee's* through the latter half of 1918, 1919 and 1920, the period of my editorship, would have revealed that the work of several writers was especially favored. The aspirant would have learned a good deal about the needs of *Ainslee's* by familiarizing himself with the serials, novelettes and short stories signed by these stars.

Since I used so little nonfiction material, comparatively few articles were submitted. Amateur writers would sometimes send me accounts of personal experiences, with the comment that they were "as romantic," or "just as thrilling," as fiction. This showed a thorough misconception of the art of entertaining by means of narrative. Happenings in real life can be utilized by the clever teller of tales. He rearranges them and provides a climax wherever one is needed. But in their original sequence they never form a story. They are merely chronicles, devoid of plot. Were this not so, the morning newspaper, with its varied record of strange events, would be as fascinating as a magazine.

Of course, I rejected practically all the articles sent in. But really good work imposes itself, in spite of office rules against the form in which it is cast. I found myself unable to refuse a certain essay on perfumes, another on an old house, two on the frills and fancies of love. They were short, and certainly pleased many more readers than they disappointed.

In my estimate of ten thousand manuscripts rejected in two and a half years, I do not include poems. Heaven knows how many poems I turned down. Probably five thousand. The magazine had always been hospitable to verse. Consequently, a great deal of it came in. I was especially interested in maintaining a high standard in this field. Poetry is regarded in too many offices as being merely "filler" material. I did not see why it should not be featured. To get what I wanted, however, I had to invite the best poets to become contributors. The daily crop of unsolicited verse was, nearly all of it, incredibly bad.

The average rhymester seems to have a passion for topical subjects. This is very well if one is contributing to newspapers, which can publish within a few days of the event celebrated. A monthly magazine goes to press a good many weeks before it appears on the newsstands. In 1918, every mail brought me stanzas dealing with the activities of the A.E.F. in France. In 1919, the favorite theme was the westward bound transports. After I had read for the thousandth time that the boys were "coming home," followed by a line that invariably ended with the words "across the foam," the mere sight of a soldier poem drove me to distraction.

To summarize, I rejected ten thousand prose manuscripts and half as many poems, because:

First: The great majority were not good enough to be published in any magazine.

Second: Of the remainder, some were not in line with the magazine's policy; some, though another editor might have bought them, did not appeal to me.

How to Plot a Story When You See It

Thomas H. Uzzell

December 1923

Sight of a striking picture, a brief conversation with a chance acquaintance, or even a dream of some great ambition in life has, let us say, given you a sudden desire to write a story. You have a good "story idea." If you have the story-telling gift, you want to expand that idea so that, when written up, it will have the unity and the dramatic "punch" which will make it acceptable to a magazine. Given one of these good ideas, how should you effect the needed expansion?

"How to plot a story when you see it" I have taken for my title because I want to emphasize the latter half of it. If you really "see" the idea, namely, *understand* it, I don't think you'll have much difficulty making it into a good plot. Understanding, remember, is not feeling; understanding is grasping a thing intellectually.

Let's consider this business of the intellectual grasp of story ideas. I can illustrate by taking concrete examples. A student came to me saying he wanted to write a story about his dog. By discussing the matter with him I saw that he was very fond of a hunting dog which he owns. The chief *feeling* which his story idea aroused in him was affection for this rather remarkable pointer. This feeling he wanted to express in his story. If he did no more than feel intensely, he might sit himself down to his typewriter and stare at it for hours without being able to write a single word. He needed a *thought* about the idea of love for a dog which would show him what step should be first, what second and so on.

He really began to understand his idea when I showed him that the thing the reader would be interested in was not so much the dog as *his love of the dog*. The emphasis of the story would be on a quality of his own character. The story, in other words, would be a *character story*. We then got to work to invent a scene in which the hero of the story, because of his love of the dog, all but gives his life to save the dog's life. Such action proves dramatically that the man loves the dog. This plot was written up, and the resulting manuscript has just been sold to the *Pictorial Review*.

A few years ago (to use another example) a friend of mine told me jokingly that he had bought a straw hat. It fitted nicely, he laughed, the day before when he bought it, but the next day it didn't fit; it was too small. The solution of the mystery was that after he made his purchase he got a bump on the side of his head by colliding with a piece of furniture; the bump increased temporarily the size of his head!

This struck me as a good story idea. The *feeling* it gave me was humor; we laughed at the occurrence. When I came to make my plot, however, I had to analyze it to *understand*. To do this I asked myself: "What is the nature of the episode? What will the reader be interested in if I expand it?"

Well, it is clear surely that the interest here is not in character as in the case of the dog story; the only quality of the man involved was the nature of his scalp which made it expand when struck, and this manifestly has nothing to do with his character.

No, the interest here was in a *peculiar happening* or *event*. My problem, therefore, in making my plot was simply to expand the episode, changing the characters as much as I chose to make the same effect more dramatic or intense. The question I asked myself then was this: "Under what circumstances could a bump on the head seriously affect the whole life of some man?"

At this particular time, mobilization for war was under way, and I very soon decided that a bump on the *top* of the head might be the one thing which, by adding a fraction of an inch to a man's height, decided his entering the war and losing his life. This plot I used and sold the story.

The above two examples present two distinct kinds of story interest. Here is another example which presents a third: Before we entered the war everyone was discussing formulas for world peace. I was then just out of college and remembered that one day the professor in the sociology class said that the one thing which would make men quit killing each other was to let a third party come along who would kill them both if they did not combine forces to oppose him. This struck me as a fine story idea. I thrilled over its possibilities. If I had done nothing but thrill, however, I doubt if I would have gone very far with it.

I reasoned thus: What is the nature of the interest in this prize idea? Clearly enough it is not interest in any one man's peculiar character. It is not yet an interest in any precise event or bit of action. I soon saw that what I was thrilling over was a bit of theory about life, a philosophical abstraction, if you will. The theory was this: Men will cease fighting each other when menaced by dangers greater than those they present to each other.

Having made sure of this fact, the making of the plot was comparatively easy. I simply had to think of two men locked in mortal combat and then turn loose on them some hideous horror which would make short work of them unless they combined their forces to make short work of it. The most horrible danger I could think of was poisonous spiders. If the men were fighting in a closed room and tarantulas and scorpions were turned loose on them — there! the plot was made. I wrote it up and sold it to the *Saturday Evening Post*.

Now there is a fourth kind of story interest under which some story ideas may fall, namely, a strong interest in setting, or as some call it, "local color" or, still more accurately, the "atmosphere" of a place. Since not one story idea in a thousand belongs to this category and since plotting them is rather difficult, I shall merely mention this classification in order that you may know it when you see it, and, until your skill as a plotter is greatly improved, avoid trying to handle it.

The above illustrations are intended to show you that the way to plot a story once you see it is to make sure, first of all, that you *do* see it. Seeing it involves analyzing it and analyzing means classifying. You must learn to classify your story materials.

Our first problem is to reduce the chaos in which story ideas generally occur to us. We must find some order of classification for the phenomena of life itself. No classification can obviously be of much practical use to the writer unless the categories are very few. Research into this question has disclosed the fact that all story effects can be put under four heads according to the materials from which they derive. The emotional effect of a story may be produced by:

1. Emphasis on character
2. Emphasis on an event
3. Emphasis on a general truth
4. Emphasis on setting

To make the use of these classifications quite clear to you, let me set down a few miscellaneous story ideas and classify them for you. The classifications enclosed in parentheses will indicate what your first step should be in plotting stories beginning with ideas such as these.

1. A poor mother faces the predicament of bringing up her baby in poverty or of giving her to a wealthy neighbor who will provide for her every want upon the condition that the mother relinquish all claim to her. (Complication.)

2. A professor of mathematics has the reputation of being "cold," unromantic, with a machine-like mind. Although his students do not know it, he has been married three times. (Character.)

3. A young girl has been to so many petting parties and has philandered with so many boys that she feels she has no real affection left for any man and can never honestly marry. (Thematic.)

4. A golden chalice has been stolen from the altar of a church, and two sisters devote themselves to a long search for it as a holy pilgrimage. (Character.)

5. A robber who breaks into a house in the daytime is stung by some bees and is later caught by his being identified through the slight wounds caused by the bees. (Complication.)

6. An explorer is so overcome by the desolation and loneliness of a great desert that he falls into despondency and kills himself. (Atmosphere.)

These four classifications are *kinds of material*; they are not story patterns nor even effects. A given effect could conceivably be produced by any or all of these different kinds of material. The stuff of narrative is human conduct; all human activity, in short, is composed of *people*, *actions*, *places*, and *ideas* about people, actions and places. The four categories are scientific rather than artistic groupings. They are ultimate divisions.

Much practice will be necessary to make this analytic scheme your own; you may not even sense its value until it begins to operate automatically without your being aware of using it. For some time, doubtless, this method of seeing and plotting stories will seem clumsy and mechanical. This is inevitable in the mastery of any new process. For a time at the beginning you must be laboriously conscious of every step, in order that some day you may be unconscious of them; in no other way can you win your artistic freedom.

The Author and His Style

Louis Dodge

January 1924

I have an idea that more young writers go stranded on the reef called "style" than on any other dangerous place along the shores of fiction. I believe there is almost no such thing as style at all, in the common use of the word; yet most of the ambitious young writers I have talked to reveal to me the fact that they believe in this bothersome myth and are fearfully misled by it.

If I were asked to advise a youngster on this subject I should put my conviction in language something like this:

"In order to write well, begin every sentence with a capital letter and end it with a period. Put in the necessary number of commas, colons, semicolons, dashes, and the rest of them — and *say something*."

There never was a good story in the world that had nothing new or fresh or true or original in it. I can't conceive of a bad story possessing these qualities.

The things a writer says — they constitute his style. When you find a writer who has a dull style, you have found one who has little or nothing to say. When you find a writer with a captivating style, he is always one who has something to say to you — something you did not know, or something that had slipped into the background of your consciousness and which you are glad to be reminded of.

Much is said of Joseph Conrad's style. Certainly he has a magnificent style; but this is not due to the fact that he distorts or juggles the English language. It is because he has a great deal to say and that he is one of the few men living who have taken the trouble to express the things he knows. Conrad is Conrad because he has sagely observed the effects of the sea in calm and storm upon men of various types, and also the effects of isolated places upon the human mind. And he reports these things to us as simply as he knows how. I venture to assert that when he writes he doesn't give a thought to language, but concentrates instead on the fact, the episode, the scene he wishes to place before his reader. He says something. If he uses striking language (as he often does) it is because no other language would express his ideas or paint his picture.

Robert Louis Stevenson has been referred to more than almost any other writer of our time as a stylist. I doubt if the word would have pleased him. He was an exact writer, and due to various causes he preferred to write of subtle things. Sometimes his entire picture was dark (as in "The Master of Ballantrae") and sometimes it was charmingly bright (as in "An Inland Voyage"), but it was always subtle. As a result of this he was often driven to the necessity of finding a word which would have had no place in the vocabulary of a person dealing with obvious things. But I think the fact remains that Stevenson was always bent upon placing his idea before his reader as simply as possible.

It may be that when the young writer is advised in relation to style the word actually meant is *manner*. But the distinction between the two words ought to be made plain.

Certainly there is an excellent manner in using words, and there is a bad manner. Macaulay had a very excellent manner, as perhaps we may all agree; he liked to use simple sentences and the words he chose were sober. Carlyle, on the other hand, employed a very bad manner. He put too much burden on his reader by forms so involved that even clear meanings became obscure. Meredith, among the novelists of our day, was a chief offender against good taste in his latter years. The reader of "Lord Ormont and His Aminta" feels the uncomfortable effects of his wanton jugglery. It requires a perverse mind to enjoy the eccentricities.

It may be charged that a literary manner and a literary style are one and the same thing. There is, however, a difference, as I understand the words.

After all, books or stories are like people; and we like people for what they are and not for what they seem. A story which says nothing (but does it well) is like a person who is faultlessly clad and good to look at, but who calls and says a few conversational things in a careful manner and goes away leaving an effect of strain. After the advent of such a person, how restful and good it is to welcome the friend who drops in informally and brings a real message of warmth, of positive meaning, of an original point of view. Better a beggar with a real tale of woe than a great diplomat who wears a mask.

I am not sure I have made my meaning clear, but as one who walked in the dark for years as a result of incomprehensible axioms on the subject of style, I wish I might impress upon the ambitious young writer everywhere this rule: Do not think so much about how you are to say a thing; charge yourself rather with the high duty of choosing a good thing to say.

The writer who is ever to scale the heights will first learn, pretty thoroughly, the lessons of grammar and syntax and etymology; and then he will forget that there are such things, just as a great general forgets that he wears epaulettes, and he will consider this shibboleth the firstly and secondly and thirdly and the finally of his purpose:

Say something.

If a paragraph or a sentence appears in his story and is found to say nothing, he will take it out relentlessly, no matter how pretty it may sound to the ear or how much distinction it may show to the eye. It is an intruder, it is an assassin which destroys the reader's interest and the writer's purpose.

If you have an honest desire to write, don't clutter your page with "intriguings" and "acid tests" and other borrowed plumage. Your reader will have seen those things before; and he will be your reader solely for the purpose or in the hope of finding something fresh and new. To use the phrases of others is to mark time. If you want a hearing, hold fast to the one rule:

Say something.

Poetry and Verse: A Distinction

Thomas Kennedy

December 1926 - January 1927

I f the confusion about the nature of poetry were merely an academic one, we might well let it alone. That is to say: If only the accurate use of a word were involved, we might be justified in leaving the question to purists while practicing poets continued with their writing.

The trouble is that the confusion goes deeper. Many people strive for excellence in metrical structure, feeling that once they have attained that desirable result, the whole battle will be won. Many people who have attained metrical perfection—or something approximating it—wonder despairingly why their poems are not more successful, or go on writing verse that is not, and never can be, poetry, blaming their critics, the editors, for willful perverseness.

The truth is that verse, in and of itself, is not poetry. The only exception is that verse superlatively well done sometimes becomes poetry through becoming something more than verse. Poetry is not meter, or rhyme, or alliteration, or assonance—in short, it is not music in words.

The truth is—and every successful poet comes to realize it sooner or later—verse is merely the form of expression habitually associated with poetry because it is peculiarly well fitted to it. Poetry itself is a spirit or an essence that may, or may not, infuse what is written in verse. A definition of such a rarefied substance is difficult. We may say tentatively, however, that poetry is the interpretation of life in terms of beauty through the medium of words. Or we may go further and suggest that it is the spirit of strangeness and wonder; of strangeness added to beauty, that somehow manages to get itself expressed in words, as in other mediums. Whoever fails to recognize and apply this principle will not be a poet, however much he may excel as a versifier.

Now, I feel sure from many of the specimens of verse sent me for criticism that this idea is a new one to many who are trying to write.

Nor would it be particularly surprising if it were to arouse skepticism or even protest. Suppose we look, then, at a specimen of perfectly good verse that is not poetry at all.

> King Henry the Eighth to six spouses was wedded:
> One died, one survived, two divorced, two beheaded.

Some of us may recall the rhyme used for memorizing the list of English kings, beginning:

> William the conqueror, William his son,
> Henry, Stephen, and Henry; then Richard and John.

These lines are good enough verse so that we might not be inclined to criticize them at all severely. They are useful, in that they help us to remember important facts. They are not at all unpleasant to the ear. Will anyone seriously contend that they are poetry?

When we speak of beauty, as we did a moment ago in our attempt at definition, we mean really whatever gives us pleasure; that is, whatever appeals favorably to our emotions. The appeal of the lines just quoted is primarily to the intellect. They make use of our sensuous feeling for rhythm merely as an aid to memory in retaining facts. We do not read a list of the English kings for any pleasure that it gives us; nor do we follow in bald summary the marital adventures of Henry VIII to gain aesthetic satisfaction. The aim of these lines is merely to present facts, but the purpose of poetry is far different.

If we admit, as I think we must, that the purpose of poetry is to give pleasure through appealing to our sense of the beautiful, certain things become apparent. To most of us, beauty is entirely a thing of emotion; therefore, it comes to us entirely through our physical senses, being concerned exclusively with what we can see or hear or touch or taste or smell. Read this sonnet by James B. Kenyon:

Supplication

O God, and dost Thou mock us when we cry?
    And wilt Thou look upon our sharp distress
    Neglectful of our utter helplessness,
Nor heed nor help us tho we were to die?
O takest Thou no thought for those who lie
    Stripped and half dead with wounds and weariness
    Among life's thorns, and wilt Thou pitiless
Look on our hurts and pass us coldly by?

O Thou, who, in Thy Son, didst feel the blow
    Of palm and spiteful scourge, the speechless pain
Of loveless solitude — Thou who dost know
    The unutterable pangs of being slain
Of love for love — O end my bitter woe!
    Yea, let me die, if so to die be gain!

If the poem does not strike us as a remarkably good one, the reason surely does not lie in metrical weakness. Nor can we say that it is insincerely written, or without a high theme. Why is it not more successful? Possibly we might answer this question by deciding which lines are the best. Is it not true that, whenever the writer achieves a strong line, he does so by getting away from the abstract words that fog his emotional effect in most of the poem? Can we not feel for the man, "Stripped and half dead with wounds and weariness," even when "sharp distress" and "utter helplessness" leave us not particularly moved?

After all, there may be something in this theory that what appeals to our emotions is only what our senses can apprehend. A picture means more to us than an abstraction, because it makes us feel more. Specific terms and concrete imagery — these are the things that appeal to our emotions, yet even to this statement there are exceptions. Here is part of a memorial poem for William Jennings Bryan. Although the lines abound in abstractions, they do have a good deal of concrete imagery. What is the matter with it? Why does it strike us as bad?

Great were the battles that he fought for those who labor long,
And splendid was his service on every moral plain,
Magnificent the mace that helped to crush the crowning Wrong
And stay the plague of Drink's vile and malignant reign!

His soul was only combative and militant for Good,
In Statesmanship sublime he strove that cruel wars should cease,
He wisely wove and welded well the bonds of brotherhood
And knit a score of nations in noble pacts of peace!

Anyone can see, I think, why "service on every moral plain" is not particularly appealing to the emotions, however much the intellect may approve it. Abstractions leave us cold. What, though, is the matter with the concrete words rather plentifully scattered through the lines? Why do they not produce more of an emotional effect?

Simply that they are not the words to appeal to our imagination. Even an admirer of Bryan would have a hard tussle before he could make his imagination picture his hero astride a war horse, clad in medieval armor, brandishing a mace or battle-ax. He would have difficulty for two reasons: First, because the imagery is incongruous with the subject; second, because the imagery has been used so often that it has become stereotyped. We have heard these same figures of speech applied so often to so many men in so many differing situations that they no longer mean anything to us emotionally. Our imaginations have been prodded in this particular quarter so often that they no longer make the slightest response to the stimulus.

We may conclude, therefore, that in order to stir the imagination, and through it the emotions, concrete imagery must be, not only congruous to the subject, but also fresh enough to strike us with a little of surprise, to present to our imaginations a picture that is new. In following this conclusion to its logical results, we discover that much verse intended to be poetry is nothing of the sort because it is merely a pale ghost of what other poets have said. The man who objected that he had found Shakespeare only a mass of stale old quotations was, of course, mistaken only in that the familiar passages are borrowed from, instead of by, the great playwright.

A large part of Shakespeare's imagery has passed bodily into the living language. Making it was an exercise of the creative function; repetition of it is nothing of the sort. Every great age of poetry produces a vast bulk of important work that overshadows the generations that follow. Many of us are still living in the shadow of the nineteenth century, still unconsciously influenced by the poets of that important period, still revamping the diction and the imagery that belonged to that period. The poets of that time invented their diction and imagery to express the spirit and interpret the life of their own age. If we wish to create, and not merely to imitate, we must do the same thing for our own time and country; and if we fail to do this, we are merely shadow-posts, echoes of true poets.

Always when I have made these statements to a group of students, objectors have arisen. Some of them are people with a love for poetry but without a spark of the creative impulse; others are people who feel within themselves an aptitude for philosophical thinking, and who believe that philosophy must be told in abstractions because its underlying ideas are abstract.

For them a little confronting of hard facts is usually salutary. Consider two versions of several ideas:

Abstract. Life is short and ends in death.

Concrete. We are such stuff as dreams are made of, and our little life is rounded with a sleep.

Abstract. We cannot get beyond the reach of infinite love.

Concrete. I know not where His islands lift their fronded palms in air; I only know I cannot drift beyond His love and care.

Abstract. It was a dark and stormy night.

Concrete. The wind was a torrent of darkness amid the gusty trees.

Abstract. She was beautiful and strange.

Concrete. She learned her hands in a fairy tale and her mouth on a valentine.

All of the above concrete examples are quotations from verse, though printed here as prose. An even better example may be had by giving the abstract equivalent of a short poem and printing the concrete version. I choose one from Stephen Phillips that ought to convince even the philosophically minded.

Abstract. We wrong our love and those for whom we feel love by quarrelings and dissentions. Suppose we were deprived of the opportunity of forgiving and being forgiven, how would we feel?

Concrete:

My dear love came to me, and said:
"God gives me one hour's rest
To spend with thee on earth again:
How shall I spend it best?"

"Why, as of old," I said; and so
We quarreled, as of old:
But, when I turned to make my peace,
That one short hour was told.

These examples ought to be convincing. It only remains, therefore, to see how various poets have applied these principles in their work.

While we are forbidden to borrow the imagery of other writers, we can legitimately study and imitate their technique. Our problem, now, is to see what other poets have done, in order that we may make our own as much as we find useful of their method, rather than of their subject matter.

In the study of poetry about physical things, we can do no better than to go to the great lover of material beauty, Keats. Here is the first stanza of "Ode on a Grecian Urn":

Thou still unravish'd bride of quietness,

Thou foster-child of silence and slow time,
Sylvan historian, who canst thus express
A flowery tale more sweetly than our rhyme:
What leaf-fring'd legend haunts about thy shape
Of deities or mortals, or of both,
In Tempe or the dales of Arcady?
What men or gods are these? What maidens loth?
What mad pursuit? What struggle to escape?
What pipes and timbrels? What wild ecstacy?

Notice the wealth of specific details. Not only does the poet express in concrete and suggestive imagery what he says by way of address to the urn, but he presents to us, by many specific and concrete words, a complete picture of the urn itself, or at least of the significant part of it, the frieze of figures carved on its sides. This treatment is no more than what we might expect, when the subject treated is entirely objective.

When the writer draws generalizations from the concrete, when he has an abstract idea to express, we might, at first, expect to find his clear-cut imagery fading into cloudiness. We might go on with this poem, but I think the principle will be emphasized more if we quote from another by the same writer:

In a drear-nighted December,
Too happy, happy tree,
Thy branches ne'er remember
Their green felicity.
The north cannot undo them,
With sleety whistle through them;
Nor frozen thawings glue them
From budding at the prime.

The underlying idea here is an abstract one, but the poet has tried, wisely, to be concrete in detail: December instead of winter; *green* felicity; north, a suggestive word, instead of cold; branches, instead of indefinite thou. It would have been easier to express the idea with less concreteness and precision; the point being, that the poet actually was at pains to avoid any such indefiniteness as that.

The poem from which we have quoted certainly is relevant enough to the principle of letting the abstract thought be inferred from the concrete details. In the following extract from Tennyson's "St. Agnes' Eve" we

find, even more definitely, the use of concrete details to evoke a spirit
or mood, nowhere explicitly stated:

> Deep on the convent-roof the snows
> Are sparkling to the moon;
> My breath to heaven like vapor goes;
> May my soul follow soon!
> The shadows of the convent-towers
> Slant down the snowy sward,
> Still creeping with the creeping hours
> That lead me to my Lord.
> Make Thou my spirit pure and clear
> As are the frosty skies,
> Or this first snowdrop of the year
> That in my bosom lies.

Even in the prayer of the saint, we have three lines of concrete imagery to one line of abstract thought. The rest of the effect of loneliness
and contemplation and spiritual exhaltation is accomplished entirely by
the selection and arrangement of concrete imagery. No doubt I have
repeated that phrase so often that some readers will begin to tire of it.
I wish it were possible to repeat it so often that no would-be poet could
ever forget it.

So far, we have quoted from poets who were to a considerable degree
interested in the things of this world. What will we find in one who lives
in a rarefied region, that apparently has nothing to do with material life?
Let us return to Shelley as a perfect example. Perhaps after seeing a
few specimens of his work, we may conclude that all poetic ideas must
be expressed in concrete terms—even abstract ones.

The whole poetic drama of *Prometheus Unbound* is an allegory of the
struggle of the human soul to free itself from self-inflicted, debasing
superstitions about the nature of God. It is not God that Shelley attacks,
but humanity's idea of God. Every character in the drama represents a
spiritual idea or force. We need not particularize further than to explain
that in the character of Asia is represented the spirit of love and beauty.

Remember that the lines to follow are addressed to a spirit. Here we
expect abstraction. Let us see whether we find it:

> Life of Life! thy lips enkindle
> With their love the breath between them;
> And thy smiles before they dwindle

Make the cold air fire; then screen them
In those looks, where whoso gazes
Faints, entangled in their mazes.

Child of Light! thy limbs are burning
Thro' the vest which seems to hide them;
As the radiant lines of morning
Thro' the clouds ere they divide them;
And this atmosphere divinest
Shrouds thee wheresoe'r thou shinest.

Fair are others; none behods thee,
But thy voice sounds low and tender
Like the fairest, for it folds thee
From the sight, that liquid splendor,
And all feel, yet see thee never,
As I feel now, lost forever!

Not only are these lines addressed to a spirit, but to an invisible one. Many an earthly lover might despair of such concreteness, in addressing a flesh-and-blood mistress.

Equally significant is any part of Shelley's "Hymn to Intellectual Beauty"—as abstract a topic as poet ever attempted to treat in words:

The awful shadow of some unseen Power,
Floats tho' unseen amongst us,—visiting
This various world with as inconstant wing
As summer winds that creep from flower to flower,—
Like moonbeams that behind some piny mountain shower,
It visits with inconstant glance
Each human heart and countenance;
Like hues and harmonies of evening,—
Like clouds in starlight widely spread,—
Like memory of music fled,—
Like all that for its grace may be
Dear, and yet dearer for its mystery.

In the treatment of this most abstract of all possible topics, Shelley cannot write for three lines before a sure instinct leads him directly into concrete imagery, and keeps him in that safe path. Thereafter, the succession of sharp little pictures pours on and on, with seldom a lapse into abstraction. It reminds us of Sir Arthur Quiller-Couch's comment on Shakespeare, who, he said, could not even mention an abstract quality without at once linking it up to a concrete detail.

Even the most skeptical should be convinced that, whatever is meant by beauty as an abstract term, its manifestation in poetry is confined almost exclusively to concrete and suggestive terms, usually expressed in the form of verse. The verse and the imagery are two distinct parts of poetic technique, either of which may exist apart from the other.

The "Had Horrors"

Laurence D'Orsay

July 1927

M any years ago I sat in an office in New York City, in the *role* of a disciple at the feet of Gamaliel. Gamaliel was the most famous fiction magazine editor of that day and many subsequent days and also the best-beloved—a keen-minded, good-hearted man, who gave their first chance to many men and women now among our most popular authors. As I desired to sell Gamaliel some stories, need it be said that I listened, eagerly and respectfully, to all the priceless pearls of wisdom that fell from his lips, inscribing them indelibly upon the tablets of my memory?

To us there entered one of the staff readers, a clever but inexperienced chap whom Gamaliel was just then breaking in. He carried in his hand a manuscript, and slapped it down on the desk, eyeing it balefully as a cat eyes a mouse too tough to chew.

"That's the story of Silas Sniffkins," he explained, mentioning a name known to all fiction readers today, "the one you sent back to him to fix over. Something's wrong with it still. He's got a good opening now, and a good finish. But somehow it doesn't register. I don't know just what's wrong. It's a cracking good story, but he seems to take too long to get to the meat of the thing after his dramatic start."

Gamaliel picked up the manuscript and glanced over the first three pages with an expert eye. He took but a few seconds, and it struck me, as I watched him, that he was looking for something which he expected to find. And he found it, for he nodded his head sagely.

"Plain as your Grecian profile," he told his loyal vassal. "Sniffkins has a bad attack of the had horrors."

"What are the had horrors?" the staff reader asked curiously.

"They usually have 'em," Gamaliel declared, "and it's a good thing to have 'em young, just as children have measles and mumps. They think they must stop the story for a time to tell the reader all about what the hero and his heroine and the villain *had been* doing before the reader ever saw them. Just look at this." He handed me the first sheet of the story.

"A good situation," I commented, after reading it. "Immediate suspense. He has the reader guessing right at the start. Anybody would want to turn over the next page to see what happens."

"Yes," Gamaliel agreed, "but he wouldn't find out. He would have to wait till he got to the end of page four. Sniffkins leaves 'em hung up in the air. He starts his puppets working for a page, and then he drops the strings and gives us a lecture about their past lives—a solid wad of narrative retrospect covering nearly three pages. Just look at the damn thing! *Hads* and *had beens* scattered all over page two and page three as if he'd shaken them from a peppercaster! Well, Sniffkins isn't an incurable. He's got the makings of a good writer. I'll explain to him that the reader doesn't care what *has been* happening to the characters before he meets them: He wants to know what's going to happen to them next."

In the absence of a Gamaliel to give them a shot of hope, many clever but inexperienced writers, who are selling *some* of their stuff, wonder why they don't sell the rest of it. What's the trouble?

If a story has strong and well-sustained entertainment value, an editor will overlook many technical flaws. But one thing he will *not* overlook, as a general rule, is a bad attack of the had horrors—a stodgy lump of bald and undisguised retrospect on the second, third and fourth pages. For that is destructive of entertainment value at the critical moment when, having caught the reader's attention by a good opening, the writer should strive to hold it by going straight ahead along dramatic lines. It is as if the chef offered you a slab of cold and greasy suet pudding after you had polished off the hors d'oeuvres, instead of serving some appetizing and nourishing soup.

Well, the suet pudding, in all its hideous and repellent nakedness, is usually in the second place on the menu of these stories which won't sell. First comes a good opening, showing you the characters in a dramatic situation which tells you what kind of people they are and what they are up against. Then, instead of going ahead and letting them fight out their fight, whatever it may be, the author stops to tell all about them, what they have been doing for the past few years (perhaps, in exaggerated cases, from the cradle) and how they came to be in that particular place and in the particular relation which they bear toward each other.

The proper way to handle retrospect is to ditch nine-tenths of it. But you must have some, of course, in almost every story—although you will notice that nearly every modern stage play manages to get along with a microscopic quantity. The thing to do with this irreducible mini- mum of explanatory matter about antecedent happenings is to link it up with your actual moving story—that is to say, with action, with dialogue, and with the thoughts running through the minds of the characters. In this way you can weave the whole thing into one pattern, and connect what is past with what is present and with what is going to happen. And you can make retrospect *entertaining*—take the curse off it com- pletely—if you associate it with characterization and with the presenta- tion of the dramatic conflict and the interesting human problem which that conflict is to solve.

Homer and Euripides never knew the canons of the short story or the requirements of magazine editors, but they *did* know how to present a story so that it would interest people from the start and keep on inter- esting them to the finish. The modern writer who wishes to succeed, to sell consistently instead of occasionally, should study their methods and the methods of other authors who were eminently successful in their day. Those methods, of course, must be adapted to modern require- ments; but the art of entertaining people is basically the same in all ages. Homer and Euripides, remember, *entertained the multitude*.

Each of these two eternally famous authors produced a masterpiece which involved a great deal of retrospect and depended on that retro- spect for much of its dramatic effect and its entertainment value. Let us see how Homer handled his retrospect in the *Odyssey* and what he accomplished with it.

> *Tell me, Muse, of that man, so ready at need, who wandered far and wide, after he had sacked the sacred citadel of Troy. Many were the men whose towns he saw and whose mind he learnt, yea, and many the woes he suffered in his heart upon the deep, striving to win his own life and the return of his company. Even so he saved not his company, though he desired it sore.*
>
> *Now all the rest of the princes who had fought at Troy were at home, and had escaped both war and sea, but Odysseus only, craving for his wife and for his homeward path, the nymph Calypso held in her hollow caves, longing to have him for her lord. All the gods had pity on him save Poseidon, who raged continually against godlike Odysseus.*

After those five introductory and explanatory sentences, which tell so much in such brief space, the story swings into *action*, significant and vital action—the gods and goddesses, gathered in the halls of Zeus, discussing the plight of Odysseus, and Zeus deciding to rescue him from Calypso. You will notice that Homer had a very mild attack of the had horrors—an attack so mild that it was a gracious visitation rather than an affliction. In those five sentences he links retrospect entertainingly with characterization of his hero and with statement of his hero's problem. He has to account, at the very start of his story, for a big slice out of the life of Odysseus—nearly ten years. But he is far too wise to give his auditors a dull, lengthy and particular account of what Odysseus *had been* doing during those ten years. He gives a most entertaining story about that later on, after he is perfectly sure he has interested his audience deeply in Odysseus by what Odysseus has said and done and suffered *in dramatic action before the eyes of that audience.*

Euripides opens *Medea* in a manner which has been copied by innumerable writers of melodramas. In those old Victorian plays which inspired the ten-twent'-thirt' productions, so popular in this country in ante-movie days, it was the regular thing for the faithful old butler to appear at the rise of the curtain, and say to the new parlor maid, "Today the young squire comes of age, me lass. Well do I mind that stormy night, twenty-one years ago, when his sainted mother, now with the angels in glory, put the little bundle in my arms, and told me—." And so on.

Similarly, Euripides has Medea's faithful old nurse in front of Medea's house in Corinth, at the opening of the play, telling the audience all about the position of affairs. She starts with retrospect—with brief and beautiful references to the well-known story of Jason and Medea and the winning of the Golden Fleece. In that brief retrospect Euripides is careful to begin his wonderful characterization of Medea, and coming from the lips of the old nurse who loves her so dearly, it cannot be otherwise than sympathetic characterization. But this retrospect is cut to the bone. It simply amounts to saying to the audience, "You know the old love story of Jason and Medea. Now, this is what is going to happen to them next when they are well on in years." Most of the nurse's retrospective speech is devoted to statement of the problem and speculation over the dreadful solution which it may have.

> But now, the world is angry, and true love
> Sick as with poison. Jason doth forsake
> My mistress and his own two sons, to make

His couch in a king's chamber. He must wed:
Wed with this Creon's child, who now is head
And chief of Corinth. Wherefore sore betrayed
Medea calleth up the oath they made,
They two.

The fearless soul of Euripides is daring now the monstrous and the terrible—a story so dark and dreadful that even the Hellenes, fond of tragic themes and plots though he knows them to be, may well recoil from it. He is going to make Medea kill her two little sons because Jason has deserted her for another woman, and he is going to make Medea a sympathetic character and keep her so. A gigantic task, truly, and one which genius only could perform. Euripides sets about it at once, planting the sympathetic characterization in that opening retrospective speech by making the nurse suggest that Medea can't help herself, being what she is.

Methinks, she hath a dread, not joy, to see
Her children near. 'Tis this that maketh me
Most tremble, lest she do I know not what.
Her heart is no light thing, and useth not
To brook much wrong. I know that woman, aye,
And dread her! Will she creep alone to die
Bleeding in that old room, where still is laid
Lord Jason's bed? She hath for that a blade
Made keen. Or slay the bridegroom and the king.
And win herself God knows what direr thing?
'Tis a fell spirit. Few, I ween, shall stir
Her hate unscathed, or lightly humble her.

Practically speaking, in a story which would seem to involve a frightful amount of retrospect in its very nature, Euripides gets out of his difficulty competely by making his initial retrospect almost wholly statement of his problem and characterization of his protagonist, the two things being inseparably woven together by the fact that the problem is conditioned by the kind of woman Medea is.

This is how master craftsmen handle retrospect, making it entertaining, useful and significant, making it *advance the story* instead of *break the story*. If a chunk of bald narrative retrospect—the hads and the had beens—seems to be demanded by the nature of the case, a competent and experienced writer takes it for a danger signal. He begins to wonder whether he is approaching his story from the right angle and telling it in a correct and entertaining manner.

THE SEARCH FOR THE RIGHT WORD

Fred Kelly, the humorist and the author of the dog's only book of philosophy, *You and Your Dog*, was a guest of his friend, Booth Tarkington.

"A few nights ago I sat in the attic workroom of Booth Tarkington at his home in Indianapolis while he told me how discouraged he becomes over his work," says Kelly.

" 'Are you ever conscious right at the time,' I asked, 'of doing something that's pretty good?'

" 'No,' Tarkington chuckled, 'it all seems fairly bad. You know, writing is about the most discouraging job of all. One knows so well what he is trying to express but the words aren't available.'

" 'This afternoon I tried to write a paragraph or two describing a certain scene in northern Africa. It was as vivid in my mind as if it were still spread out before me. I tried to make it equally vivid to readers. But when I groped for crystals all I could pick up were just a few smeary words—a meaningless mess. Yet all the time I knew the right words were somewhere if I could only find them.'

" 'Will you keep at it,' I asked, 'until it does suit you?'

" 'Oh, it will never suit me,' he replied, as he slid farther down in his chair with a weary sigh. 'I'll still feel that I could do it better and think how well somebody else could do it.'

"As I came away, I thought: So long as he has that attitude toward his work, no wonder it's good!"

Three Secrets of Successful Fiction Writing

J. Everet Courtney

February 1928

Though by no means representing the "whole story" of successful fiction writing, the three ideas presented herein are named as "secrets" because other, more technical, things sometimes crowd out thought of these vital and necessary considerations of story-creating, without which the writer is badly handicapped. What is worse, he sometimes fails to discover the real reasons for his apparent inability to "sell," these reasons often being among the very trio of "secrets" mentioned.

The first and most important of these is *impressions*. There is humor, spontaneity, convincing characterization and such, which spring from impressions. Impressions are the life of salable stories.

Of course, we all register impressions, but in widely different degrees of intensity. The freshness of these impressions has much to do with their value to the writer. This freshness and intensity can be cultivated, where they do not come naturally, by alertness and constant interest through observation of people about us; just as impressions can be dulled, stagnated, by disinterest and a souring viewpoint toward life. The writer who hopes for success, and for continued success, must keep his impressions active, alive, always. For, be his technique ever so brilliant, without that ability to interpret impressions in terms of freshness and humanness, his work will quickly wither and die of artificiality and monotony.

Nor can the fiction writer allow his view to grow blasé through long contact and experience. A fiction writer may easily fail through a lack of experience in the ways of life, but he might also fail later on because of being "too close" to these things, perhaps with a jaded taste as a result.

An illustration of this is seen in the play critic's case. He, no doubt, knows a great deal on the subject — and yet usually his ability to, himself, create a successful play or story is practically nil. And, not infrequently, the intermittent playgoer could write a better, truer impression of a new play than these critics, if the truth were known. This is because he has not been fed up, so to speak, by too much experience. He still retains the freshness of early impressions. It is, therefore, this danger of a jaded palate for impressions that the seasoned writer must guard against. Above all, he should avoid becoming a cynic.

Next in importance in our trio of "secrets" is that of *mingling* — getting out and about with other folk — doing things, hearing things, picking up firsthand news and impressions and ideas about life. In this way the writer not only has a good chance to pick up threads of good plots, but he avoids that fatal "hermit style" of narrow, stunted writing which almost always betrays him.

Writing, particularly fiction writing, is a profession of keenest competition. The successful businessman does not attempt to conduct his business without mingling with persons and matters connected with his profession. How, then, can the writer, facing just as keen or keener competition, hope to produce successfully without this assistance?

Sympathy is the third of our "secrets." It is scarcely necessary to tell even embryo writers that this does not apply to sympathy for self, which, in all callings, generally marks the last stage on the way down and out. The kind of sympathy here referred to is sympathy toward others and life in general. In short, a genuine heart interest in our fellows.

Interest and sympathy of the sincere sort extend naturally to story characters as seen by readers. Such characters live and breathe and convince and entertain. They are real because you yourself understand them and live in and with them. You believe in them, and so do your readers.

Without that sympathetic touch, however, your characters become mere puppets. Their reactions — if, indeed, they have any — are stiff, unreal, unconvincing and, of course, unentertaining. When you find a yarn "dragging" as you attempt to write it, the trouble may be a lack of heartfelt sympathy already described.

1930s

How to Write Mystery Stories

S.S. Van Dine

The Writer's 1930 Yearbook

The detective story is a kind of intellectual game. It is more — it is a sporting event, and the author must play fair with the reader. He can no more resort to trickeries and deceptions and still retain his honesty than if he cheated in a bridge game. He must outwit the reader, and hold the reader's interest through sheer ingenuity. For the writing of detective stories there are very definite laws — unwritten, perhaps, but none the less binding; and every respectable and self-respecting concocter of literary mysteries lives up to them. Herewith, then, is a sort of credo, based partly on the practice of all the great writers of detective stories, and partly on the promptings of the honest author's inner conscience. To wit:

1. The reader must have equal opportunity with the detective for solving the mystery. All clues must be plainly stated and described.

2. No willful tricks or deceptions may be placed on the reader other than those played legitimately by the criminal on the detective himself.

3. There must be no love interest. The business in hand is to bring a criminal to the bar of justice, not to bring a lovelorn couple to the hymeneal altar.

4. The detective himself, or one of the official investigators, never should turn out to be the culprit. This is bald trickery on a par with offering someone a bright penny for a five-dollar gold piece. It's false pretenses.

5. The culprit must be determined by logical deductions — not by accident or coincidence or unmotivated confession. To solve a criminal problem in this latter fashion is like sending the reader on a deliberate wild-goose chase, and then telling him, after he has failed, that you had the object of his search up your sleeve all the time. Such an author is no better than a practical joker.

6. The detective novel must have a detective in it; and a detective is not a detective unless he detects. His function is to gather clues that eventually will lead to the person who did the dirty work in the first chapter; and if the detective does not reach his conclusions through an analysis of those clues, he has no more solved his problem than the schoolboy who gets his answer out of the back of the arithmetic book.

7. There simply must be a corpse in a detective novel, and the deader the corpse the better. No lesser crime than murder will suffice. Three hundred pages is far too much pother for a crime other than murder. After all, the reader's trouble and expenditure of energy must be rewarded.

8. The problem of the crime must be solved by strictly naturalistic means. Such methods for learning the truth as slate-writing, Ouija boards, mind-reading, spiritualistic séances, crystal-gazing and the like are taboo. A reader has a chance when matching his wits with a rationalistic detective, but if he must compete with the world of spirits and go chasing about the fourth dimension of metaphysics, he is defeated *ab initio*.

9. There must be but one detective — that is, but one protagonist of deduction — one *deus ex machina*. To bring the minds of three or four, or sometimes a gang of detectives to bear on a problem is not only to disperse the interest and break the direct thread of logic, but to take an unfair advantage of the reader. If there is more than one detective the reader doesn't know who his co-detector is. It's like making the reader run a race with a relay team.

10. The culprit must turn out to be a person who has played a more or less prominent part in the story — that is, a person with whom the reader is familiar and in whom he takes an interest.

11. Servants must not be chosen by the author as the culprit. This is begging a noble question. It is a too easy solution. The culprit must be a decidedly worthwhile person — one who wouldn't ordinarily come under suspicion.

12. There must be but one culprit, no matter how many murders are committed. The culprit may, of course, have a minor helper or co-plotter; but the entire onus must rest on one pair of shoulders: The entire indignation of the reader must be permitted to concentrate on a single black nature.

13. Secret societies, camorras, mafias and the like have no place in a detective story. A fascinating and truly beautiful murder is irremediably spoiled by any such wholesale culpability. To be sure, the murderer in

a detective novel should be given a sporting chance, but it is going too far to grant him a secret society to fall back on. No high-class, self-respecting murderer would want such odds.

14. The method of murder, and the means of detecting it, must be rational and scientific. That is to say, pseudo-science and purely imaginative and speculative devices are not to be tolerated in the roman policier.

15. The truth of the problem must at all times be apparent — provided the reader is shrewd enough to see it. By this I mean that if the reader, after learning the explanation for the crime, should reread the book, he would see that the solution had, in a sense, been staring him in the face — that all the clues really pointed to the culprit — and that, if he had been as clever as the detective, he could have solved the mystery himself without going on to the final chapter. That the clever reader does often thus solve the problem goes without saying.

16. A detective novel should contain no long descriptive passages, no literary dallying with side issues, no subtly worked-out character analysis, no "atmospheric" preoccupations. Such matters have no vital place in a record of crime and deduction.

17. A professional criminal must never be shouldered with the guilt of a crime in a detective story. Crimes by house-breakers and bandits are the province of the police departments — not of authors and brilliant amateur detectives. A really fascinating crime is one committed by a pillar of a church or a spinster noted for her charities.

18. A crime in a detective story must never turn out to be an accident or a suicide. To end an odyssey of sleuthing with such an anti-climax is to hoodwink the trusting and kind-hearted reader.

19. The motives for all crimes in detective stories should be personal. International plottings and war politics belong in a different category of fiction — in secret-service tales, for instance. But a murder story must be kept *gemütlich*, so to speak. It must reflect the reader's everyday experiences, and give him a certain outlet for his own repressed desires and emotions.

20. And (to give my credo an even score of items) I herewith list a few of the devices which no self-respecting detective-story writer will avail himself of. They have been employed too often and are familiar to all true lovers of literary crime. To use them is a confession of the author's inaptitude and lack of originality. (a) Determining the identity of the culprit by comparing the butt of a cigarette left at the scene of the crime with the brand smoked by a suspect. (b) The bogus spiritualistic séance to frighten the culprit into giving himself away. (c) Forged

fingerprints. (d) The dummy-figure alibi. (e) The dog that does not bark and thereby reveals the fact that the intruder is familiar. (f) The final pinning of the crime on a twin, or a relative who looks exactly like the suspected, but innocent, person. (g) The hypodermic syringe and the knockout dope. (h) The commission of the murder in a locked room after the police have actually broken in. (i) The word-association test for guilt. (j) The cipher, or code letter, which is eventually unravelled by the sleuth.

Write With Simplicity

Albert Payson Terhune

The Writer's 1931 Yearbook

Brander Matthews was one of the wisest men I have known. I had the privilege of studying under his tuition at Columbia for three years. I had the honor of personal friendship with him. One day, as he and I stood at the window of his study he pointed to a drably smug-looking middle-aged man in the street below.

"If I could write that man's life story," said he, "if I could set it down just as it happened, from his childhood to this day — I would have written a greater book than any in all the literature of the world, except only the Bible."

I wondered to hear my friend and preceptor speak so vehemently. First I glanced at Brander Matthews to see if he were joking. He was not. Then I peered down the street after the very commonplace man of whom he had spoken. I could see no outward sign that the pedestrian had led a life whose story would set the world aflame. Answering my foolishly blank look of inquiry, Matthews went on:

"No, I don't know who he is. I don't know anything about him. I never saw him before. I just picked him out as an example, because he seemed to be most typical commonplace. Here is what I am driving at:

"There is no man or woman whose life story, if honestly and completely told, would not make a far greater drama than any ever written. But that drama can never be penned. Nobody has the perfectly correct vision of his or her own life and the episodes and angles of it which are great drama. The struggle on the cliff and the rescuing of beauty in distress are not the truly dramatic moments in any life. Sublime drama consists of everyday happenings and reactions, greatly described."

Being young and bumptious, I thought my wise preceptor was mistaken. To me, the life-and-death ride, the Prisoner of Zenda duel, the Hawkshaw detective clash, seemed the ideal forms of drama. Everyday occurrences and scenes did not strike me as dramatic in any way; or indeed worth writing about at all.

Thirty-odd years of study and of experience, since then, have shown me how unbelievably correct was Brander Matthews' sermonette. If I had learned to profit by it earlier in life, I might be a great writer by now; which I never shall be. If readers will have the wisdom to follow the precepts of Brander Matthews' preachment, they may save themselves many a disappointment in the attempted writing of successful stories. In other words, they should write of the simple things which they actually know, instead of going far afield for unconvincing bits of so-called drama along lines with which they are glaringly unfamiliar.

Ray Long sized up the Brander Matthews theory, in his wonted Napoleonic style, during a visit to me here at Sunnybank, a few years ago. We were discussing story writing and why the majority of aspirants fail to make good at fiction. He said: "Novices must realize that it is fifty times better to describe mediocre happenings in a remarkable way than to describe remarkable happenings in a mediocre way!"

Turn over in your memory some of the greatest short stories, and you will find how true his epigram was. For example: de Maupassant was a peerless short story writer. What were the themes of his most famous tales? Did they deal with swordplay and pistol shots and abductions and clanking ghost chains in darkly mysterious dungeons and with involvedly twisted plots? Here are the themes of two of his best short stories:

A poor clerk's wife borrows a necklace. She loses it; and spends the rest of her youth and middle age in saving money to replace it;—only to find out at last that the necklace was paste and not of diamonds.

An old countryman stoops over thriftily to pick up a piece of string. Onlookers think it is a purse he has picked up and stolen. Their suspicion weighs on his mind until his health breaks down.

Those are the outlines of two immortal stories. Not a melodramatic or an extravagant or an involved happening in either of them. One might name a dozen more de Maupassant tales which have achieved deathless fame on no subtler plots than those of "The Necklace" and "A Piece of String."

Everyone has deep knowledge of some one or more walks of life; a knowledge which he or she has mastered; and whose correct recital would make great stories. Perhaps the novice is a shipping clerk, a shopgirl, a farmhand, a garbage collector. Very well, then. There is breathlessly interesting drama and narrative force in the ten thousand details of any or all these jobs; in their setting, in the companionships formed; in the myriad bits of unusual local color. The stories written by any of these people could be made remarkable, if they would make them mirrors of life.

Will they do it? Not they. Not while they can write of dark crimes of which they have no knowledge; and of society life and of dime novel adventures and of supposedly romantic love; and of other topics on which they are wholly ignorant.

To few of us is it given to face death in single combat; to ride out water spouts at sea in leaky craft; to win a princess from the villainous prince who seeks her hand; to foil international jewel thieves or racketeers; to rescue the only daughter of a multimillionaire; to decipher the chart telling where the treasure is buried. And when we try to depict these adventures in fiction we write as unconvincingly as if we were trying to describe a visit to the planet Mars.

But to countless thousands of us it is given to know exactly how the office manager behaved and spoke and looked when Smithers reported late for the third time that week; how the grittily slippery sidewalk felt, and how the dawn wind cut the face when we shambled sleepily to work at 6 A.M. in the rush season at the store; the silly way debtors answered and behaved when we called to collect that overdue bill; the hundred different characters of the hundred different children in the school where we teach; the vapidly loquacious chatter of our fellow workers or fellow revelers; the sordidly queer little happenings of our fellow tenants in the apartment house and the idiosyncracies of the janitor.

We know all those things and many more. We know them so well and they are so much a part of our daily lives that we don't think them worth setting down in print. The few of us, who have the cleverness to realize their value, reap rich harvests.

Write well of what you know. If you can't write well of familiar things, it is a million percent certainty you can't hope to write well of things you don't know. The scene, the characters, the theme — all are right at your hand. Use them. Don't turn your back on them to stray far afield and write blunderingly of unknown things.

The Working Philosophy of a Playwright

Marc Connelly

As Told to Bernice Breen

April 1931

A ll creative writers will realize that it is utterly impossible for anyone to lay down hard and fast rules of work that will be equally helpful to another. The best that can be done is to give an outline of the difficulties which everyone encounters, and a rough chart of individual experience in overcoming them.

In dramatic writing, as in all other forms, the problem divides itself into three main difficulties. First, the problem of getting an idea of sufficient novelty and importance to serve as the basis of the play. Then, the various technical difficulties in developing the idea; and finally, the not inconsiderable hurdles that are encountered in marketing the finished product.

By far the most difficult and important work of the playwright is done before he begins to write his play. Of the numerous ideas which are part of every creative worker's stock in trade, some one stands out because it seems fresher and more significant than the rest. Right here occurs the first problem of analysis. Does it seem novel only because it deals with some sphere of existence unfamiliar to the writer? Will it seem equally new and unusual to an audience of typical Broadway playgoers, the judgment seat before which every dramatist must be measured? And if the theme and locale have been used before, will the would-be dramatist bring an emotional slant to the problem that will freshly illumine the whole theme and be convincing to the audience?

If the first flash of a theme upon the writer's consciousness meets these tests, then he is ready to lay the groundwork of his play. This brings him to the period of longest, most difficult and most discouraging work. For an idea must be thought through, and thoroughly digested emotionally, before it can be put on paper. Sometimes six months or a year will go by without a line being written. Yet the play is being built in its writer's consciousness just as surely as though it were being written in black and white. Once one has achieved artistic maturity, it will be found indeed that this invisible writing is the more indelible, for what was a lifeless skeleton takes on warmth and color and begins to live and breathe.

As the writer discovers what characters are necessary to give vividness to his theme, what setting is appropriate, how many acts and scenes are needed for its full development, he will undoubtedly find it necessary to make notes from time to time. These notes may be but suggestions around which he will build later, or they may be snatches of dialogue that have the spontaneity and charm which come from the first fresh vision of a subject.

How extensive these early notes may be is a matter for each individual to decide. The preliminary work for *The Green Pastures* ran to nineteen pages, and was the result of about six months of intensive work. However, when that was done, the play—whole and complete—was done. The actual writing of dialogue took but six days.

Without intending to seem didactic, I must emphasize that the most important thought for the young dramatist to keep in mind in constructing his play is that it is an emotional mechanism. Its primary purpose is not, as is often supposed, to make people think but *to make people feel*. Therefore, as he builds each scene, it would be well to ask himself not—what facts do I want to convey, but—what emotion do I want to communicate? Is it to be love and admiration for the hero? Then he must be made to appear splendid and generous in his relation to other characters. Is it to be a tender pity for the heroine? Then she will have to be thwarted, imposed upon or in some way treated unjustly. Thus, indirectly, a feeling of hatred is aroused toward the person who causes her unhappiness.

Obviously there must be emotional variety in a play. Any one scene unduly prolonged ceases to grip an audience, not because they have lost interest in the characters, but because it no longer feels as they feel. So that the playwright, in order to maintain interest, must weave together the different strands of feeling to produce both variety and harmony.

All of these problems must, in dramatic composition, be solved through the medium of dialogue alone. There is not the novelist's ready standby of long analytical passages. The characters must speak for themselves. Once the author has put them on paper, he cannot say a word in their behalf.

It behooves him, therefore, to perfect his technique in the difficult medium of dialogue. There is nothing for the novice in dramatic work to do but concentrate on the problems of dialogue until he is as sure of the form as he is of the keys on his typewriter. To obtain the emotional sweep and surge necessary to carry an audience along, the writer cannot be hampered by technical considerations any more than by the thought of how to form his letters.

Developing a feeling for natural dialogue is, perhaps, one of the greatest difficulties that faces the beginner. His ear must be trained to catch the authentic note in words as the violinist's ear is in music. This is a subconscious, rather than a conscious process. By mingling with the type of people of whom he is writing, and listening not too mechanically, he will gradually acquire a feeling for their mode of speech and thought that will give authenticity to his writing.

Of course, speech springs from character. Dumas, I think it was, said that on a journey, it is not half so important to know where one is going as to know with whom one is traveling. Since the playwright's preliminary work has taken care of the object of the sentimental or emotional journey that is drama, the author is now free to pass from the objective to the subjective — to enter into his characters, think as they think, and feel as they feel. They will undoubtedly surprise him, they will occasionally get beyond his control, but if they are real to him they will be real to his audience.

It is this sense of reality in the mind of the audience that must be the constant aim. People go to a play primarily to feed themselves emotionally. They seek what they lack in life. A continuous current of interest must be maintained, and even after the play is written, the dramatist's work is not done.

For each audience has to be won and held individually. Trifles of which the author is unaware can break the mood created on paper. On the whole, men are interested primarily in the soundness of the play's fundamental idea or in the development of some character; while women, who are so large a part of all audiences, are more critical of details. Even such comparatively unimportant items as an unbecoming gown or an irritating trick of speech or gesture can break the smooth emotional current which flows between the audience and the stage. Therefore, up to and after the production of a play, the author must be on guard to maintain the most important element of all — the fundamental emotional unity.

Creating "Lovable" Characters

James Hilton

March 1938

On account, I suppose, of Mr. Chips, I have sometimes been asked how one creates a lovable character in fiction. My first answer is that the worst possible way would be to take pen and paper or typewriter and say to oneself: "I am going to create a lovable character."

As a matter of fact, the process of artistic creation is mysterious, even to the creator; there is, as G.K. Chesterton once said, all the difference in the world between knowing how things are done and knowing how to do them. The artist knows how to do them; he does not as a rule care whether he knows how they are done or not. He leaves that to critics, commentators, glossarians, footnoters or his own biographer (if he is ever likely to have one)—but always with a wistful memory of Lord Balfour's remark in the British Parliament—"Gentlemen, I do not mind being contradicted, and I am unperturbed when I am attacked, but I confess I have slight misgivings when I hear myself being explained."

The only trick I know in writing is to have something to say, or some story to tell, and to say it or tell it as simply and as effectively as possible. The proverb in *Alice in Wonderland* cannot be bettered—"Take care of the sense and the sounds will take care of themselves." So far as "style" goes, I am a functionalist; if a sentence represents exactly the idea I wish to convey, I am satisfied with it. I dislike "style" that has a look or sound of having been stuck on afterward, or "style" that employs unusual words with no intention but to startle the reader, send him to a dictionary or give him the snobbish feeling that because he cannot properly understand what he is reading he is therefore improving his mind enormously. And I am ready to use any words that seem useful, whether the purists object to them or not—"intrigue" as a verb, for instance, which conveys to me a definite and needed shade of meaning between "interest" and "absorb."

Anybody can construct a dummy with an assortment of attributes attached to him like labels, and some writers have so successfully convinced the public that this is character-creating that the very word "character" has come to have a secondary meaning nowadays—i.e., we say a man is a "character" when we mean he is a little bit eccentric. Every stage actor knows how much easier it is to put over a juicy bit of character acting than to portray an ordinary person who might be you or me; and most actors know also (to their own dismay) how readily the public is taken in by this sort of thing. A genuine creation should *have* character as well as *be* one; should have central heating, so to say, as well as exterior lighting. When Sir Walter Scott introduced any new personage into his novels he usually began with the hair and finished with the heels, making a complete inventory of dress and features all the way down; the result was that you felt you might possibly recognize the fellow if you were ever to meet him and he happened to be wearing the same clothes. But when Dostoyevsky or Dickens gives you a character, you feel that you know him with your eyes shut. It is the difference between — "He had light blue eyes, lank hair, slightly stooping shoulders and wore shabby tweeds" — and (I think Morely wrote this in one of his novels) — "Everything of him was *rather*, except his eyes, and they were *quite*." Please don't take this sentence as any sort of model; it is merely an example of how a good writer blows you a petal of meaning instead of felling a whole forest for you — hoping you'll be just as satisfied, edified and instructed.

So far, you may have noticed, I have been evading the question I began with—how a lovable character can be created. Frankly, I don't know. If you have a story to tell and tell it simply and without fuss, some of the characters may be lovable and others not so; you can hardly create them to specification. But sometimes, after you have finished with them, they ring a bell in your heart and afterward in the hearts of your readers.

People love lovability—we all do. It is still human nature (even with a quarter of the world at war) to admire goodness. Our admiration, at its core, is sharp as a nerve; let them once touch that nerve, and stories have a good chance of being popular. But if there were any formula for touching it, believe me, the world of fiction would be swamped with "lovable characters." The truth is, the nerve is as secret as it is sensitive; try to create lovability to order and you will probably produce a mess of mawkishness that nobody will enjoy. The only recommendation I can give is that a writer should create the characters he has in mind and let them be lovable if they will.

Within Quotes

Erle Stanley Gardner

August 1938

I learned what I know about writing the hard way. I stubbed my toe over every obstacle there was in the path of the beginning writer. Dialogue got me down and had me almost licked. Plots knocked me all over the ring and had me hanging on the ropes. The presentation of action threw me for a ten-yard loss every time I tried to carry the ball.

But I'm still here, happy, grinning, contented, battle-scarred and making a living. I've found out enough about my old enemies so they don't knock me all over the ring now, although occasionally they land a good punch which has me pretty groggy for a while. But so far I've managed to escape the fatal count to ten — which should prove something.

So let's look at this dialogue business.

Years ago, when I realized that dialogue was one of my main troubles, I decided to take it to pieces and see what made it tick. I acted on the theory that if you want to lick an enemy, you first have to learn all there is about him. Study his strong points and his weak points. I started in with dialogue. I find that I still have my old notebooks. And, just in case you're interested, here's the way I approached the dialogue problem then, with a few supplemental notes which have been added at a later date.

Here's the way the notebook reads:

Dialogue
Object.
1. Portray character, reader isn't interested in what you tell him about the character of one of the actors in the story. He's more convinced if he finds out for himself in the way he would in real life. This is through conversation in relation to action.
2. To advance the action.

3. To avoid the historical slant.
4. Break away from author's personality.

How It Is Handled.

1. Few lines idea in art.
2. Condensation.
3. Elimination of useless repetitions and qualifications.

Perhaps Sets a Pattern.

Strained Attempt at Smartness Destroys Illusion Reality.

Poor Dialogue Destroys Pace Rhythm.

Enables Break up Subjective Dissertations to Hold Interest.

I think a writer should keep a notebook, not for the purpose of keeping plots alone, but to list points of technique which he picks up from time to time, and so he can review his own thoughts.

It's been quite a while since I worked out this first dialogue business, yet I can go back over a period of years and instantly recapture my thoughts of the moment.

I have a pretty large-sized notebook, filled with pages of self-criticism, suggestions from other authors, copies of interesting paragraphs from articles in writers' magazines, etc.

So let's put this notebook classification of dialogue under a magnifying glass and see what we have. Under Object, subdivision 1 is self-explanatory. So's 2. But 3 needs a little explanation. I had found that my stories weren't stories, but histories. I unconsciously approached the reader not from the angle of something which was happening, and in which he was an actor, but from the angle of something which *had happened*, and in which he was a tardy spectator. I'd already cataloged that as one of my faults. By advancing the story more through dialogue and less through statement I found I could eliminate a lot of that fault.

Subdivision 4 needs just a word. I used to get too much *me* in the story. It's well to be individual and show that individuality in your writing. But your characters must be individuals, entirely free of your apron strings. Don't cart them around, dump them in situations for a few pages, then pick them up, carry them into the next chapter and dump them again. Let them move under their own power and take the story with them. And the way to cut the characters loose from your apron strings is through their dialogue, their oral reactions to the things the other characters are doing.

Now then, let's detour for a moment to the "How Is It Handled" classification.

Subdivision 1. Ever notice how the artist who tries to sketch in everything he sees gets all bogged down in his own detail, how his pictures seem to lack a theme, how they shriek of such painful work that it's wearying to look at them, while some other artist makes two lines, throws in a patch of shadow, and it becomes a tree?

Well, in dialogue I found it worked better not to try to portray character and advance the story by working too much detail into the conversation. Sketch in a line and a bit of shading so that the reader sees the tree.

Subdivision 2. I found, to my surprise, that characters in stories almost never talk the way they do in real life. Listen to a friend. Figure the number of words in his ordinary conversation, then notice how you'd have to write what he said, to get it published in a story.

Subdivison 3. The characters you like don't modify what they say with a lot of qualifications. They say "yes" and "no" and "drop that gun" and "what of it." They don't say, "Well, if it appears that Uncle John is dead, and since there is no other alternative, and because you represent the heirs, I'll agree; unless, of course, it should transpire that there's a will, in which event I'll reserve the right to withdraw from the agreement."

In other words characters reach decisions (unless you're deliberately trying to portray a man who can't reach a decision). They express their decisions in a few definite words. The best illustration of this is in the movies. Go to a movie, enjoy it, then sit through the show a second time just to listen to the way the characters talk and what they say. You'll be astounded, if you haven't already consciously thought of it, to see with what few words the characters advance the plot, show their characteristics, and yet you feel that you're listening to really, truly, flesh-and-blood conversation.

You'll find that writing movie dialogue is a science, a science worked out until it has become an art.

"Perhaps sets a pattern." This was the note I used to remind myself that the reader likes to identify himself with the characters, likes to figure that he'd have said about that same thing himself — if he'd thought of it. Therefore you want to figure the psychological reactions of the reader to what's taking place in the story, and when the hero says something, be sure he says it in a way which the reader might use as a pattern, something the way he'd like to talk in a similar situation. You'll make more reader friends that way — or that's the way I figured it when I was having the session with the notebook.

Now, using so much of this framework as a basis of study, I can pick up any story written by any good author, and find bits of dialogue that fit into this same pattern. In other words, successful authors have long ago encountered these same problems, solved them and passed on to other problems. I don't say their reasoning and mine are identical, but so far as mine is correct I can ascertain that it's fairly well supported by illustrations.

Look at these examples, picked at random.

Take this from a yarn in *Country Gentleman* by Jerome Beatty:

> *"Jumping Jupiter!" exclaimed Dorothy. "You've been here two months, child, and you still believe Ed Seaver's hooey? Even the fan magazines don't print that yarn any more."*
>
> *"Well, wasn't she born on a South Sea isle and didn't she grow up among the carefree natives?"*
>
> *"She was born on a Kansas farm, that gal. I met a fellow the other day who went to college with her. He even was engaged to her—but she left him to go to Hollywood. That South Sea stuff, honey bunch, is publicity hokum."*
>
> *"Anyway, I think Bonita Belmore is just priceless—no matter where she was born."*
>
> *"She's no good. Anybody who would leave that boy for the movies—"*
>
> *"What boy?"*
>
> *"The boy from Kansas I was telling you about. The one she was engaged to. His name is Jimmy Dodd. You ought to see him, child; tall and kind of shy—and—well, he's all right, take my word for it."*
>
> *"I will. Are these manuscripts ready to be mailed?"*

Get the way the story is advanced, the way you feel interested not only in the characters who are talking, but in the ones who are being talked about? See the pair who are doing the talking without even knowing what they look like?

Or try this from *Cosmopolitan* by Margaret Culkin Banning:

> *"OK," said Mike, "But how about the bacon? Does the boy bring it home?"*
>
> *"He will. I don't have to worry about that. But even if he didn't, I wouldn't care. There are a lot of other things in this world more important than money!"*
>
> *"Name me two."*

"Figure it out for yourself," said Lily. She couldn't give him any more time. She had things to do.

Notice how cleverly that dialogue is worked in with a few swift lines and a bit of shading which makes you see a tree. Notice how it's condensed, how it gives you a picture of the characters, their environment, their problems ... and yet two people wouldn't have talked just like that. They'd have talked more, qualified their statements. There'd have been the "Well, well, well, what are you doing here? Haven't seen you for a long time, and you're looking fine.".... "You, too! Where's your wife? I haven't seen her for ages. Where are you keeping yourself these days, and why don't we have one of those get-togethers?" ... "Swell idea. The little lady was talking about you just the other day. Say, I tell you what, let's ..." etc.

On the other hand, you have to be careful with this crisp, clever dialogue. The big-name writers handle it as a barber handles a razor. It's sharp edged. Properly used it's a wonderful tool. Get careless with it and it makes trouble. Some writers try so hard to be clever they create characters which aren't convincing. Their characters talk with such brittle-sharp conversation it gives the reader an inferiority complex. It takes just a dash of swift lines, written with a delicacy of touch.

Let's look at *This Week* and see how James Warner Bellah goes about his stuff:

"So," he said, "if you'll just see your way clear to a settlement of four million dollars, round figures, we'll set the day."

Her voice was desperately low: "Do you mean to say that you are asking me to marry you — without feeling one thing for me — ?"

He said, "We're well-bred people. Love is for barmaids."

She said, "Go away quickly, Michael."

He raised his eyebrows. "I say, you Americans are frightfully touchy about money, aren't you?"

"Go away, Michael," she said.

In that scene the author was sketching in a bit of background. He wanted to show the reader the character of the girl, the thing she was trying to forget, her reason for being where she was and feeling as she did. It was a device to relieve the story from any possibility of a historical drag and make the reader feel right at home with the characters. In those few lines you've learned a lot about what the author wants you to learn, and, mind you, you've done it for yourself. He doesn't say "The girl was sensitive, romantic, impulsive, yet firm. She had been places, was wealthy, a romanticist, yet she had seen the sordid rear its ugly head when she had been expecting romance—as though some jack-in-the-box had thrust up a screaming caricature of ugliness when she had opened a box which might have contained an engagement ring." He lets you find all this out for yourself, and, as a result, you feel this girl is one of your friends, rather than a friend of the author.

Remember sometimes when an officious friend, a too friendly friend, had dwelt at length on the charms of some young woman whom he was going to have you meet? "You'll be crazy about her, Jack, my boy. She's young, willowy, a swell sport, good company, honest and sincere without being Victorian about it. She knows her way around and doesn't ask odds of any man . . . and I've told her about you, what a swell egg you are, about that time you took the ball around the end and ran for . . . ."

Let him keep that up a bit and you don't give a damn whether you ever meet the little lady. When you do, you look for the gold and the diamonds of her character and see only wistful eyes and a turned-up nose and a hint of a freckle. You think, "Oh, splash." And she, looking at you with those wistful eyes, is thinking, "So this is the big, handsome brute? I feel like telling him, 'Go cure your halitosis with Listerine. Put Mum under your armpits and wash with Lifebuoy soap. Then come back in two years. Perhaps you are perfect, but you don't look it, and who gives a whoop anyway?' "

But suppose this friend had kept his trap shut and just introduced you to a snub-nosed gal with freckles, who looked just like any other of the sex that invariably gives a right-hand turn signal when they're really going to turn left—and she'd seen you as only a big palooka with a cleft chin which she really didn't like and eyes that were like her spaniel's. And suppose you'd started talking, and found out, a bit at a time, that the girl was different and she'd learned that you had a commanding personality . . . what ho, my lads, we're off to another romance. Ike, gimme that ring out of hock and take this overcoat instead.

Or, let's look at examples from some of the action type of magazines, where you'll find that dialogue has to have a certain punch.

Take this for example:

> " . . . *beefed to Doran, and Doran tried to get Smith pulled off the case and thought he did. Then Morrow got killed. Get that?*"
> "*I hear you talk.*"
> "*Then Smith picked up a guy . . .*" *etc.*

The above is from a yarn by Roger Torrey in *Black Mask*. See how the mere statement, "I hear you talk," in answer to the question of the man who was spilling a lot of facts, shows the character of the listener, casts doubt on that of the talker, and keeps the element of mystery and suspense in the story?

Or, take this from a story by Carroll John Daly in *Dime Detective* (and any student who wants to get virility in dialogue and action can always count on Carroll John Daly having a sleeve pretty well filled with aces).

> *"Am I to understand that you have taken Richard Havermore prisoner, and that you know personally where he is, and that you intend to torture him to death?"*
>
> *"That's it exactly," he said slowly.*
>
> *And that was all. He'd made his own trap, put the cheese in it, then stuck his face in for that cheese. My gun was out again, up and down — and his lean body crashed upon the table.*

Notice how Daly advances the plot with a statement of facts, and then illustrates it with a comment on action which lifts the reader right out of the chair.

One of the best ways of handling dialogue is to intersperse just the right amount of narrative action between the passages of dialogue. That keeps the story moving and the conversation from becoming monotonous.

I can illustrate with another passage from that same story of Daly's:

> *I twisted two guns into my hands. He looked blank and chirped in a bird-like voice that could be heard all over the place: "You police — no?"*
>
> *"No is correct." Then I stepped forward, lifted my gun up and down. It was the blow with my gun that knocked him to the floor, but it was his own idea to hit it with his face.*
>
> *A voice called: "That sounds like you, Williams."*

Or, take a specimen from a story by William E. Barrett in *Detective Stories*:

> *"I'm Chet Chandler, McQuillen," he said, "and I can do you some good. Let me have your story."*
>
> *He was brisk and businesslike; a slender, well-groomed young man with level eyes and a jaw that he didn't develop by "yessing"*

people. I liked him, but I couldn't see any reason why he should be my lawyer.

"Nobody that's heard my story has liked it," I told him.

The corners of his eyes wrinkled up pleasantly.

"Give me a crack at it."

I shrugged. After all, it was no secret. I'd been telling it to the cops all night. With a cigarette burning cheerfully, I went into it again. He followed it all the way and interrupted only when I skipped over the descriptions. He wanted everything, and when I finished, he smoked quietly for a few minutes before he opened up.

"Would you be interested in learning that the fifty-dollar bill you had was part of the Baintree ransom money?" he said.

I stiffened at that. "That Missouri kidnapping?"

"Yes. Know anything about it?"

Notice that the conversation isn't really the conversation a person accused of crime would have with an attorney. It's a condensed version which, nevertheless, makes you feel you've heard a long conversation. You sense the reserved, self-sufficient character of the storyteller when he says, "Nobody that's heard my story has liked it."

And, for sheer picture-painting, character-sketching conversation, take this from a story by Leslie T. White in *Dime Detective*:

"The wagon cop frowned, moistened the stub of his pencil. "How'n hell do you spell 'malicious'?"

"Make it resistin' arrest, instead," the patrolman growled and walked away.

And if you want a nice illustration of how a little comment on the part of the author, interspersed with bits of conversation, can give added meaning and emphasis to what's being said, notice this from a yarn by S. Omar Barker, in *Adventure*:

"You're a damn fool," observed Butch Gates. His tone was impersonal, but there was no hint of either condescension or contempt in it. Then, as if an afterthought, he added: "Both of you."

These are typical examples of the best dialogue technique. Don't think they're easy to find. If you want to see the game from the other side of the fence and realize what an editor has to contend with, just pick up a few magazines and say to yourself, "I'll just pick out a few examples of outstanding dialogue technique."

Story writing has improved a lot since I broke into print. My early stories wouldn't get by today. Competition is more keen. Quality has progressed.

And, for beginning writers who are keeping up a brave front and holding a stiff upper lip, but who secretly are tired to death of getting courteously insulting slips stating that stories are returned, not because they lack merit, but simply because they are unavailable, I have one or two suggestions.

Study plot. What is it? What is its function? What is it supposed to accomplish? How is it built up? Study dialogue. Analyze it. Strip it down to essentials. Study action. What makes for action in a story? How does one get virility and sense of speed in a yarn?

Then, with those three things in mind—plot, dialogue and action—write a yarn and send it out.

See what happens.

And more power to you!

Accent on the Unusual

Irving Wallace

December 1938

I f you can get excited about the fact that Victor Hugo was born in the French city of Besançon, and that he died in May 1885, then you are either a pedagogue or a Rhodes Scholar, but you're certainly not a writer of articles, at least not articles that sell.

On the other hand, if you get a glint in your eyes and begin to tremble when you learn that Victor Hugo did his scribbling in the nude so that he wouldn't leave his desk, that he once penned a sentence 823 words long, and that he submitted *Les Miserables* to his publisher with a large question mark instead of a letter and received an exclamation point in reply, then you are definitely a writer.

And if you aren't selling, you will be, mark my word, because you have that most important of all gifts—an eye for the unusual.

Now, of course, the anatomy of an article is composed of many things—colorful English, compactness, pointed anecdotes, analysis. But the legs upon which the article stands is the subject itself; the blood pumped through the article is the amount of human interest and oddity injected into it.

And I'm willing to bet my last year's check stubs on this: If you take an extraordinary subject and give it ordinary detailed treatment, or if you take the usual subject and brighten it with unusual treatment—presuming you can write above the sixth grade or Gertrude Stein standard—you'll have a sale inside of three months. You can't fail.

I know. Because I graduated from Sunday school papers to pulps and then to slicks with the man-bites-dog formula as my textbook.

In the offices of Hearst's old New York *Examiner* there used to be a placard that read:

"What we want to arouse is the 'Gee Whiz!' emotion."

Well, there you have it. The "Open Sesame" to the feature field. Make 'em say "Gee whiz!" Either at your subject or at your material.

Now I'm going to take you into my laboratory, show you how I work. Of course, when I reveal my methods, you'll immediately go to work and cut me out of two or three markets—but what the devil, we're all one great blood brotherhood, we'll all wind up in the same asylum, so—

To begin with there was *Ken Magazine*. I read the book, succeeding copies of it, thoroughly. All the big subjects seemed pretty well taken care of by big names or by authors who were, or had been, on the scene. I realized that an attempt to buck such competition with only secondhand material would mean a rejection. Obviously, run-of-the-mill political pieces on Germany, England, Czechoslovakia wouldn't stand a chance.

So I did the next best thing. I selected an unusual subject, within the slant of *Ken*, that the big names didn't know about or were too busy to touch.

I thumbed through the drawers of my oddity file. There was a notation on a country called San Marino. The smallest republic on earth, and located in Italy. In Italy! There was my story! Democracy flourishing within fascism. A natural!

The lead came easily:

> *Buried in Europe's stronghold of fascism is a community in which Italians think and write and speak as they please, without supervision, free of Roman censorship and Mr. Mussolini's hypnotic gaze. The people are republicans and liberals, peaceful and independent, in the very midst of dictatorial Italy!*
>
> *It sounds almost impossible, but it's true. For the country of San Marino, only thirty-eight square miles in size, the world's oldest and smallest republic, is situated on the Adriatic slope of the Apennines in northern Italy, a half-mile above the sea on Mount Titano—above, also, the rolling of war drums and the clank of sabers.*

Once I had my unusual subject, and my angle, the material was just a mechanical matter of research, selection and an effort to get something really exclusive. First, I went through the periodical guide in the library, and checked back on every item published about San Marino in the last quarter of a century. Old travel, news and political magazines were helpful.

Then I scoured travel books, American and English. And finally, for exclusive information, I interviewed several adventurers and lecturers who had visited San Marino. From them, for the price of a few beers, I learned that in San Marino:

Taxes are almost nonexistent. The annual tax on a six-room house is thirty-four cents! The government receives income enough from its four industries — cattle-raising, wine, stone and stamps — to run it- self. Stamps are the most prosperous. Collectors the world over, but especially in the United States, clamor for odd San Marino num- bers — and whenever the government is pressed for cash it prints a new issue.

I sent the opus to Chicago. And Arnold Gingrich's reply was in the form of a pink check that had the same exhilirating effect as giggle water.

OK, that convinced me. I hope it does you.

Using the same method, I heaped dozens of other features on a punch defenseless public. Even the Sunday school papers fell prey. Some years ago when Don Ameche was doing *The First Nighter* from Chicago, I accepted his invite to watch a broadcast and snoop through the CBS studios. It was all quite interesting. I made a notebook full of jottings, converted them into three articles on radio — ponderously dull articles — which were all bounced with "don't forget return postage" underlined.

What was wrong? Obviously, my subjects. I was writing about radio acting. No good. Too commonplace. I poured through my notes again. A page entitled, "Sound Effects" socked me between the optics.

I threw myself at my typing machine, and batted out a minor epic on the Merlin or the Mike at CBS, the soundman who crushed a berry basket in his big hands to produce the battering of a door, who crumpled brown paper to imitate a crackling fire, who slapped his palm on a drum for authentic thunder.

It sold. To *Pioneer Magazine*. Then, again, to three others in the next three years.

When Bing Crosby first became famous, I did a piece on him. Confi- dentially, it stunk. It was an adjective-loaded recital of his deeds. No umph. No personality. Last year, putting the accent on the unusual, I did another piece on Bing Crosby. The following queeriosity injection turned it into a sale:

Up until 1935 Bing never took a singing lesson! Then, suddenly, he determined to improve himself. So he hired a teacher, slaved on vocal exercises. Something went wrong. Letters poured in from his fans. Everyone wanted to know what was spoiling his voice. He imme- diately quit the lessons, and has never taken one since.

The mellow peculiar crooning quality in his voice is due to an unusual growth in the valuable Crosby throat. If you think you have such a growth, you better trot off to your nearest radio station and take an audition.

These odd insertions gave the article a literary hotfoot. It sold, immediately, to the Catholic magazine, *St. Anthony's Messenger*.

It is even easy to score if you take an everyday familiar topic and hop it up with amazing items.

Good example was a jaunt I took through Mexico. Thirty miles outside of Mexico City I came across two gigantic structures, the Pyramids of the Sun and Moon. Quickly I pounded out an article. I drooled about the beauty of the pyramids against the backdrop of a plush blue Aztec sky. I wailed about the moon, a filmy yellow evil eye, looking down upon those ruins of mystery. Naturally, it had no more chance of selling than an essay on the fragrance of spring. It came home to mother six times.

I pondered. I decided to learn more about the Mexican pyramids. I read. The research was fruitful. There was a Lord Kingsborough who devoted his life to studying the pyramids, who penned twenty-seven volumes on them at a cost of $300,000. Kingsborough's theory was that the Ten Tribes of Israel had built the pyramids. Incidently, he went insane.

A verbal tip sent me to more books, and I learned of a French archeologist who insisted the pyramids were built atop the original Garden of Eden, and displayed skeletons of Adam and Eve to prove it.

Well, hell, there it was. Blending these facts, and more, in with description, I sold the pyramid saga to *Boy's World* at a decent price, and then to *American Farm Youth*.

At this stage, if you are in a sufficiently good mood, you might agree that unusual subject matter can often turn an editor, who consumes iron ore for breakfast, into a purring creature of goodwill and charity toward all — writers.

But already I can hear you noisily swilling your ale and hammering on the table. "Zounds!" you bellow. "It's good for you to gibber about making use of nutty facts. But how in the name of so-and-so and so-and-so are we supposed to find them?"

I don't know how you're supposed to find them. But I know how I do. And maybe that'll help.

First of all, I clip. I'm better than Stecher with the scissors. I also enlist my sister, the insurance man and the blond next door to help. We clip. All of us. Madly.

I devote an entire file cabinet — green, four drawers — to cuttings. In that cabinet reposes John Hix and Robert Ripley and Strange Food Facts and Strange Liquor Facts and two dozen others. Also, feature stories from newspapers and notes copied from a dozen magazines and more books.

I never lift the facts entire. Not cricket. But they give me tips. Hell, I read in six different places about a man who was swallowed by a whale and lived to tell the story. But nobody ever devoted more than two or three lines. I wanted to know more. I wrote inquiries, read books and the net result is "He Played Jonah" to appear in *Coronet*.

Your oddity file will eventually be indispensable. It will drive you to drink, but also to endorsing grass-colored checks. Yesterday I interviewed Alexander Kerensky, father of the Russian revolution. He was here in Hollywood. I could send out the piece as a straight interview. But I'm not taking the risk. I'm doing plenty of peek-a-boo on his past, and when the article goes out, it will be filled to the gills with wonderment and the bizarre.

I'm looking through my files now. This minute. Looking for a good snapper ending that'll lay you in the aisles. Let me see. Here's a note on a gent labeled Reverend Santa Claus who resides in Slater, Missouri. So help me! And what about the fact that Christmas was banned in Massachusetts for twenty-two years. Oh, you know that? Well, maybe this'll do it. Saint Nicholas, who lived and expired in Myra, Asia, was Patron Saint of the Thieves! Underneath the latter fact is the quaint notation, "Merry Christmas" — and though it's not at all unusual, the same to you!

Down With Modesty

Phyllis A. Whitney

August 1939

I have been selling with some regularity to the love pulp, confession and juvenile fields, and during that time a number of nice editors have said a number of complimentary things about my stories. But the most repeated comment is this: "We like your characters. They're human, real and attractive."

How did the transmutation come to turn the trick? And couldn't other people learn it a bit more quickly than I had—since my characters hadn't always had reality in life?

When the answer hit me it threw all the odds and ends that have been drifting about in my mind into their proper places, and made the whole thing dovetail perfectly.

The thing that has always discouraged me in articles on depicting character is the admonition to Write About Life. From the way these fellows talk you can't help but think that the only possible way to be a writer is to spend your time hanging over the back fence, or talking to strangers on street cars, or getting Aunt Susan to tell you about her lost love. Then all you need to do is gather up your notes, literal or mental, and pack all that material into a story.

I've tried. I've wept with Aunt Susan and listened wholeheartedly while she poured out her soul. I've felt warm and virtuous and self-satisfied because she seemed to find comfort in talking it out to me. But could I get it down on paper and sell it? I could not!

I couldn't even finish the story, because on page three Aunt Susan was as dead as her lost love and there was no use in committing murder twice over.

So I thought it was me. I just wasn't a "normal" writer, since I couldn't go around gathering the sorrows of the world to my bosom in order to relay them to a palpitating public. It frequently amazes me to discover how much more my neighbors know about me than I do about them.

There are two kinds of writing minds, and they arrive at the same result by different routes. One kind can slip under Aunt Susan's nice gray pompadour with no effort at all; the other insists upon staying strictly behind its own pompadour. Mine is the latter type.

I want to be the whole show all the time. *I* want to play heroine, and the minute Aunt Sue starts trying to steal my act, I lose interest and the story goes cold in my hands. I want to write about *me* and not about the policeman on the corner, or the beggar who buys an apple for the horse. I am all my own heroines and some of my more attractive villainesses. Call me an egomaniac, or any other high-sounding term you like, but just remember that I am in awfully good company and my name — if only you and you and you would own up — is legion.

Yet the oldest advice in the world — and to a beginner the most brutal — is "write about yourself."

It looks so easy and it isn't at all. The beginner starts off in bewilderment, sounding vaguely like William Saroyan (but not enough so), and you can't sell *that* to the pulps. Then after a while he just stops writing because he can't figure out how to get himself into a pulp story. Or even into any kind of story.

So I'm going one step farther. I'm going to tell you *how* you can write about yourself, and what you can use for a handle to get started. If you're not selling, you need to know. If you are selling, you know subconsciously, but it's surprising how it speeds the thing up once you're consciously aware of what you're doing. I'll bet all the boys and girls who turn out the big wordage are aware of it.

We must begin by admitting boldly to ourselves that we are pretty swell people, that our virtues are countless and that we're not appreciated nearly so much as we should be. You'll be surprised how easy it is to convince yourself. Then when we start on the next story idea, we take one of these virtues which we prize so highly in our secret souls (and which our friends neglect) and endow our hero or heroine with it.

To return to Aunt Susan. If I had been a bright little girl, I'd have recognized that the story lay not in the lost love, but in the girl who was listening to Aunt Sue's story.

I can see myself this minute, listening warm-heartedly and generously, etc., and my sympathy is at once drawn to that girl and I could put her in a story with no trouble at all. Then, by some mysterious legerdemain, Aunt Sue would fall into place so that I could write about her too. Probably because I could visualize her thinking of *me* as sweet and unselfish and—oh, you can't pile it on too thick! And the nice part is that you can be perfectly shameless about it.

We never can be shameless about our virtues in real life. When someone says we are clever or unselfish or something, we are forced to cast down our eyes and murmur deprecations. We'd never dare admit the truth of such statements, no matter how thoroughly we agree with them.

But in fiction there's not the slightest danger of ever being caught. In my stories I can be self-sacrificing in the best heroic tradition, or I can be a "brave little thing," or I can go about enveloped in mystery and glamour, yet there's no need to hide my blushes when the story comes out in print, because no one is going to suspect that I was writing about myself. Self-sacrificing, brave, glamorous—*me*? I can hear the assorted guffaws of my friends. But they don't know, you see, and I do.

You see, I needn't actually possess all the virtues I lay claim to and that I write about. I need only be firmly convinced that I possess them. And so far I have yet to find a virtue I can't convince myself I possess.

I am a little speck of this and a little mite of that, and when I turn the creative (I use the word politely, not literally) microscope upon those mites and specs, I get—a check for a hundred dollars.

These virtues may even be qualities which look decidedly like faults to other people. So long as I can glorify them to myself, that's all that's necessary.

Step into the laboratory for a moment while I write a scene. First I'll give it to you as it might actually have happened; as the girl's husband might have seen it.

I can't remember now what she was sore about, but she was plenty mad. And when she gets mad her nose gets red, her hairpins come out, and her voice goes up. She stood there and yelled at me and stamped her foot. I said, "Sh! the neighbors!" and she screeched, "If you treat me like this, the neighbors ought to know!" So I laughed and that did it. She picked up the thing nearest her and threw it at me. Missed, of course. But at least a man would have picked up something that could do some damage, like a milk bottle, maybe, or a can of spinach. But she, glaring at me with a you-brute-I-hope-this-maims-you look in her eyes, picked up—a loaf of bread. I ducked and it hit the wall. The wrapper broke and slices flew every which way, and she burst into tears.

That, probably, would be the truth of the matter, but fortunately we don't have to worry about truth in fiction. Now let me go on with the scene, coloring it in my own mind so that it might be used in a story.

She was so angry she was trembling, but she did wish she hadn't thrown that silly loaf of bread. It would be sliced bread, at that. Still, she was a little proud of herself too. She'd been quite magnificent in her anger and her points had gone home with what she felt sure was a barbed wit. Come to think of it, she'd been courageous to stand up to him at all, considering that she was so little and that he could squash her with one thumb if he ever wanted to.

She put up her chin and waited a moment for it to stop trembling, before going into the bathroom mirror to see how she looked. That was a little disappointing, because the effect wasn't quite so magnificent as she had hoped. Some of her hairpins were coming out and her nose was decidedly pink. She went back to the kitchen and sat sadly down on the floor among the bread slices and began to roll little pellets of dough between her fingers. When she heard his step on the porch the tears spilled over and she wept softly and not too unhappily. She knew she looked little and pitiful and appealing, and that when he came in to kiss her she would forgive him.

Sickening, isn't it? Yet I could make quite a real person out of that girl because I'd be seeing her as I wanted to see her.

It works in all sorts of ways. Assume, for example, that you are one of these tall and lanky gals with a longing to be petite. So you make your heroine a fragile little thing whom the hero can tuck under one arm with no trouble at all, and for some 5,500 words you have the time of your life. Yet in your next story you're likely to find yourself one of these Diana-like affairs who goes striding gloriously through life, treating smaller women with the utmost scorn.

In last week's story I was feminine and docile and yielding. In this week's I am an impregnable fortress and the hero has a heck of a time. But I enjoy it straight through, and because I can find in myself little snatches of all these contradictory characteristics and can sympathize with each one in turn, I can make my heroines come to life.

What would I like my hero to say to me? Ah! there I can go to town. Real, live heroes are so durned inarticulate, but let me get one wedged in my typewriter, and can I make him talk!

Listen, you hombres who write westerns! Next time you get stuck in a place where there has to be a love scene (because the editor said, "love interest"), try it yourselves. Think about the last attractive blond you met (or if you like 'em dark, that's all right too). What would she say to you in a love scene? I mean what would you *like* her to say?

What virtue or characteristic of *yours* would you like to have fascinate her especially? All right, give that characteristic to your hero and when the love scene comes along you may surprise yourself by how real it will be. And how real—surprisingly—the girl will be. And all because you started thinking about her consciously in connection with yourself.

There's too much modesty in the world, anyway. Down with it!

Now let's take *your* case. You came home from that bridge game last night and your wife remarked rather bitterly that Mrs. Tremont was only trying to be friendly and you didn't need to shut up like a clam for the entire evening. You don't argue with your wife. You know better. But the injustice of the accusation rankles bitterly.

You thought Mrs. T. a silly old hen, and you don't like to talk unless you have something to say. So your next hero is strong and silent, and the idle chittering of females leaves him unmoved. Until he meets a woman who knows how to be quiet, admires the wise things he says when he does speak, and respects his silences. The story will be good because you'll understand that fellow through and through, and by the time it's written the rankling will be gone.

Or *your* case. That girl who came to your house last night and waited while you read her manuscript. She was a wistfully charming little thing in her rose-colored dress that set off her dark hair so nicely. She was young and eager and she listened with such flattering attention to every word you spoke.

The radio was playing dreamily in the background and you two were quite alone in the living room. (Your wife was out in the kitchen washing dishes.) Now, you are a decent sort of guy. While you have had your moments, you are good backbone American stuff, and you are fond of your wife and your home and the whole pattern of your life. But that doesn't mean you can't appreciate a charming picture when you see one.

It might even cross your mind (though only fleetingly, of course) that it might be a pleasant experiment to kiss that soft, trusting little mouth. Naturally you don't. If you did, the girl would be shocked and leave your house at once. Your wife would be shocked and leave for Reno. Your life would be completely disrupted and you'd get no writing done for at least six months. If ever. And all for a sample of lipstick. Better frustration than fervor.

So after a while the girl takes her manuscript and goes home. The story was pretty bad anyway, but she looked nice with her long, slim legs and the graceful way she moved her hands. And you sigh and go off to bed.

But *are* you frustrated? Not you. You are a writer.

The next morning you have a rendezvous with a girl in a rose-colored dress. Three double-spaces down on your typewriter. And this time there is no normal timidity to hold you back. You are a man of action. You handle the situation as an expert should, and are not at all surprised when the girl returns your interest. After all, you're the hero, aren't you, and you take such things for granted. Miraculously your wife doesn't leave you, for miraculously you have no wife. At the end of a number of hours you love, leave or marry the girl, according to the dictates of your plot, and she's off your mind for good.

Whereupon your wife conveniently reappears and summons you for lunch. You sit down to a plate of your favorite beef stew and find yourself ravenously hungry. Inhibitions? Frustrations? Suppressed desires? No, thanks — not for you.

Instead you very neatly knock off two birds with one stone. By putting yourself into your stories you not only make your characters real, sympathetic and dimensional, but you also fool your subconscious into thinking you are doing a lot of things you shouldn't do, and thus keep it both contented and caged.

POSTSCRIPT TO *DOWN WITH MODESTY*

I had forgotten that I'd ever written this piece, and I read it with some astonishment. This is not *my* "voice" today.

I was a very young thirty-three then and had not yet published my first book. Now I am ninety and writing my seventy-fifth book. That is quite a gap.

However, though this writing seems a bit slangy and skittish, I was making some good points about using ourselves and "bits and pieces" of our lives. I know myself a little better by this time, and I have collected many more of those bits of experience. And I use them in my writing — as all writers of fiction must.

At least I showed a sense of humor, and I was practicing what I preached — that loaf of bread! I really did throw a loaf of sliced bread at my husband (in a rage) in those long ago days. (An action which seems slightly undignified to me now!)

It had been interesting to go back and visit a young, beginning writer — someone whom I hardly remember.

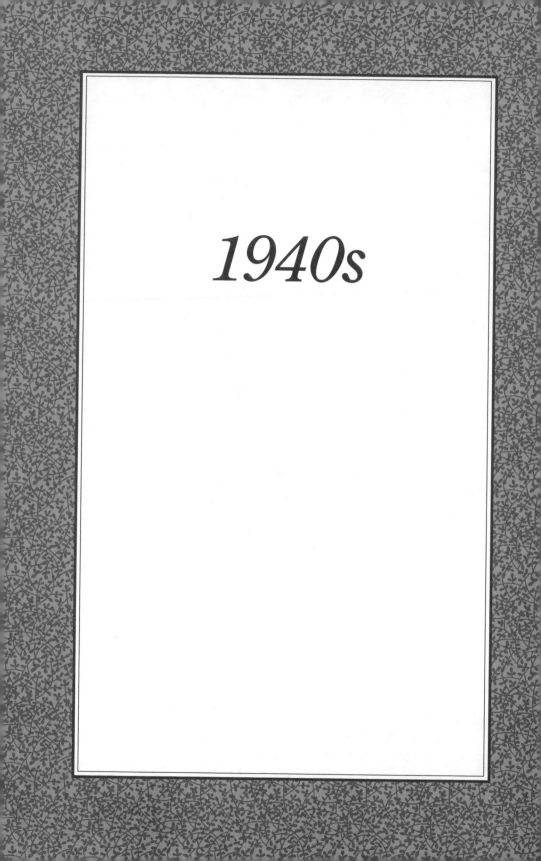

1940s

Setting the Pace

Arthur Gordon

July 1941

W hat makes a good story good?" That's a question writers must ask themselves constantly if they want to succeed at this tough trade of freelancing. They must ask themselves, and they must also answer themselves, because nobody else is going to tell them.

Oh, an editor may say pontifically—as I sometimes do myself—"A good story is one that carries the reader, and a bad story is one that the reader has to carry." But this is no help unless you know *why* the good story carries the reader and *why* the bad one doesn't.

That "why?" is a pretty big one.

One thing, however, must be plain, even to the beginner with hardly a hundred rejection slips to his credit, and that is the fact that the boring point of his readers is very low. The reader's attention is like a restless sheep; it will wander at the slightest provocation, or even at no provocation at all. Furthermore, once this attention is lost, even for a moment, it rarely comes back. So the art of storytelling boils down to capturing the reader's attention at the outset and holding it like grim death all the way through.

This has been said before, but it's everlastingly true. I know, because besides freelancing now and then I am an associate editor at the big women's magazine *Good Housekeeping*. I read Lord knows how many stories a month, and if the manuscript doesn't hold me, I don't hold it—long.

"All right," you say, "but how can we make the manuscript hold you—or any other jaded editor?"

I have noticed, after reading manuscripts professionally for several years, that there *is* something which nearly all successful stories have in common, something which I call *pace*. I call it *pace* because I can't think of a better word to convey the idea of constant, unflagging, steady *progression* from the beginning of the story to the end. Call it what you will—suspense, drama, or whatnot—it's the vital force that keeps the story moving through the reader's consciousness against the natural inertia that's working against it.

I call it pace, and in this article I want to give you one specific tip that may help you solve the endless problem of setting the pace in your stories and keeping the yarn moving at that pace—or even an ever-accelerating one—right up to the last line.

The tip is this: *Plan each scene of your story as if the scene were a complete story in itself.* Think of each scene as a dramatic episode in which the suspense mounts exactly as it does in the story itself, an episode finally terminated with a sharp, pungent curtain or punch line which will carry the reader over the lapse of time or change of background into the next scene, which then builds up in the same way. Emerson said once that every poem should be made up of lines that are poems. Well, every story should be made up of scenes that are stories.

The length of the scene, of course, and the number of scenes in the story will vary with the style of the individual writer. In general, it seems to me, action stories need short, terse scenes, while character development and subjective, stream-of-consciousness stories can develop more leisurely, in longer, more elaborate sections. But this is a dangerous generalization. The only safe one is that if the scenes in a story are successful, the story is likely to be too.

Another advantage of this scene technique is that it forces you to outline your story in advance, a dull but very necessary chore. The road to hell is paved with writers who start a story—and sometimes I think this is the rule rather than the exception—without knowing the end of it. I have heard of writers, and even known a few, who deliberately get their characters into situations and then "let them work themselves out." But the editor is usually just as bewildered as the characters by this hope-for-the-best technique and he, after all, is the one who buys the story.

The other day I came across some of my original story outlines—I mean the very first thought-sequences on paper. Some were written on the backs of old envelopes; others were typed in presentable fashion. Perhaps the most typical was one called "Family Affair," which eventually appeared in *Good Housekeeping*. It was a story with only three major characters: a young husband, his wife, and a pretty fellow office worker named Midge whom he invites for a weekend at his home in the suburbs—without consulting his wife in advance. The minor characters were the two small children of the young couple, a maid named Opal, a dog called Mrs. Chips, and an ancient automobile named Lazarus.

The outline wasted no words. Here it is (if I can read my own writing) verbatim:

Family Affair

1. Young husband gets off train Friday night. He is a commuter, hot, tired, worried about something he has to tell his wife. Wife fails to meet him, but finally shows up. She has been at beach. He resents this, and they bicker about it. He learns she has overdrawn her checkbook again. More quarreling. He finally says he has asked Midge Roberts, pretty co-worker, down for weekend, arriving next day. Wife blows up, walks out on him.

2. Husband struggles all Saturday morning with unfamiliar routine. Puts baby to sleep on porch. Struggles to entertain older child. He's too proud to phone his friends to find out where his wife is. Finally goes to station to meet office gal in terrible thunderstorm.

3. She arrives. Is surprised, but not displeased to find wife missing. She is pretty, fairly hard-boiled, unsympathetic. Definitely not the mother type, she nevertheless tries to play that role with the children. Various misadventures befall her. But that evening she gets into evening clothes, looks luscious, begins to tell husband his wife doesn't appreciate him. He loves it. She does a job on him, and somehow he finds himself kissing her.

4. Maid comes in, says baby is sick. Husband, terrified, finds baby red in face, very hot. He can't find thermometer. Midge is no help at all; he finally sends her for the doctor. Just after Midge leaves, the wife reappears. She hasn't been far away, has been keeping an eye on her husband. She takes one look at baby, diagnoses case as bad sunburn, nothing more. Husband, penitent and vastly relieved is forgiven. Midge goes back to town. Family life is too much for her.

This, I realize, is pretty crude, but it is the first of the many painful steps in getting a story ready for marketing. I do not show it here as a model outline—far from it. I merely show it as an example of story-planning in terms of scenes *from the very beginning.*

That sort of planning can be apparent in even the sketchiest outline. Another story outline of mine has exactly sixty-three words, to wit: Boy, member of family of camera fiends, lives in ski resort village. To village comes New York glamour girl, escorted by crack Austrian skier. Boy meets girl, hates Austrian, gets into ski race with him and loses—because Austrian trips him at a crucial moment. Boy's peppery old aunt is only witness; she clinches her story by producing camera evidence. Whereupon boy wins girl.

"Heavens," you may say at this point, "how could such a hackneyed and obvious plot ever sell anywhere?" Well, that fact is that it was too hackneyed for the big magazines. But the *Toronto Star* bought it. And, as you can see, no great effort was expended. It was just a matter of draping a few presentable ornaments on a very weather-beaten framework.

So much for "plotting" in scenes. Now, what about the far more difficult task of making the scenes good ones?

One requisite for writing good scenes is the ability to recognize bad ones. One way to do this is to select a random scene in one of your unsuccessful stories—not the *climax* scene, because you've probably made that as dramatic as possible already. But choose a fairly important one. Now, mentally divorce it from the rest of the yarn. Then begin to ask yourself questions. *Is it really necessary?* Does it drag? Does the dialogue (if any) quicken toward the end? Could it be shorter? Does it seem hurried? Could you add some twist, some bit of repartee that will close the scene with a snap and send the story whirling on its way?

Questions like these, honestly asked and answered, may prove both embarrassing and useful. Embarrassing because they reveal the weaknesses of your story technique—useful because they enable you to improve it. And don't excuse yourself by saying, "Oh, I can't judge my own work." Nonsense. Every successful writer can and does judge his own work. If he didn't, the work wouldn't be successful.

The last lines of a scene are the most important. Every actor and every playwright knows the value of a good curtain line. The same is true in magazine fiction. I have heard it argued that too many curtain lines break the continuity of a story. I don't agree. If you hit the reader with a good, solid punch line at the end of a scene, you knock him right into the next scene, which is where you want him. Here is a crude analogy. Did you ever, as a child, amuse yourself by spinning a wheel of your upturned bicycle? Well, if you did, you didn't take hold of the wheel each time and shove it ponderously forward. You gave it a succession of smart slaps—and it went much faster.

Of course, a curtain line isn't absolutely essential. Here is a scene in which there is none. It's a fine scene from a fine novelette—Ketti Fring's "The Man Who Waited."

By the river that night George was sitting on an old forgotten bench, waiting. A few cars passed, and finally one of them stopped, and he knew it was she, the way the car's door was banged to so firmly, with so much spirit. That was Fremy, all right. Every night she did it that way. He loved that spirit, and it made him sick to think how he was going to have to deaden it tonight. But it had to be. He couldn't go on letting this girl be so crazy about him. He couldn't tell her why, either. He couldn't take the chance. His conscience, his sense of duty, was one thing he wouldn't allow to be interfered with. And Fremy being as she was, and in love, would be capable of trying anything.

She never knew in what mood she would find him, so always she approached a little cautiously. Tonight the curve of his body, the dangling arm, the drooped chin — tonight he looked miserable and a little mean, maybe. No matter, though — she had to say it at last.

"George?"

"Yes." He nodded her the word, but without addressing it to her with his eyes.

"George, there's something I want to tell you. I couldn't wait to get here to tell you tonight. I've got to tell you. I know I shouldn't, but it's on my heart's tip-tongue all the time. I can't help it, and I know it's — "

"Go on, say it," said George, stretching. It was almost as though he had yawned right in her face — more, in her heart. Yes, that brutal. "Go on, say it. You love me."

The chill of it stunned her, so that she caught her breath and gasped a little.

Fremy had been born a lady. She hadn't quite lived it down. She had been trying hard to, because she hated ladies, ladies and their sachet packets. But tonight, in this hurt, the lady in her blood stiffened and made her rise and turn and go away, through the trees, back to the car.

In the car, still for a moment she waited. Waited in a dreadful silence. He must come after her. Of course he must. He must explain that it was just a mood, that it was just — well, something.

She watched through the trees for a movement, a sign. But it didn't happen that way. There was no movement, no voice calling. Nothing. After a while she started the car and drove away.

There is no curtain line in that scene, yet it is very vivid, and the last line has a finality about it that puts a definite period to the episode. Here is another example that does have a punch line at the end; this is taken from my "The Wolves of Darkness." The situation is this: A married man, who has been having an affair with a woman, decides to break it off and go back to his wife. But before he leaves, the woman asks to see him once more, so he stops at her apartment . . . .

Serena was waiting for him, as she had waited so many times since that rainy night in July. Now the apartment was no longer strange to him; it was as intimate and familiar as Serena herself. Now it shared their secret, had shared it from the beginning. It was almost, he thought, as if the apartment expected them to be lovers. But this time they did not kiss, did not even touch hands.

"Sit down, Jonny," Serena said; "I have something to say to you."

He sat down warily, watching her as she leaned against the mantel, stretching her arms along it in the sinuous feline gesture he knew so well. Her face was quite calm, her voice unhurried. Watching her, he felt the old attraction tugging at him. But he sat still, waiting.

"This afternoon," she said, "I wrote a letter to my husband in Washington. I told him I was leaving him—for good. He has known about us, of course. But he always assumed that I would come back to him. Now I have told him that I am not coming back."

Never moving, Jonathan said, "Why did you tell him that, Serena? Why this sudden burning of bridges?"

She moved impatiently away from the mantelpiece. "Because I would rather be with you," she said.

"You know that's impossible," he told her. "I have a wife and child. My loyalties belong to them."

She laughed a little at that. "I should say your loyalties are some-what divided now."

He shook his head. "Don't go sentimental on me, Serena," he said angrily.

Her eyes narrowed a little as she turned and faced him. "You expect to see your wife tonight?" she said.

"Yes."

"Will you give her a message for me?"

"Perhaps," Jonathan said, and a small chill wind of premonition blew between his shoulder blades.

"Tell her, then," said Serena, "that in due course I am going to bear a child. Your child. Tell her that for me, will you?"

Most authors, of course, "write in scenes" whether they are conscious of it or not. One advantage of consciously using the scene technique is that it helps a writer with the troublesome element of time. The action of a story frequently covers days, if not weeks or even years. Many writers find these transitions awkward, to say the least. I have had beginners say to me despairingly, "But how can I get my characters over this time lapse? I'm so afraid the reader won't be able to follow me."

This self-consciousness on the part of the writer is more likely to destroy the continuity of the story than any so-called time lapse. But by planning the curtain lines of the scenes to coincide with the time breaks, the writer can avoid this mental hazard. It helps the reader, too, to sense the climax and prepare himself subconsciously to go on with the story in a different set of characters — with no hesitation at all. But remember, the scene itself has to be a dramatic entity; if it ends lamely, the transition may seem forced and awkward.

Most of what I have said here will seem obvious to the experienced magazine fiction writer — and perhaps even to the beginner. But as an editor, I have long noticed that the most obvious rules are usually the ones that writers most cheerfully ignore.

So when you think back over this article and say to yourself, "Writing in scenes. Why, of course. How elementary!" just stop for a minute and take out your latest story — the one that didn't sell — and go through it *scene by scene*, honestly checking the dull ones, the ones that drag, the ones that end tamely. Mind, I say honestly! Then count the check marks. Then say, "How elementary," if you still want to!

Plots the Triple-O Way

John Nanovic

The Writer's 1945 Yearbook

There's more than one way to skin a cat. And there's more than one way to build a plot.

That's where the trouble began. If there were only one way to build a plot, and no other, then writing a story would be fairly simple. You would build a plot exactly according to the rule of plot building. But somebody found that there were variations in building a plot, and, by careful work, these variations gradually grew up into different methods and systems of plotting, and writing troubles grew accordingly.

Generally, the more complicated a plotting system can be, the more perfect it is considered. If your plot structure can, by means of subheadings, Roman numerals, Arabic figures, capital letters, parenthetical divisions, look quite complicated, and cover everything you have in the story from the opening sentence to the word count at the end, then you're in business as the Plot King (two for ten dollars).

Right now, let me stick my neck out. I will not argue about the quality of such plots. The only trouble is that editors (and I've had a dozen years being one) do not generally buy plots for publication.

The purpose of a plot is not to be impressive, but to be practical. A fancy plot may look like something to the writer, but the editor never gets a chance to see it, so he is not at all impressed by your great efforts in that direction. The plot is simply a reason for writing your story. If it gives you a good, strong reason, a solid base, you have a good chance for a story. If it doesn't, you're in trouble.

Perhaps we can start on that basis. The plot is merely the framework of the story; it is not the story itself. Therefore, let us make the plot be no more than a framework; let us leave the trimmings, the angles, the color, to the story writing. Let us give the plot only the essentials of the story.

Plotting is simple if you can only keep it that way.

Plotting can be brought down to just three little words — the Triple-O of story plotting.

Here they are:

1. Object
2. Obstacles
3. Outcome

That is your story, no matter how you twist or turn it, or how you color it. Your hero sets out to get something. The obstacles that are in his path are the things that make your story. The outcome of his battle with these obstacles gives you your climax.

You can compare this to almost anything you want, and you'll get the same result. In a race, it's your start, the distance between the start and the finish line, and how the runner finishes that means anything to you. If you are building a tunnel, it's the object of digging through that mountain; the obstacles in your path, and the success of holing it through.

The fact that this is so simple makes it look weak. The fundamental purpose of a plot is not to write your story for you. It is merely to give you a purpose in writing. It doesn't give you all the trimmings; it doesn't give you any of the trimmings. Purposely so. You furnish the trimmings to suit the particular story that you are writing in the story itself, not in the plot.

It is surprising how effective the system is, too, when put into practice. It serves equally well for a short-short or a novel. You simply add to any of its points, to add to length or strength.

On novel-length stories, the Triple-O is just a start. When Lester Dent gets to work on a Doc Savage novel, he doesn't start his writing with just this plot germ and base 40,000 words on it. Dent has this own method which completes the job of putting Doc through his exciting experiences. But the Triple-O is the base.

1. OBJECT

Clark Savage, Jr., read his father's will in which a double-crossing act of a former partner was revealed so that Clark Savage, Jr., might avenge the act.

2. OBSTACLES

The only way to avenge this was to find the guilty partner and prove that guilt—proof that had to be gotten from the land of the ancient Mayans. The obstacles that beset Doc were many, both natural and those put in by design by the villain. Whether these obstacles were two or two hundred depend entirely on how Les Dent wrote his story. He could stretch a few incidents out, or he could use his fertile imagination to advantage, as he did, and sow obstacles by the hundreds.

3. OUTCOME

Doc overcame the obstacles to his goal. He uncovered the evidence that cleared his father's name and got the heritage that was there for him when this was accomplished.

Neither Les Dent nor any other writer will begin to write a novel on such a skimpy outline of action. This, of course, is *not* an outline; it's a plot. Once you've built your plot, you can dress your outline as you will; either very complete, or just hitting the high spots of your story. What you do with your outline depends on your method of writing.

Only, for goodness sake, don't kid yourself into thinking that an outline is a plot. Your plot is basic, like bread. Your outline is the dinner, with all the courses in place.

Walter Gibson, in doing *The Shadow* novels for the past fourteen or fifteen years, starts with a no more complicated plot.

As an example, *The Shadow* gets a message asking for protection. We have the object—to protect whoever it is seeking such protection by removing the menace.

The obstacles? Attempts on the part of the villain to kill The Shadow; attempts to kill the victim; false clues; perhaps another crime to mislead The Shadow.

The outcome? Arrest and disposition of menace in one way or another.

Walter Gibson may start with this bare plot, but his outline is more complete. Gibson sometimes spends as much time on preparing the complete outline of his story as he will in writing it, but the essential plot, as shown here, is the guide for the outline; it is the theme, the thread, which keeps the whole story together, no matter what cross-plot or counter-plot there may be. If you keep the Triple-O in mind, you'll be certain to keep your cross-purposes in the story in line with its theme.

For the quickest, most forceful example of just how effective this method of plotting is, use it for a short-short. That's all you need; nothing else. You want the purpose or object; you want the obstacles in the path; and you want the outcome. Whether the outcome is a straight one, or whether it's got a kicker in it, is immaterial. Your method is the same. It is essential.

This plot-construction method doesn't hold the author down hard enough to the job at hand; it may let him stray. If it does, I believe that is good for the story, because it lets the author's mind stray along the channels which suit the story best while it is being written. *It does not bind the writer to a predetermined style of writing; nor to a stiff and hard plan of action.* There is enough room for him to bear down on a new angle that may come up, because he is certain of not losing his main theme.

The Triple-O serves as a continuing thread on which your story hangs. Because it is so simple, there is less chance of your straying from it. And because you need not put too much attention on that part of your story, you can put it on the writing, or characters or background, or whatever you wish.

And, no matter what sort of story you wish to write, you have only that one method to follow. It is adaptable to any type of story that you like to do.

You may be a faithful follower of the well-known "thirty-six" situations, or you may prefer any one of the other forms of creating plots, of picking out the circumstances from odd pages of a book, or by successive drawing of cards, each with its own situation. Or you may prefer the method of reading several papers, carefully noting any situations which might lend themselves to story ideas.

Whether you use card indexes, scrap books, personal experiences or whatever it is, the Triple-O will give your plot idea a base to stand on. It will cement your thought firmly; it will make it so broad that you can place on it any other thoughts or ideas that may come to you.

And if you've ever struggled with a plot that calls for "Event Number 1" or "Situation Number 5," or anything like that, when you felt, all the time, that the story should be one that depended on its mood, rather than on its physical structure, for success, you'll realize the advantage of using this broad base, and then writing the story as you wish to write it, without regard for the proper sequence of situations or any of the other routine things.

So long as you establish, in the opening of your story, the object of your yarn, you will be in a position to go ahead and write it in whatever mood you wish because all your writing will have to be for the sole purpose of obtaining that objective.

What could be simpler? You have just one thought, one goal, to write to. How does your hero get what he's after? How does each successive victory bring him closer and closer to his goal?

To test this plot method further, try it in reverse. Take any good story that you've read, and bring it down to these bare essentials; then you'll see how extremely simple, yet how very effective, the Triple-O method can be.

What Happened?

Pauline Bloom

March 1945

That's the first thing people want to know. What happened? What happened? A small knot of people becomes a larger and larger one. Why? Because everybody wants to know what happened. After they are assured that something has indeed happened, is happening and will continue to happen, they ask, "Was the girl pretty?" "Was the boy brave?" "Did right triumph over wrong?" "Did it all end happily?" Otherwise, they don't care. Truly, they don't care.

This doesn't apply merely to the vast millions who buy the pulp and comic magazines and the comic strips, but to readers of fiction at all intellectual levels. Whoever your audience, the "What happened?" in a story is the most important ingredient, and that is what you should measure first into your mixing bowl, before you even begin to think of the other materials.

There is no substitute for story value. From the pulpiest of bang-bang to the classics which have survived centuries of competition and changing literary fashions, fiction is weighted primarily for its story interest. And that's as it should be.

If you take a long view of fiction down through the history of literature, you will see that the stories which are still read, and which will continue to be read for many years to come, are those in which things have happened. Scheherazade, Homer, the anonymous compilers of the Bible as well as Fielding, Dumas, de Maupassant, Tolstoy, Dostoyevski, Dickens, Ibsen—all were expert craftsmen who built their stories on firm foundations of sustained conflict.

In each of these periods there must have been long-haired dilettantes who labored over a piece of mood or a fragment of a character. But their work has lacked the vitality necessary for survival. We hear an occasional piece of music which offers rhythm, nothing but rhythm. We see paintings which are studies of texture, just texture. Such art representations have their catalytic function, their period of usefulness, but they are too anemic to endure. The very lifeblood of fiction is conflict and the events which grow out of that conflict.

Characterization, pace, style, atmosphere and all the other bugaboos which keep writers awake nights all have their place, but it is not first. The story comes first. It is very easy for a young, impressionable writer, in his horrified recoiling from "mechanics," to develop such an infatuation for any one of these other writing elements, that he becomes blinded to honest, basic story values. This is a healthy, normal phenomenon if it happens early in a writer's life and lasts a short time—like puppy love. But anyone old enough and mature enough to earn his living by writing must discard this adolescent point of view and go about the serious business of learning his trade.

How, then, shall we make this story element strong enough? My personal experience is that the most outstanding feature of a story is the one which precipitated the writing of it.

If I become intrigued by a character and submit to his blandishments, I know I'm doomed. Struggle as I may, the result is not a story but a character sketch, and there is not much market for a character sketch. True, there's always the *New Yorker*, but how many writers do they support? Every dilettante, every beginner in the country, writes *New Yorker* pieces which never appear in the *New Yorker*.

If I start with mood, an atmosphere, a pervading tone, I'm just as lost even when I do achieve a good piece of writing. Editors don't want a piece of good writing which has a mood. And don't blame the editors. Readers, too, don't want a good piece of writing which has a mood. But they all want a good story with a well-sustained, integrally motivated mood. The way to build such a story is to start with the story, not with the mood.

"But," you will say, "suppose I get a really good idea for a character, a situation, a story atmosphere, or anything else of that sort. Are you suggesting that I just throw it away?"

My answer is no, don't throw it away. File it away either in your mind or in your notebook, and forget about it. Leave it to your subconscious. Have no illusions to its salability. File it away and forget about it. It is only a small fragment of a story which you cannot use, until the exactly right time comes for using it. Wait until this time comes.

Start your story plan with a conflict, a good, vital conflict between your main character and a powerful force either outside or inside of himself. Let the nature of this conflict dictate the main characteristics of your chief protagonist. Let the nature of your conflict dictate the subsidiary characters, the pace, the length, the atmosphere, the treatment, the style, the mood, the beginning, the middle and the end.

If these subsidiary elements do not come immediately to mind, you rummage through your files for what you need, just as a creative hat designer will first block a hat body into one certain shape and style, then look through boxes of feathers, ribbons, flowers and whatnots which will be exactly suitable to the already blocked hat—suitable in line, texture, color, mood, etc. You hold your developed conflict in one hand, and you try out various items of character, situation, mood, backgrounds, atmosphere, until you find exactly the right ones.

Here's how it works out with me in practice:

I sit down at my typewriter, roll in a fresh sheet of yellow paper, shut out of my mind all the gnawing little details of personal existence and decide to build a story. Conflict. Well, suppose I take the conflict in a man's mind between his love and loyalty for his wife, and his integrity as a human being under her growing domination.

This conflict immediately gives me several clues to the two main characters. Pa is not a Caspar Milquetoast, but an intelligent, warmhearted human being who has merely been following the road of least resistance. Ma is not mean or vicious. She has just fallen into the habit of thinking herself infallibly wise—always.

Pa being the person he is, his rebellion should come about as the result of an injustice or injustices inflicted not only on himself, but on someone else too. Who? His own child, his son, who is clinging to an adolescence he should have outgrown years ago without the pressure of his mother's thumb. A girl? Yes. Ma doesn't approve of the match.

But there should be some wider implications to add vista and importance to the story. Suppose the woman has somehow made herself a power in the community and has then abused that power?

At this point I remember a clipping which I had filed away several years before. It had to do with a postmaster who summarily moved his post office to some outlying district most inconvenient to everyone in the village but himself. I checked with a lawyer friend and discovered that under certain conditions the law would be on the postmaster's side.

Further rummaging revealed the fact that there were interesting variations between the rate of pay, qualifications and duties of postmasters depending on the location of their office.

So Ma is the postmaster of a small, fourth-class post office which she rules with an iron hand in a steel glove. She says no, Willie cannot marry the girl he loves, and Willie hasn't the gumption to stand up to her. When it suits her convenience, she picks up the post office from the village and moves it into her gas station five miles out, putting in a stock of soft drinks and frankfurters on shelves erected by Pa and Willie.

Pa doesn't like it, but the habit of twenty-five years is on him, and Ma is a handsome, basically good woman, an inspired cook, and is most interesting to study in her maneuvering mood. There. Pa is a kind of an introspective, thoughtful person, though a simple, uneducated one, and he certainly needs an outlet with the kind of life he leads. Something not highbrow, of course, but that would still enable him to outwit his clever wife.

My eyes roam to the bookshelf over my desk: *Roget's Thesaurus, Bartlett's Quotations, World Almanac* — that's it. Pa is addicted to the almanac. He spends leisure moments marveling over this informational potpourri. This hobby crams his head with odd bits of knowledge which at first only irritate Ma, but which eventually prove to be her doom.

Pa gives her plenty of rope. It is she herself who twists it around her own neck with her stubbornness. He lets her move the post office. He lets her pull wires to promote it from fourth class to third class so that she can appoint him her assistant. But when she discovers that whereas as fourth-class postmistress she just rode along on her original appointment, her promotion to a third-class postmastership promptly subjects her to a civil service test, things are not so good with Ma. She is not the civil service test type.

With the help of the wisdom and knowledge acquired via the almanac through the years of his henpecked existence, Pa emerges as a third-class postmaster. He moves the post office back to the village where it belongs, leaving the house and the gas station to Willie and Pearl, who are about to return from their honeymoon, also through Pa's subtle machinations. And a subdued Ma reaches for the almanac so that at the next examination she can perhaps qualify as Pa's assistant. This story, under the name "Ma Flunks Out," appeared in *Woman's Day*.

As you see, the conflict is boss. The conflict dictates everything. If it does, all the other story elements fall neatly into place. There is movement. There is a good story.

Start with a conflict, and develop your story floor by floor. This done, you can turn to the decorating, the actual writing and embellishment of the story.

At this point and at this point only you can pamper your temperamental whims, use your own particular methods for courting inspiration. She will respond, don't you fear. But never, never give her free rein during the building process. That part of the job is just not her province. Not only will she botch it all up, but she will bewitch you so that you will be unable to see the most glaring faults in the structure, and you will cordially hate any person who points them out.

The things which you as a writer want to say, the values which you want to convey, will come through much more effectively through the medium of a story which is based on conflict, in which each event grows inevitably out of the last and pulls the reader just as inevitably into the next development in the unfolding of the story.

Whether it's a three-year-old begging for a story, a high school freshman with an armful of comics, a maid waiting impatiently for the latest confession magazine, or Einstein absorbed in a detective book, they all want to know exactly the same thing.

When a reader — any reader — looks at the first page of a story — any kind of story — the question in his mind is, "What happened?" It's your job as a writer to tell him what happened.

The Ten Deadly Sins

David X. Manners

August 1946

Five days a week, seven hours a day, I sit at an editorial desk in one of New York's largest publishing houses. Often, it seems I sit there longer than that, particularly when the manuscripts are bad. And they do get fragrantly bad at times. Yet, willy-nilly, after I read a story I write a report on it, including a comment which I hope may be helpful to the author in the future.

I do that, partly out of the goodness of my heart, but mostly because my house needs stories urgently. And so, where I might be tempted to pass off my comment with a simple, "lousy," "terrible" or "this smells," I restrain myself and try to point out exactly the shortcomings that keep the yarn from ringing the cashtill.

A well-known psychiatrist once said that the only way we know what normal human behavior is, is by observing abnormal behavior. By tagging the bad, he asserted, we automatically set up the standards of what is good.

Why not follow a similar tack and derive what a good story is by studying the ones that have gone off the trolley? With that approach in mind I checked over my rejection slips. Analyzing them, I found that certain basic faults occur over and over in the stories that make editors doze, along about four in the afternoon.

Let's start right at the beginning of a story.

1. IT HAS NO NARRATIVE HOOK

A narrative hook is called by many different names, but all it means is that there's something interesting or intriguing at the beginning of the story to catch your interest and make you want to go on to page 2. It's important that the hook be in the first paragraph, or better yet, right in the first sentence. It's a basic gimmick not only of fiction writing, but of all writing, yet it's surprising how many authors — professional ones too — often forget it.

There are a variety of ways in which interest may be won at the beginning of a story. The most common way is by indicating that someone is in a jam. I've done it in some of my own stories in just so many words: "Joe Blotz was in trouble." That's enough. For nothing intrigues the human race so much as to hear someone is about to get his ears cropped, and they'll be sure to go on to page 2 to get the gory details.

Another way to hook interest at the start is by unusually striking writing or description. I remember a Dorothy B. Hughes's novel that begins by comparing a certain character's eyebrows to caterpillars writhing. That's probably not anything near what she actually wrote, but it will give you an idea of what I mean.

Another trick that you can use is just the reverse of the trouble one. In this case, you picture your character as sitting on top of the world. Everything is just perfect. Nothing could be better. In fact things are so good it's pretty clear to magazine readers that it won't last long until trouble develops.

Still another way to cadge interest is, strangely enough, by starting off with a simple statement. You might say, "Women are ornery creatures and cause nothing but grief."

Make the statement, and then lead into your story. Any statement will do. They don't have to be true.

There are plenty other methods. Study stories you like, and you'll see how they do it. And you've got to do it. You can be subtle about it, if you wish, and in slicks you will be, but it's got to be there.

2. IT'S CONFUSED

You start reading this story and you can't figure out what in the devil it's all about. The author himself probably didn't know what he wanted to say. Or maybe he achieves confusion by throwing a dozen characters at you in the first page. These characters will invariably each have a first and last name, and be called by one part of the time, and the other the rest of the time.

Another trick is to have all your characters have similar sounding names. Jack Jordan, James Yordan, Zack Jackson and Mack Jason should be enough to give any reader the willies. I got these out of an actual story that came in my editorial pile.

Still another good source of confusion is to keep back facts from the reader. Conceal things. Don't tell him what the hero's background is, or what he's up to. Some writers think they are being literary and pretty hot stuff by being devious. They'll probably cool off while chewing on a rejection slip.

3. IT'S TRITE

I once had an art teacher who would upbraid me for painting a model's blouse red when it was red.

"What's the idea painting that girl's blouse red?" he'd say. "Everybody knows it's red. Get the other colors in there—the purples, the whites, the blues."

Stale writing has no punch because it repeats to the reader what he already knows, adds nothing. The writer doesn't think when he writes tritely, and the reader doesn't have to think when he reads it. Use words that aren't threadbare and the reader will have to think what they actually mean and he'll get a picture in his mind. And it will sound convincing. If you go to the trouble of saying that the heroine's eyes are cold as old pewter, the reader may believe you. If you say her eyes are cold as ice, he probably won't. He'll think you're just repeating what you read someplace else.

Go through your stories after you write them and pick out hackneyed words, phrases and dialogue, and replace them with your own stuff.

Some would-be Steinbecks, heeding the advice to be fresh, go in for outlandish, obscure, strained writing. Read the market you aim to write for. You'll probably conclude that their stories have a lot of trite stuff in them. OK, you'll wind up with plenty trite stuff in yours, too, even after you try. Read better stuff than you're writing. It may have a salutary effect on your typewriter's elimination.

I'm not going to say much about plot except that peanuts to pretzels, you won't sell a trite plot unless it has at least something fresh about it, a fresh character, a fresh background or a fresh angle. Good writing and handling can save a trite plot—but don't presuppose your writing and handling are in that favored class. Play safe—be fresh, and get slapped with a check.

4. IT HAS WEAK CHARACTERS

They're usually positively gutless. What you're writing about is supposed to be real life. So why not get your characters from life? Many writers merely repeat the characters they read in other authors' stories and come up with dummies. Characters must act at least a little bit like the way human beings do.

Characterization is partly description, but it's mostly what goes on inside a person and makes him tick. These inner workings come under the label of motivation. A character's motives should seem like the genuine purposes of flesh-and-blood people of the kind we meet in our everyday life.

I remember, in a J.P. Marquand book, characters described in brief phrases like "she was a pale blonde in a yellow sweater." Accuracy, not verbosity, is the important thing.

Characters will seem superficial if you don't give the reader some idea of their background and what they've been doing all the years of their lives up to the time they appear in the story. It may not be necessary to go into this detail except for lead characters and even then it may often be taken care of in a sentence or two, but it's important. The point is you should know your character thoroughly, and if you do, the reader will feel that he does, too.

The reader likes to identify himself with your hero or heroine. He expects them to be everything he would like to be himself. Your hero must never be narrow, selfish, bigoted, cruel, inconsiderate, crooked, deceitful or any of the other things that flesh is heir to. He must not be goody-goody. Give him a few foibles and shortcomings. Make him seem like a guy you'd like to come home to—and maybe your reader will decide to know him too.

5. IT'S BADLY PACED

Many stories start off with a great infusion of bang-bang right in the first paragraph, and the action continuing fast and furious thereafter. That's bad. We haven't had a chance to get acquainted with our characters yet and decide if we like them or not, and so the action is meaningless. We don't know who to root for.

In different magazines you'll find a degree of difference in the pacing. But in all of them you'll find they give you a chance to get your bearings before the bang-bang commences.

One common form of bad pacing is when a story is static. This means that nothing happens. The story doesn't move along, and the reader's interest does—in other directions. Too long explanations, particularly at the beginning, make a story static. Good stories very often are begun close to the middle or ending, just before a dramatic point where the reader's interest can be quickly and securely won. Then the explanation is trundled in—in small and painless doses.

Often you can pare down that explanation. If it stops the flow of the story you better find ways of introducing it elsewhere where it won't. Ask yourself: Is that explanation necessary?

6. IT'S SLOPPILY DONE

It takes more enthusiasm than an editor brings to his job to read a script with filled in "Es," "Os," "Gs," single spacing and no margins.

7. IT'S REPETITIOUS

It's loosely written. The author uses a lot of words to say what he could have said in a few. What's the point of reading over again what you already know?

Someone once said that authors should write their stories as if they, and not the publishers, had to pay for every printed word they wrote. That's good advice.

8. IT HAS NO "BUSINESS"

Story business merely is all the little tricks and technical data or unusual angles that give your story a sense of reality and of having something to say. It includes background and factual material that you can either get out of books or gain through firsthand experience. Flavor your story with spot knowledge of the locale.

Would you like to know how an editor does it — that is, how an editor gets "business" into a story that doesn't have it? A friend of mine, Ralph McGinnis, edits *Farm Quarterly*, the new, colorful farm magazine. He received a good technical article on how to raise pumpkins. It was right as rain, but it read like everything else the Department of Agriculture puts into its booklets. There wasn't anything in the vernacular. It read as though no one who ever raised pumpkins had anything to do with the article; even though its facts were accurate. In a good farm article you should be able to smell earth and sweat and animals, and this one smelled of an office desk. So McGinnis pulled twenty proofs of the article and sent it off to twenty men who made a business of raising pumpkins. (He got the names by asking a seed house.) He asked each one a provocative little question in order to flush some sort of reply. Fourteen men answered and from their letters he picked up forty sentences which, when professionally sprinkled into the article, gave it the flavor of its subject matter. He gave what we editors call "the business." In fiction and articles you want the authentic flavor of the subject matter; and it's even better when you're reporting it as though you are seeing it for the first time, as one sees the green countryside when coming out of a hundred-mile tunnel.

9. IT HAS NO TWISTS

"Twists" means when the opposite happens to what the reader expects. Every page or so may not be too often to have a minor twist. Nothing will jog flagging interest like a good twist or surprise.

Have a character show up who is supposed to be dead. That's a twist. Have a gem turn out to be a fake. That's a twist. If you want an easy way of getting a twist, just have your hero do the opposite of what you expect. If he wakes up and hears a woman screaming outside his door, you'd expect him to go out and see what's the matter. Have him turn over and go back to sleep and you'll have your twist. Of course, you'll have to explain why he goes in for this unorthodox action.

10. IT HAS NO SNAPPER

George M. Cohan said you should always leave them laughing. In stories you always want to leave your reader with a warm glow, satisfied that the story is complete and that everything is taken care of.

To write *finis* to your story you'll need a punch line. Study published, good stories and you'll know what this punch line is. In short-shorts it's often a surprise ending or unexpected final twist. Sometimes it's just a clever little bit or snappy dialogue. But it's got to be there.

That winds up the many reasons why a story that goes to market may return.

In greater or lesser degree the reasons apply whether you're writing a soap opera for TV, a screenplay, or the next great American novel. Good luck!

Write It Simply

Eugene M. Fisher

March 1946

Once, when I was an eager cub reporter, the city editor of the Honolulu *Advertiser* gave me a Bible to read and quizzed me now and then just to make sure I studied the book.

That editor had no interest in my attitude toward religion. He didn't even care about my off duty morals. He was teaching me to write and chose the Bible as a textbook. Most editors in those days were setting specific rules for reporters—telling them just which details had to go into the lead of a news story. My editor had other ideas.

"The lead is nothing more than a trap to catch the reader's interest," he said. "Make it set the atmosphere for your story. Make it indicate the character of the story. Keep it short, so the reader can grasp it quickly. Put some punch into it. Make it hit him between the eyes. If he wants to know all the who, what, when and where, he'll read on. If he doesn't read on, you haven't written a good lead."

There was more.

"Write simply," he insisted—and that's where the Bible came in.

There is no finer writing in the world, he reminded me, than some of the passages in the King James version of the Bible—and you'll seek in vain there for long, "flowing" sentences. You won't find many words of more than three syllables.

As a reporter I remembered and tried to practice his methods, and seldom was any story of mine altered on the copy desk. But later as a freelance magazine writer, I forgot those rules, or thought they didn't apply to smooth-paper authorship. From the "little" magazines, from *Cosmopolitan* and *Saturday Evening Post*, and from almost everything in between, I accumulated one of the nation's largest collections of formal and informal rejection notices. For years my sales were less than enough to pay for the postage I was using.

Then I tried my hand at westerns, and in 1930 I sold a story to *Ace*

High, after I had revised and rewritten the tale twice along lines laid down by the editors.

When I read my final draft of that story I made a startling discovery. The writing *Ace High* wanted was the same simple, direct writing I had first learned in Honolulu.

For the pulps I did that sort of writing thenceforth, but in stuff aimed at the smooth-paper books I still tried to make my sentences "flow." I sought rhythm. I tried to avoid what I thought was the "jerky" style of the pulps — and slipped inevitably into the long-sentence habit again. When the "better" magazines turned my stories down I rewrote them and sold many of them to my pulp markets.

That went on for years. Then the editor of one of the country's top fiction magazines wrote me a letter. He had seen in a pulp book one of my rewritten stories he had rejected.

"If you had written it that well for me," he said, "I should almost certainly have bought the damned thing."

So now I know. Now, when my few remaining hairs are graying fast, I have learned again that the best writing is the simplest writing. I know that this is true for *Esquire* and the *New Yorker,* for *Blue Book* and *American* and *Rangeland Romances.* It is true for *Science and Mechanics,* which I edit myself.

The simplest writing is the best writing because it has the widest appeal. Any mind, however erudite, grasps the simple things most quickly, understands them most readily and retains them longest. If you and I have read a sentence twice to seize its meaning, the author has fallen down on his job.

Let's dig up a few samples to illustrate this matter of construction style. May I be the first guinea pig?

I sent off to one of the best smooth-paper magazines a story with a western setting. It opened like this:

> *Already the swift and sudden Arizona night had fallen, and yonder in the west, where only now, it seemed, the mountain peaks had stood out sharp huge purple needles, the distant range was lost in universal blackness. Somewhere, not far away, a coyote howled weirdly and the man swung about with a sudden start, one hand racing for a gun as if some long-awaited danger were actually upon him; then he shrugged his wide shoulders and cursed himself softly.*

Seventy-nine words, not counting several uses of the indefinite article. Two sentences, one of them held together artificially by a semicolon. Two subordinate clauses. Eight commas, to keep ideas from running together in a meaningless mess. Awkward construction. The very length of the sentences destroyed the sharp picture I wanted to draw of a man in constant danger.

Here's how that opening looked when I "wrote it down" (as I thought) for *Ace High*:

> *Only now, it seemed, the western peaks had stood out sharp as huge purple needles. Already they were lost in the blackness of the sudden Arizona night.*
>
> *Not far away a coyote howled, weirdly. The man started swiftly up. One hand raced for a gun, as if some long-awaited danger were actually upon him. Then he shrugged his wide shoulders and cursed himself softly.*

There is the opening that would have sold that story elsewhere for better pay—if the whole tale had been as well written. Sixty-three words. Six sentences. Two paragraphs. Only four commas. Only one subordinate clause.

Here is the opening paragraph of a "how-to-do-it" article recently submitted to *Science and Mechanics*:

> *Facet cutting is the art of enhancing the beauty of transparent gem stones by developing symmetrically arranged flat surfaces that reflect and refract light to reveal the gem's true brilliance and color. Such work demands somewhat more specialized equipment than cutting the rounded or cabochon gems described in an earlier article of this series and makes a greater call on the lapidary's skill, but the amateur who is willing to invest patience, intelligence and effort in his hobby can do it, and his reward will be the creation of glowing beauty.*

The author knew what he was talking about. We wanted the story, and we bought it.

There was plenty of meat in that first paragraph, too—altogether too much meat in one big piece for any reader to chew and swallow at a single bite. Two sentences. Ninety words tied together with conjunctions, prepositions and commas. When the story got into type it looked a little different:

> *Facet cutting is an art. It enhances the beauty of transparent gem stones—and that is its purpose. Facets are symmetrically arranged flat surfaces that reflect and refract light to reveal the gem's true brilliance and color.*

Such work demands somewhat more specialized equipment than cutting the rounded or cabochon gems described in an earlier article in this series. It makes a greater call on the lapidary's skill. Yet the amateur who is willing to invest patience, intelligence and effort in his hobby can do it. The creation of glowing beauty will be his reward.

The author's first sentence became a paragraph of three sentences. His second sentence, broken into four, made a second paragraph. In the edited version, sentence length averages 13.6 words against the original sentence length of 32 and 58 words, respectively. The whole thing can be more readily grasped. The plan and purpose of the story become clearer.

We can easily find published examples to illustrate my thesis. The first was taken at random from Adria Locke Langley's *A Lion Is in the Streets*:

Verity felt like a tightrope walker trying to balance herself with two umbrellas. One, a huge emotional umbrella, and the other a small umbrella of good sense. The good-sense one was very small, it sometimes seemed to her. No larger than a Victorian face shade. Yes, she thought, that's probably it—just a complexion saver. One umbrella was never put wholly away while the other was relied upon. She couldn't let go of either one; so she swayed this way, then that, feeling always a little insecure, a little annoyed with herself.

That paragraph is easy to read and it's easy to grasp. It paints a clear picture of a woman torn between what she thinks she should do and the things her emotions demand.

This example was chosen from the first chapter of Marguerite Steen's *The Sun Is My Undoing*:

It came, before dusk had fallen, like a lightning shaft that drove deep into the foundations of civic propriety. Hercules Flood, founder and owner of the timber company which, in the fashion of more prosperous provincial businesses in those days, had extended its activities to London, and its reputation throughout the shipbuilding trade of England; notable contributor, no less in his private than in his public life, to the fame and dignity of his city; pillar of commercial probity, distinguished officer of the Society of Merchant Adventurers, shipowner, alderman, magistrate, sheriff, sometimes church warden; benefactor of the poor and terror of local miscreants; celebrated patron, not only of more serious exploits, but of the Ring, the Sod and all sportsmanlike activities of the district; last but not least, father of the distinguished abolitionist light of Methodism, and eminent man of affairs, Mr. Jason Flood—Hercules had died of a stroke, at the height of a drunken orgy whose descriptions, as time wore on and invention surpassed itself, transcended the utmost bounds of human possibility.

The word count is 171, and all but eighteen of those words are strung together in one confusing, jumbled sentence. Not one person in fifty, I am convinced, could read that paragraph once, quickly, and come up with an accurate statement of the detail it contains. Any reader who cannot summarize, for himself, a paragraph after the first reading obviously hasn't grasped all he has read. A writer whose work can't be grasped quickly has failed in part of his purpose.

That paragraph is, in my opinion, very poor writing, and the fact that *The Sun Is My Undoing* became a best-seller does not invalidate the criticism. It became a best-seller in spite of spots of poor writing. The story had other qualities that outweighed its awkward telling.

That very fact offers a vital moral: Good writing of itself will never sell a manuscript. There has to be real virtue in the story. But good writing may very well tip the scales in favor of a run-of-the-mill yarn that otherwise would never get into print.

Robert Gunning, of Columbus, Ohio, makes his living conducting "readability" surveys for the larger newspapers. His precepts are being adopted by newspaper editors throughout the country. Reporters are being schooled to make their copy more readable—and Gunning's chief emphasis is on simple, clear writing.

He grades every story—local, state, wire, even the editorials—on the basis of its readability. His grading system is based on the reading capacity of persons who have completed a given number of years of formal schooling. Thus a 6 means that anyone with a sixth-grade education should be able to read and understand the story at once. Anything graded 12 is beyond the grasp of persons not high school graduates.

Writing material that Gunning might grade a 6 is not, of course, a goal for every kind of writing at all times. But it will suit our purpose more often than not. Perhaps the best book of psychology, *Mind in the Making* by James Harvey Robinson, is easily within the realm of almost everyone's understanding, and it is the lucidness of the book that made it great.

Reader's Digest, by Gunning's system, rates a 7 consistently, and *Reader's Digest* is one of the most popular and widely read magazines in these United States. The editors of that book not only condense but also simplify the material they use from other publications.

For myself, I have certain rules that I try to follow—not slavishly, but with judgment. Few of my sentences run to more than twenty words, none to more than thirty. Seldom do I let a paragraph exceed sixty words. I never use a polysyllable if there is any monosyllable to carry my meaning. Every manuscript must be held to a minimum wordage, regardless of the method of payment.

As an editor I have never tried to fit reporters or contributors into a pattern that is strictly my own. Each writer's style is his own, and must remain so. But editors will continue to revise copy—and a story well and simply written, needing no revision, is always hailed with gladness.

Why not try a test on one of your own unsold stories . . . the one you think is good . . . the one that makes you wonder why the editors turn it down?

Go over it again. Strike out every word, every phrase, that does not actually advance the action or play some other *vital* role. Cut sentence length to the bone. Trim paragraphs, or split them, or both.

Now start from the beginning once more. If you have used words like "stertorous," kill them and try words like "hoarse." Simplify your words as well as your sentences.

Rewrite and retype the manuscript. Pick a likely market and send your story on its way once more.

If there were any accurate way of checking results among those readers of *Writer's Digest* who may try this plan, I should like to wager a new hat (I do need one, myself!) that a considerable percentage of these rewritten stories will be accepted.

How to Become a Character

Louis L'Amour

The Writer's 1949 Yearbook

Every story is a story of character and the conflict of characters with each other or with a situation.

Whenever a person is confronted by an unfamiliar or trying situation or with a striking adjustment of his or her feelings to a situation, there lies a story.

There are three essentials to every story: a character, a problem and the rewards awaiting the solution of the problem. Settle on these three points and your story has begun. The problem and the reward are purely secondary to the conflict of the character with the difficulties presented by the problem.

I shall attempt to set forth as simply as possible the methods by which character is presented.

"Take a good handful of human life," Goethe advised, "though all men live it, few there be that know it."

In this statement lies the unfailing interest people have in the reading of fiction, for they find in stories the reactions of people like themselves to situations the reader either has faced, may be compelled to face at some future date or likes to imagine himself facing.

The advice of Socrates to "know thyself" is of utmost importance to the writer, for no matter how much we like to imagine ourselves as unique and distinctive individuals, we are all much of a type. If this were not true, then all national advertising, movies, radio programs and national magazines would be foredoomed to failure.

This basic identity of feelings and emotions is of first importance to the writer, for by his knowledge of the feelings of one man he may have a key to the feelings of all men. The difference is rather in degree than in kind.

Five methods are usually used to express and develop character in fiction. Most competent writers use them constantly. These methods might be described as character development by Explanation, Speech, Action, Reaction and Effect.

Explanation: *In delineating the character by explanation, the author himself explains the character by a description of his appearance, dress, mannerisms, attitude, speech and background or any part of these phases.*

Certainly one of the finest examples of this method is the description of the borrower of "The Necklace" in de Maupassant's story of that name. Too extended to quote here, the characterization is often suggested as required reading for all writers, and the story itself is in every sense a masterly example of the storyteller's art.

Although all of us use this first method of presenting characters — by describing them ourselves for the reader — it is a method which the beginner frequently overuses. The beginner does this so often that the editor considers it his hallmark.

When an editor has a pile of manuscripts to read, and after reading the first hundred words of a story and finding there nothing to delight his eye, he will frequently break the story to page 5 or 6 to see what he can pick up. If his eye rests on something like this, which it does in even more times out of ten than you would believe possible, he gives up on the script:

> *Sally thought to herself that if he felt that way about it, she would leave him this day. Raised from early childhood to believe that honesty between man and wife was the cardinal virtue of the home, Sally had no other choice because of her background. She could not live with and respect a man who lied to her.*

The situation is "good story," the conflict is a reasonable one, but the author doesn't trust his characters. He stops the show, comes to the center of the stage, and tells you, the reader, what the characters think and why. The reader senses this overt attitude on the part of the author, this insistence that he wants to talk, and the reader does what people generally do with any me-first person. They go someplace else. To characterize by synopsising the action, by outlining the character's motives and desires, by distilling the give and take of conversation and boiling it all down into one fine capsule for the reader, etiolates the charm and vivaciousness of what you have to say.

To quote an example of the expository method of characterization from my own work, here is a paragraph from the story "Old Doc Yak," published in *New Mexico Quarterly Review*.

He was a man without humor. He seemed somehow aloof, invulnerable. Even his walk was pompous and majestic. He strode with the step of kings and spoke with the voice of an oracle, entirely unaware that his whole being was faintly ludicrous, that those about him were always suspended between laughter and amazed respect.

Another danger to be avoided in presenting character by this method is a letdown after presentation. For instance, the above character must immediately speak and act to illustrate the author's description.

Brevity is the quality most to be sought in illustrating a character by explanation.

Speech: *Character is illustrated through speech.*

"As a man speaketh, so is he." By dialogue the story is advanced while the speech itself describes your character.

Dickens, one of the greatest masters of character delineation, often gave a character some typical word usage or manner of speech, some peculiarity of phraseology, so that whenever he spoke he might be instantly recognized by the reader and need be designated in no other way. Character actors often use this method.

One of the finest examples of characterization offered on the screen in many years is that given by Walter Huston as the old prospector in *The Treasure of Sierra Madre.* To anyone who has known old prospectors, and I have known many of them, that was vivid characterization.

Certain actions or speeches such as the Lone Ranger's "Hi, ho, Silver!" or Sherlock Holmes's "Elementary, my dear Watson" are now symbols known to millions. The characterization of Holmes is also established by his playing of a violin while solving crimes, his deer stalker's cap and his pipe.

Your reader learns much about your character from his words, but he will also learn from his dress and from his actions, and the effect he has upon those around him. Above all, once the character is established, he must be consistent. He must act and react according to his own characteristics; he must be the kind of person you originally made him and must not deviate or the story won't "ring true."

Most of the outstanding figures of history deliberately used mannerisms to identify themselves. Napoleon, for instance, is tagged by his hat and by his habit of carrying one hand in the front of his coat, Lincoln by his beard and frock coat, Teddy Roosevelt by his teeth and his glasses as well as his expression, "Bully! That's just bully!"

Action: *We know people by their responses to situations.*

Expressed simply, characterization is merely the business of showing what kind of person the actor is. The less you duck this business the more of a character you have.

Character may be betrayed by small things as well as great. Little, unconscious gestures or mannerisms may reveal a feeling or an uncertainty.

Every action, no matter how seemingly unimportant, is an expression of character. The failure to act may be a more perfect illustration of character than an action.

Characterization is a continuous process. If the actor is modified by the story's action, as is often the case, then this change in his character must be logical and due to the events or impressions of the story itself.

In real life, character is a variable and plastic thing, yet not so much so as is often believed. For the purpose of the novel the writer may use a variable character. In a short story it's a dangerous thing to do, for the secret of the short story is single effect, and the writer has no time within the limitations of the form to present very many variations in character.

The dominant character trait and the single effect are the standard techniques of the shorter forms of fiction.

Reaction: *We may illustrate character by showing the reactions of the character to people and situations.*

A story that illustrates all phases of characterization is Jack London's very fine "The Mexican." From the very opening of the story when the Mexican appears at the headquarters of the revolution, his character is manifest. He is scarcely more than a boy, yet filled with a driving, bitter purpose from which nothing can make him deviate. One feels this Mexican must have been steeled in the fires of hell itself to become so hard, so implacable. He appears from nowhere and wants to join the revolution. The others are suspicious of him, and finally one gives him a job washing the floor.

> *"It is for the revolution?" the boy asked*
> *"It is for the revolution," Vera answered.*
> *Rivera* looked cold suspicion at all of them, *then proceeded to take off his coat.*

The non-italicized line above indicates the Mexican's reaction. And later on:

> *Rivera's eyes burned venomously, but he made no sign of acknowl-*

edgment. He disliked all gringos but this gringo he hated with an immediacy that was unusual *even in him.*

His feeling is evident everywhere in the story but is most clearly shown in his reactions to others and in the dialogue that grows from those reactions.

Here, in a quotation from a *Saturday Evening Post* serial, "Murder for Millions" is an excellent paragraph of characterization by Nancy Rutledge:

> *Father. Everlastingly, father. Sometimes Chad* hated *Horace Trimbal even more in death than in life. Almost he could hear Horace's chuckle, malicious and a little dry.*

The first three words are an obvious expression of irritation, sharpened by the word "hated," betraying his true feeling for the old man he has murdered but whose spirit persists in confronting him on every hand.

It is a good idea to read through several stories and select from them passages of character delineation and underline them so that the idea can be grasped clearly, particularly the characters' first thoughts, first speeches and first reactions. Given good strong characters and a situation trying to them, a story will almost build itself, it will evolve from their conflict with each other or with the situation.

Effect: *Many characters are most plainly seen through their effect upon those around them.*

An example of this is my own story "Dutchman's Flat" which appeared in *Giant Western*. In this case the protagonist does not show himself in person until the very end of the story, as in a novel of the twenties, *Jonathan Scrivner.* Until that time he is seen entirely through the eyes of others. Lock, a stranger in the country, has killed a man friendly to the local ranchers, and they are out to find him and hang him if he is not killed in being taken.

They believe him to be a no-good specimen and possibly a rustler. They also believe that he shot their friend in the back. As they ride along, following his trail, the true pattern of Lock's character becomes manifest. He is no tenderfoot; he thinks of his horse; at one point he could have killed several of them and he did not. Later, they find a spring he had walled up. It is not the act of a shiftless man, but of one who thought of others, of one who planned ahead. Gradually, despite themselves, they began to have grudging admiration for him. He deliberately makes pursuit easy, he prepares a fire for them, leads them to water, he deliberately breaks branches and drops them in the trail, and he marks arrows in the sand. It irritates them, angers some of them, but despite that the feeling gradually works into their minds that Lock is not the sort of man to shoot another in the back, and before their final meeting with him they are ready to listen to his side of things, which they would not have done earlier.

The character of the pursuers is established in the first part of the story, and their individual characters emerge as the story progresses:

They were men shaped and tempered to the harsh ways of a harsh land, strong in their sense of justice, ruthless in their demand for punishment, relentless in pursuit. From the desert they had carved their homes, and from the desert they drew their courage and their code, and the desert knows no mercy.

These are the pursuers. Yet such men have a respect for the virtues their life demands. They recognize and respect strength, courage, the knowledge that enables a man to live, and which they very soon realize their quarry possesses.

"He's no tenderfoot." Kesney expressed the thought that had been dawning upon them all in the last two hours. "He knows how to save a horse and he knows a trail."

Yet their original misunderstanding of his character remains, partly due to the facts expressed by one of the riders.

". . . Squattin' on that Sorenson place looks plumb suspicious, for no man can make a livin' on that dry as a bone place. Ever'body figures no honest man would squat on such a place."

They ride on and find a place where a little water has been spilled from a canteen.

"Careless," Neill said. "He'll be needin' that water."
"No," Kesney said. "He was pourin' water in a cloth to wipe out his horse's nostrils. Bet a dollar."
"Sure," Hardin agreed, "that's it. Horse breathes a lot better. A man runnin' could kill a horse on this Flat. He knows that."

No western man who can read such signs has to be personally acquainted with a man to know the sort of person he is. There are indications that cannot escape a man who has followed trails, and the pursued invariably betrays himself as does Lock to these men. As they follow him they begin to understand him, to read from his tracks the character of the man they follow.

They corner him at last in an old mill, but he warns them not to attack, and explains the shooting so that they can understand how it happened. Yet they are still unsure and are resentful of his tricks along the trail. Despite their watchfulness he escapes the mill. One of the men remarks that they will find him at the ranch.

> *And somehow they were all very sure he would be. They knew he would be because they knew he was their kind of man. He would retreat no further than his own ranch, his own hearth.*

The pursuers ride on but the tumbled-down old Sorenson place has changed. The small valley is green with a planted crop, the roof has been patched and a new corral built. All around them are evidences of hard work and thought. Again they are impressed that this was not the manner of man they had believed. During their hesitation, and their amazed study of the ranch, he comes up behind them, and covering them, suggests they ride down to the ranch and have breakfast, after that, away from his wife, they can settle their difficulties.

All of this is presented through the eyes of the ranchers who followed him. For a saddle tramp or rustler they had no respect, but this man was like themselves, with their own rugged virtues and their own rough humor. His wife welcomed them, not knowing who or what they were, and following breakfast they troop outside, vaguely uncomfortable.

> *Hardin looked up. "Lock, was that right, what you said in the mill? Was it a fair shooting?"*

Lock assures them it was, and explains as he had explained the night before in the mill.

> *"All right," Hardin said. "I reckon that's good enough for me. You're a different sort of man than any of us figured."*

One danger, aside from the mere matter of space, that must be avoided is the danger of saying too much. If a girl is beautiful, it is much better to merely say she is beautiful and to describe her effect upon others, the effect of her beauty upon the hero, for instance.

The five methods of characterization listed do not give the writer a knowledge of character. For that he must go to school of life itself. There is no other way.

By all means practice. Study people you see around town, at your work, your lunch hour, anywhere they happen to be. Try to put them in words, try to decide what is their dominant trait, try to find a phrase to describe them. Notice their mannerisms. Be sure of one thing, the screwball, the fellow usually considered a nut, the odd number of the gang ... he will prove the most fascinating. The eccentric is always intriguing.

Above all, if you devote a lot of time to the study of characters and the company of screwballs, someday you may overhear someone talking of you, and they will say, "Him? Oh, he's a character!"

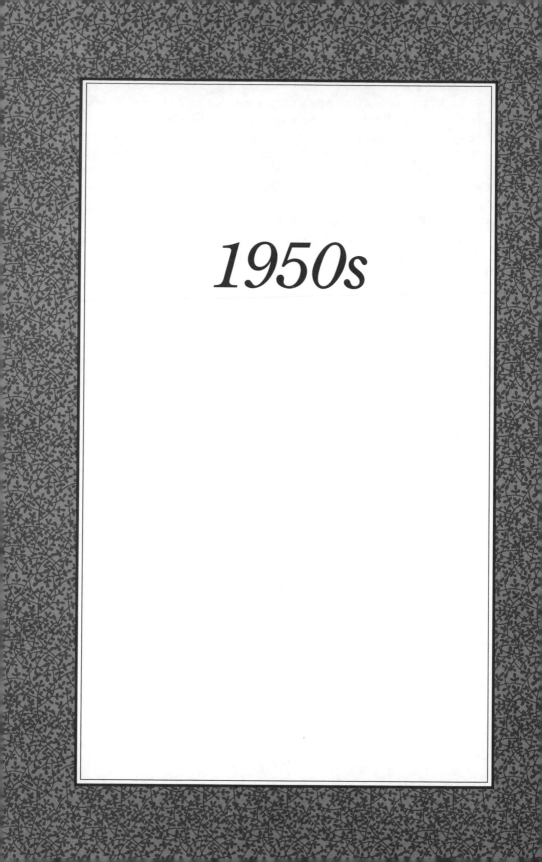

1950s

Only One "Must"

Mildred I. Reid

February 1950

Despite the seemingly countless rules of which you have heard, there is only one must in creative writing — or any other writing for that matter. You must transfer an emotional experience to the reader. Every other rule may be broken. Every other rule is broken, knowingly by professional writers, perhaps unknowingly by new writers.

Of course, one can most readily transfer an emotional experience if he does follow at least a few of the most fundamental rules of writing. One of these is reader identification. If the reader cannot in some manner identify himself with, or be in sympathy with, some character in a story, his attention is very likely to wander. Unless you do put an emotion over to the reader through this character, your story will not be remembered and the reader is not going to care much what you have to say.

Suppose we analyze this business of transferring an emotional experience to the reader. It sounds far more awe-inspiring than it actually is. Since we quite obviously do not habitually go about overcome by the deeper emotions — the more dramatic emotions such as fear, anger, hatred, sorrow — what are the other emotions we might be feeling?

Certainly frustration may be one — and a popular one with writers! And how about anticipation, amusement, pleasure, hopelessness, pity, envy, agitation, helplessness, humility, timidity, boredom, gratitude, jealousy, avarice, antagonism, greed, pride? And the diametrically opposed emotions will constitute a second list. Any thesaurus will supply still more.

You see, there is sound psychology beneath this one must of all fiction — this transferring of an emotional experience. It is because our fiction attempts to approximate real life and also because humans rarely go about in an emotional vacuum that you must create an emotion within the reader, an emotion which is threefold, for it first must be felt by the author, next by the protagonist, and last by the reader.

We cannot interest a reader if we do not give him something as demanding of his attention as are his own emotions. For an emotion is more compelling than a thought. Thus, your fiction must woo the reader's emotions more than his mind. It must give him an emotional experience potent enough to banish his own present emotions.

There is no doubt that only by constant repetition does a child learn his ABC's; the singer memorize the words of a song; the pianist master his notes. So, a writer may read the admonition to appeal to the emotions and senses, read it a dozen times perhaps, and then one day, after he has read it often enough—its meaning suddenly clicks. Then, he wonders why the idea did not get across to him at the first reading. The answer is that awareness wasn't ripe enough to flower into definite knowledge.

Hundreds of times I have told writers that most commercial fiction has its best chance of selling if it has a satisfactory ending. The reason is that the reader will be able to feel the emotion of satisfaction—and this is a pleasurable emotion, an emotion we enjoy experiencing.

Pleasurable emotions, oddly enough, are not always emotions about pleasant things. Granted, we feel pleased when the worthy protagonist achieves his purpose in a story. But we may also be pleased when the villain receives the punishment he deserves.

It may be helpful for new writers to make a list of some of the elements in life which may arouse the emotion of pleasure within the reader. And for those who have known that they must transfer an emotional experience to the reader, but have felt too inexperienced to do so, it may be a relief to note that the simple, little emotions in life are fully as salable as are the stronger emotions.

A few of the simple emotions which a writer may arouse in his reader are pleasure, satisfaction, admiration, sympathy and sometimes even recognition of a pet theme. Nostalgic stories carrying the reader back to his childhood are an example of tapping the fountainhead of the emotion of pleasure. And humor stories arouse the emotion of gaiety. And stories of right triumphing over wrong arouse satisfaction.

So, since most commercial stories do have right triumphant over wrong, it is almost more difficult not to arouse some sort of emotion within the reader than it is to do so, considering the wide range of emotions of which humans are capable. However, the trick is to be certain *before* you write a story, with just *which* emotional experience you are going to overcome the reader. For there will be one basic emotion, you know.

The word "one," as you know, signifies singleness, reiteration of some one purpose or idea or emotion. The principle of unity in any piece of art springs from the psychological need of conserving the reader's capacity for attention. It is difficult to attend to more than one thing at a time, thus this need for transferring but one basic emotional experience in a short story.

Whether we transfer the emotion of amusement over something humorous, recognition of something with which the reader is familiar, surprise over an unexpected ending, or satisfaction over an expected one makes little difference. Any of these emotional approaches is salable. But that we do transfer some sort of emotion will make the difference between a sale and a rejection slip.

Satisfaction is one simple little emotion which may be courted in a multitude of ways. For instance, you may take your reader on an emotional pilgrimage through:

1. Satisfaction because a well-known truth is reiterated. (After reading this sort of story the satisfied reader sagely nods his head and thinks: "Truer words were never spoken!")

2. Satisfaction because the worthy protagonist achieves that for which he strives. (Here the satisfied reader is happy that earnest effort was rewarded.)

3. Satisfaction because a wrong-doer is punished. (After reading this type of story, the satisfied reader thinks: "Well, it served him right!")

4. Satisfaction because a nostalgic story recalled the past. (The satisfied reader grows mellow with his dreams of the past.)

The mere planning of a story ending which will definitely create a feeling of satisfaction within the reader is not too difficult a thing to attempt, assuming that one is possessed of the basic instinct for presenting a bit of action in a neat pattern, that is, for making the characters act out the story. And, of course, there are those magazines which like the surprise twist story. So, if you are capable of springing a surprise on the reader, you may have twofold satisfaction.

Naturally, emotions must be clear-cut, with the writer furnishing the signposts which will guide the reader to the specific emotion the writer sets out to transfer. How does the writer guide the reader to one specific emotion? By reiteration, of course, as in the following sentences:

"John did not notice or care what she wore."

"There were so many niceties husbands ignored."

"She prayed he would never know such hurt as his blithe indifference brought her."

"Was it asking too much for a wife to expect faithfulness from her husband?"

All these sentences add up to one emotion — pity, pity for a neglected wife. And each sentence is what I term a signpost, a subjective signpost in the above instance, since she is thinking. But, in addition to her thoughts, there would be little acts on the husband's part — also signposts — to force the reader to realize that the husband is worthless and that the wife is to be pitied.

So, to guide the reader to one specific emotion, we give him repeated proof — but in different words and actions — of cause for a specific emotion. Reiteration in different words which have the same connotation is what finally penetrates the reader's awareness and breaks down his inattentiveness and lack of emotion. Furnish him with a cause for an emotion, and he'll more than likely feel your story.

The next time you hear someone say that you must adhere to a single point of view, that you must have conflict in a story, that you must maintain suspense, respect the good advice, but put it in second place where it belongs. Concentrate on the one thing which you must do. Transfer an emotional experience to the reader, take him on an emotional pilgrimage, and he will read your story and come back for more like it.

1 Brain + 1 Brain + 1 Brain = Viewpoint

Morry Hull

July 1951

About twelve years ago I asked my friend Paul E. Triem what viewpoint is. Paul had written large quantities of everything except poetry, and his wife writes that.

He said, "Morry, the reader is helped gently to a stump, from which he can see. That's his viewpoint."

I said, "Why a stump?"

And Paul said, "Because a stump won't move."

That sounds elementary, but Paul was talking to a writer with one degree, one published novel (six unpublished), and no magazine experience.

In the years since then, I have found slick-magazine professionals who don't know that much about viewpoint. One who appears regularly in the slicks read a story aloud, asking for criticism.

I said, "It won't sell. Who's the reader?"

The writer said, "What do you mean, who's the reader?"

"With whom does the reader of this story identify himself? Whose pants, whose skirt does the reader wear? Which person is the reader?"

"Well," the writer said, "the reader has to sympathize with all the characters. The reader, you might say, is the mouse in the corner."

It would have been too unkind to say that mice don't buy magazines. But in any discussion of viewpoint, it is necessary to start with the assumption that the reader should, and will, refuse the role of mouse in the corner. Your short story is a cross-section of human experience in which the reader wants to share. He can't have a very high stake as a spectator in the bleachers. He must *be* one of the people in the story. This is known technically as identification, letting the reader move for the duration of the story into the heart and soul of one character.

Shortly before this viewpoint discussion, Dwight Swain and I were over at my place building him a table on which to write "Drive North and

Die" for *Mammoth Western*. I was keenly interested in "Drive North" because it was a tricky viewpoint job. If I remember correctly, Dwight was asked for a multiple viewpoint story.

The novel, 70,000 words in length, starts out as author-omniscient, the writer telling the story from his own viewpoint. When four bad men murder an innocent man on the prairie, Dwight characterizes them all, for all time, in five words: "They didn't even bury him." Here is the omniscient author speaking directly to his readers.

From that point, the novel is handled by the multiple viewpoint technique — one chapter through the eyes of one character, the next through the eyes of another, until the story has gone the rounds of the lead characters. Then the first character's viewpoint takes hold once more, and the tale goes around again. Each chapter, of course, ends nicely primed for the next chapter's viewpoint.

Dwight Swain is good at viewpoint — and it takes a fine technician to handle omniscient or multiple viewpoint successfully. With the former, the writer's style has to be so pleasing that the reader would rather stay with him than become identified with one of the characters. For instance, Ludwig Bemelmans, because of his humorously sophisticated style, has been able to use omniscient viewpoint to good effect in some of his short stories. With multiple viewpoint, the author is in constant danger that his reader, faced with the thoughts and feelings of too many characters, will cease to care about any of them. Even Dwight, who is a good technician, usually writes according to the rule: "Nothing the central character can't see-feel-know or -hear."

"But what about the woman who comes in on page 7," you ask. "How can I show the *real* her to the reader through somebody else's eyes?" The woman is in the story for one reason only, for the effect her thought and influence have on the viewpoint character, with whom the reader is by now hopelessly identified. So if the viewpoint character is Miriam, you don't say:

> *Looking down on Miriam from the banister, the woman thought, "With five words to her husband I can destroy her as I've threatened to do."*

You say:

> *Somehow Miriam couldn't feel alone. She looked up, and there was the woman staring down on her from the banister. A chill ran*

through Miriam, for she knew the woman was remembering her threat, thinking again of carrying it out.

The woman is now vivid but her place in the story is valid because we feel her impact on Miriam, and this is Miriam's story.

Although viewpoint should not shift, it can expand. If you want some of the woman's feeling to seep through in order to give your story depth, portray her sympathetically — through Miriam:

In spite of her deep hatred for the woman, Miriam could not help feeling a certain sympathy. After all, she, Miriam, had everything. The woman had nothing — no husband, no home, no background, maybe even no future.

In my wife Ruth's and my double-length story, "I Love a Catholic," which appeared in *True Story*, Margy is a Protestant girl in love with a Catholic boy. The story is as much his as hers, but Margy is the reader-identified character. Margy is the reader, and there can be no viewpoint but hers. After Mike has left the Catholic church to marry her, they try to be married by a justice of the peace. Here's the scene:

Then the justice was opening a black book. He had never seen us before, but he was going to marry us.

"Either of you ever been married before?"

We shook our heads. Mike's face was grim.

Then suddenly the justice said to Mike, "Wasn't you at Jack Riordan's funeral last year?"

Mike said, "Yes."

The justice said, "Seemed to me you was there. Catholic, ain't you?"

My heart stopped. I wanted to cry out, "Look out, Mike!" I just stood there, tense. Out of his Irish heart, from way back down the years, Mike said, "Sure, I'm a Catholic."

His jaw was jutting out. His face was paling a little. That's when I saw the J.P. smile, a secret sort of smile as though he were saying triumphantly to himself, "Now I've married a Catholic, even."

That was all, just that smile. But the mighty Catholic church had been dirtied.

However thoroughly you feel what is going on in Mike's heart, you see and feel only through the suffering of Margy, with whom you, the reader, are identified. The viewpoint has been extended as far as possible — but it has not shifted. The lead character remains the interpreter.

In a *True Confessions* story, "Behind Closed Doors," Carol, the central character, sees what happens to Joanie. The gang has let Joanie into a secret high school society because she has a car they like, but on initiation night she has to pay dearly for some of her past two-timing with the "sisters' " boyfriends. If the reader were merely a spectator, what happens to Joanie would be — well, too bad. But the reader is bound up in the story through identification with a friend of Joanie's, the viewpoint character, Carol, who is on the spot. What happens to Joanie, then, is just plain terror:

> *I couldn't take my eyes off Joanie. I could almost see her heart beating, her big brown eyes hoping, trying to be sure, in the awful silence, that she had played this thing right.*
> *Marion broke the silence very gently. "Virgin, Joanie?"*
> *Joanie colored, then lost her color.*
> *Marion said, "Who?"*
> *Joanie flicked a smile on and off again. Her face twitched. The rest of us, there against the wall, were beginning to tremble, holding our breath.*

Although Joanie is not the viewpoint character, she is the whole show at this point, and it would be easy for the writer to let his reader off the stump. We stay right with Carol, however, as the action moves forward until the climax of the scene when Joanie takes a brutal beating:

> *Pledges who had already been sick got sick again. Harriet got up and went to the kitchen. She couldn't stand it. Barbara got up and followed her. I just buried my head in my hands and tried not to listen. They weren't paddling Joanie. They were kicking and beating her.*

Our viewpoint restrictions are narrowing; we are on a stump we cannot leave. Suppose our viewpoint character is a thick sort of person who couldn't see or feel deeply enough to give us a story with good, rich depth.

That's a reasonable complaint, but consider for a moment the nature of the viewpoint character. He is a composite person, made up of himself, the reader with whom he's identified and you, the writer. His own story-brain may not amount to much, but he's got three brains. You can gently, delicately, give him all the intelligence you assume the reader to have, because he and the reader are one. You will never ruin a story by letting your reader be smart.

For consistency, you can let things *dawn* on the not-too-bright viewpoint character. You can make his knowledge come hard to him. If he has to grasp something on page 14, let him start puzzling it out on page 9, like this:

> *He couldn't understand how the helpless little blond from Mobile could make a man like Jamison turn pale, how that cute little kid could be dangerous. He frowned. He couldn't get it, and he couldn't shake it off his mind.*

Or you can give the viewpoint character an attribute which, for the moment, brings his viewpoint up to standard. For instance:

> *He'd never been to college, but he'd been around the docks, and he could tell the damn thing wouldn't float.*

In this sentence, the writer gave his lead character an attribute, his experience around the docks, that justified the man's gust of gray matter. Gunnison Steele (Ben Gardner) had just died, and Dwight Swain and I were disposing of a couple of tons of his old pulps when we came across that quote.

Ruth and I call that a good device and we recommend it, although we don't use it. Our work is founded on truth, and for us truth is lost the moment we play the slightest trick on a character. What our characters in *True Story* and *True Love Stories* would not grasp must go ungrasped. This is the fate of the first-person-experience writer.

While we will not distort a character's viewpoint, or magnify it, we can and do reveal to the viewpoint character much that she herself is incapable of thinking. Any thought she cannot have by herself can be given to her in dialogue by somebody else. From then on it is her thought and she can draw from it the deductions she needs. Let's take a quote from the opening of "I Was a Drip," the novelette in *True Story*:

> *As I remember it now, nobody even said goodbye.*
> *Oh, yes, Katherine Hastings did. She said, "Bye, Sue. It's going to be tough, buying my own movie tickets." I remember I stood there thinking, is that all?*
> *That was all. It was plain in her smile, as she turned and left me.*

Sue now has a view of herself she did not have before. She has learned something about herself from somebody else, and her character has begun to change. This is expansion of viewpoint through character work in dialogue.

One of the most common faults in the work of beginning writers is inconsistency of viewpoint with character. When we're struggling to work out a solution, it is so easy to go back a few pages and let Herman say something a shade different from what he would naturally say—then Hilda could see things in a different way, we could leave out page 15 altogether and-the-story-could-close-on-page-30 with . . . . Characters too often react not from their own viewpoints, but from the viewpoint of the writer in the woodpile who's suddenly decided to pump the whole story down a plot line the characters know nothing about.

In one of my stories, I had a character with a hot temper who had to appeal to a girl who loved cool-tempered men in order to bring the story to a close on page 27. The girl was present at an argument where the man would naturally lose his temper.

> *"How does it feel to get caught ratting on your best friend?"*
> *Anger boiled in his deep chest. But a faint trace of Mary's cigarette smoke touched his nostrils, reminding him. He said, smiling, "My friend, you use fairly strong language."*

In that version of the story, the man fit the plot. He made it easier for me to team up a hot-tempered hero with a girl who loved cool tempers. But my characterization was inconsistent. If you are dealing with real characters you can't plot them. All you can do is record what they do and say as you follow them around. I had to let the hot-tempered man be what he was. The rewrite went like this:

> *"How does it feel to get caught ratting on your best friend?"*
> *Anger broiled in him, like a fire struck by a hose. He roared, "What are you yakking about? You want a bang in the mouth?"*
> *Then, in the stunned silence, he saw the disillusion, the shock, in the girl's eyes. He thought, "Oh-oh. I've done it, now!"*

Can he get himself out of this mess by page 27? If he can and does, the writer has a real story. Human experience is gripping because of the natures of people and their viewpoints. Establish a character and his viewpoint in a tough situation, then *let that character be true to his own nature*. You'll get a plot. In fact, you'll find that viewpoint is the first key to plot.

"Drive North" is long since done, Dwight has left, and I'm working away at the homemade table. Thousands of dollars worth of Swain's Westerns and our confessions have come off this table. It's a fixture around here, like Paul Triem's stump.

How to Plot a Novel

Patricia McGerr

January 1954

I n July 1951, I put a clean sheet of paper in my typewriter and tapped out these words:

Ellen stirred uneasily in her bed. In a hazy suspension between waking and sleeping she had difficulty remembering where she was until, opening her eyes, she could see in the half light of dawn the familiar objects of her own room. Not fully roused from her dreaming, she moved her gaze from the cluttered dressing table to seek, as she so often did when she woke at an unusual hour, the smooth counterpane of the other twin bed. Only this morning it was not smooth. The spread was neatly folded at the foot, the blanket was pushed aside, nearly fallen to the floor, and the sheet half covered, half revealed a broad bare back. Oh, God! she thought. A man. Not here. Not in the home of my children.

The anguish of the thought brought her fully awake, and she knew at once where she was and why and all the things she had known when she went to bed. Her eyes climbed upward to the man's neck and hairline, above which the crisply curling black tangle was both strange and well known, as if she had brought the memory of it from the depth of her dreaming. This is Edward, she told herself. My husband. The father of my son and my daughter. He has a right to sleep in that bed, where for twelve years no man has lain. And because she was so unsure about what rights he did now have, she repeated half aloud, "This is Edward. My husband."

Then I put the paper in a cardboard box and labeled the box "The Missing Years." In July 1953, a novel with that title, opening with those words, arrived in the bookstores. The work procedures followed between those two midsummer dates were learned the hard way, through trial and error on six previous books. By setting them down here I hope to provide a shortcut for you who are about to begin your first novel.

When I wrote the first words of that seventh book I had my basic idea and nothing more. I wanted to write the story of a wife whose husband deserts her and, twelve years later, returns. Why he left, why he came back, what happened to her in his absence, what kind of people they were—these were things I had to find out. I could go ahead and write the book, thinking it out as I went along, facing each problem as it came up. Or I could put off the writing until I had made careful preparations and solved every problem in advance.

I used the first method on my first book (*Pick Your Victim*, 1946) simply because I didn't know there was any other. I thought of the idea on a Sunday, started to write it on Monday. My only guide was a listing of the chapters with each one summed up in two or three words like "Whipple Drinks," "Beauty Contest" and "Bertha Goes Overboard." But the work I failed to do in the beginning added up to much more work at the end. That book had to be almost completely rewritten twice before publication.

Then I heard about outlines and, except for minor revisions, the initial draft has been the final one for every book since the first. After trying various ratios, I've concluded that the best results come from dividing my time, roughly, 25 percent for preparation and 75 percent for writing. *The Missing Years* was in the works for eighteen months (don't let those July to July dates mislead you—during the last half year it was being edited, printed, etc.). This meant that more than four months went by before a third paragraph was added to the first two. By that time the box was bulging with material.

The first step was to get a clear idea of the story I wanted to tell, how much ground I wanted to cover, what points I wanted to make. A novel should have not a moral exactly, but some significance. I had to decide what was to be the significance of this book and how best to get it across. For several weeks I sat and thought, lay in bed and thought, took long walks and thought. I also did what I could in the way of pump priming. I read dozens of books about marriage, broken homes, careers for women, everything even remotely related to my theme. I read them not so much for the facts they contained as for the ideas they stimulated. More useful even than the reading was the talking. "What should a woman do when her husband walks out?" became my favorite conversational gambit. The debates and discussions it started furnished many fresh slants and provided a good index of the problem's interest value.

At the end of this period I was ready to write the synopsis—a 5,000-

word summary of the main plot line. It made no attempt to arrange the story in sequence as it would appear in the book. Rather it was divided into general headings, with each aspect of the heroine's problem dealt with separately, even though they would overlap and dovetail in the final writing. One section, for instance, dealt with her economic progress, another with her emotional pressures, a third with her social embarrassments.

The plot on paper, the next step was character. Of course I don't suggest that you can plot in a vacuum, without regard to your characters, or that when you go on to your characters you will stop thinking about your plot. It is more a matter of focusing on one while the other simmers in the background. In working on the characters I have found it useful to do three separate jobs on each one: (1) straight biography; (2) physical description; and (3) psychological analysis.

Number 1 is a "Who's Who" type collection of the principal facts, dates and places in the character's life, including family background, education, jobs, marriages, military service, etc. Number 2 sets forth the details of height, weight, coloring and dress, with a special note on any idiosyncrasies, mannerisms and manifestations of nervousness or excitement. Both these are relatively brief and factual.

The third sketch is much longer, more comprehensive and by far the most important. I try to get down not only what kind of a person this is but also what made him that way. It is not enough to say a man is ambitious. I must also discover the early roots of his ambition and the goals toward which it is directed, as well as the ways in which it is shown. The more complex the character, the more difficult will be this part of the novelist's task—and the more imperative that it be properly done.

The most complicated character I ever dealt with was a man named Larry Rock (*Follow, As the Night*, 1950). I had to make him capable of cold-blooded murder and yet able to hold the heroine's love and the reader's sympathy. To accomplish this paradox it was necessary to go way back to his childhood and trace the pressures that had twisted his ego, made him at once vicious and lovable. I wrote reams about him that never got into the book—or got there only by implication and suggestion—but this writing helped me to understand Larry and, more important, to pass this understanding along to the reader. I was recently reminded of my struggle by a letter from a French producer who is turning the book into a movie. Larry is giving him a hard time too. "I can cast the four women with ease," he wrote me, "but I am determined to find for Larry an actor who can walk the thin tightrope between hero and villain."

In creating the husband of *The Missing Years*, I had a comparable difficulty. To clarify and emphasize it, I wrote myself this note of warning: "My main problem is Ned. I can probably cope with Ellen. But the essential thing is to make Ned attractive not only to Ellen but to the reader. On the reader's ability to understand his pull hangs the story's whole motivation. And if the reader is to find him attractive, *so must I.* Hence, it is not enough to make him a charming weakling who may appeal to some women but not to me. There must be in him enough strength to appeal to everyone. My problem is this — to reconcile the qualities that attract with the qualities that make him capable of deserting a pregnant wife and child and then returning to them. I've got to make him behave like a complete heel and yet not lose all reader sympathy. Can it be done? It must!"

For the effort that went into this characterization I felt rewarded by the verdict of the critics. What I was trying to do and how it was brought about is most fully expressed in *New York Herald-Tribune's* review: "Perhaps the best portrait is that of Ned Clement. In him Miss McGerr has created a completely recognizable individual. He has charm, he has an appetite and a flair for life; he rebels against the bit and rein. Marriage meant responsibilities and these he accepted but not the price of snuffing out the spark of his vitality. To his wife, brought up in a conventional, affluent home, he was a gay companion, a tender lover but not a good provider, or, rather, not a steady one. As he himself ruefully put it, he continually let her down. 'You've got neat ideas,' he said. 'I don't know whether you brought them from home or got them out of books. And the trouble is, I'm not neat. I can't fit into any patterns. I'll work at it though, if it means so much to you.' "

My heroine was easier to handle since a deserted wife and mother is a natural for sympathy. I find a note of warning about her, however, this one dealing with the vital problem of reader identification. "The reader," I reminded myself, "must have a real emotional response to her problems, her love affairs, her children. The woman reader should be able to put herself in Ellen's place, to become involved in her troubles. The man reader must feel protective toward her. So while she must have faults, be somewhat to blame for the breakup, it must be always human weakness, never a shrewish temper. Since the story is told from her viewpoint, her own recognition of her faults can help hold sympathy."

Does it seem that I am giving too much attention to the element of character? In my opinion, it's a point that cannot be overemphasized. On the strength of your characters your whole novel will stand or fall. If you know and understand them thoroughly, they will do much of your work for you. Much of your plot trouble will disappear because they — by reason of the kind of people they are — will react to circumstances in specific ways and thereby carry your plot forward.

A key scene in *The Missing Years* was that leading to the desertion. To make a man who is not a villain leave a wife pregnant and penniless is a tricky problem. Given a different couple, it might have been impossible. With Ned and Ellen, it evolved naturally. What I did was set his gambler's spirit in conflict with her craving for security and let them take it from there. It was in character for him to quit his job on a whim, equally in character for her to protest. The logic of his subsequent actions is summed up later in the book:

> *With the complete picture now before her (thus ran Ellen's thoughts in retrospect), she could understand his leaving her, could see it as a kind of chain reaction in which each step made the next imperative so that once the motion had begun there could be no turning back. His intentions, when he drew the money from the bank, had been good if unwise. His reaction to losing it could have been predicted. The one thing he could not do was take help from Ellen's mother. Rather than face this, he went away. And, having gone, each month he stayed made his returning more difficult. So many arguments had centered around her thrift versus his irresponsibility that he could well believe she placed security above all else, that until he could bring her this he had better stay away . . . . He—being the kind of man he was, faced with a certain combination of circumstances—could hardly have chosen any other course.*

This dependence of plot on character can find illustration throughout the book. There's one part in which Ellen steps momentarily out of character (under the dual pressure of a report of Ned's infidelity plus an unfair besmirching of her own reputation) to go off on a weekend with another man. With the trip barely under way, her native sense of virtue and conventionality reasserts itself and, since the man is an important contact, presents a serious problem. I stayed strictly on the sidelines. You got yourself into this, I told her, now let's see if you can wiggle out. I was quite proud of the way Ellen handled the situation.

Dialogue is particularly an outgrowth of character. If you are a writer who finds dialogue difficult to write, your real solution may lie in getting on more intimate terms with your characters. Once you make people breathe, it's not so hard to make them talk. First, of course, you must have the actual "meat" of the scene clear in your mind — the information the dialogue is to convey, the action to which it must lead. But the words they use, the reasoning they follow, the way they express their ideas will, in each case, be inherent in the characters. If you've gotten inside your hero, you'll find yourself speaking his lines aloud, saying them first, then writing them down.

There are many ways, for instance, for a man to announce he's left a much-needed job. Ned, being Ned, puts it jauntily: "I quit — resigned — turned in my badge — whatever you want to call it. Me and the government of this sovereign state won't be keeping company any more." Again, his curtain speech, the line on which he slams the door, is not only typical of his casualness but takes a parting shot at her practicality: "So long. Don't wait up. You'll only waste the electricity."

When the twin jobs of plotting and characterization are done, you have finished a creative phase. The next steps are more mechanical. I find it practical to make three outlines. The first is chronological — a time chart showing each year covered by the novel. This lets me see at a glance where my characters are and what they are up to at a given time. It helps too to keep their ages straight, which is particularly important in the case of children. On the chart I also note significant events that occurred in the real world during each year in order to avoid such anachronisms as a too-lavish dinner table during food rationing and to take advantage of dramatic values inherent in the times. (In *The Seven Deadly Sisters*, for instance, some effective suspense grew from "bumping" one of the sisters from a plane when my chart showed a period of high-priority travel.)

The second outline might be called climactic, since it is based on the theory that a book needs dramatic peaks at reasonably regular intervals. It is useful to visualize the novel as a magazine serial broken into four or five installments, with each one ending on a rising note. This outline can be very brief, like the five installment one for *The Missing Years*:

   I. Return, Marriage, Desertion
  II. Life with Mother, On Own, First Man's Proposition
 III. End of First Man, Juvenile Delinquency, Second Man's Proposal
 IV. End of Second Man, Daughter's Fantasies, Third Man's Proposal
  V. Return of Husband, Dilemma, Decision

Such an outline is uninformative. But it serves as a key to grouping parts of the plot so that each section has action, interest and meaning, plus some element of suspense (in this case, romantic) that will carry over to the next section.

The final outline is a chapter-by-chapter breakdown. Its main object is not to repeat details of action already contained in the general plot summary but to make clear the particular function each chapter is to serve—how it forwards the plot, what it reveals about the characters, what light it throws on the novel's significance. The length of the summations depends on the complexity of the chapters. One of the few from *The Missing Years* that is short enough to quote goes like this:

Chapter Two

This chapter will go back to their college days, establish their respective character and relationship leading up to their marriage. In this it should be stressed that they are both very much in love—this must be well demonstrated here as a foundation for everything that comes later. Then will come her pregnancy, the scene with her mother, the gambling house. The primary purpose of this chapter is to get Ellen and Ned established as individuals and as a couple. Here must be shown what makes them close and what will later drive them apart. At the end of the chapter they can be confidently awaiting the birth of their first child, secure in their love and their roulette winnings.

So now (Does it seem forever? It's been four months.) the note box is filled, the fun is over and the book has to be written. It may be personal eccentricity or detective-story training but I prefer to start with the last chapter. Once it is down I know exactly where I am going and am better able to find my way there. The end provides a guide to what must be explained, emphasized and suggested in the rest of the book. After the last chapter comes the first and, finally, a bridge between.

By the time I get to the body of the book I usually find that I have in my note box the big dramatic scenes—the ones in which people shout, shoot or make love. Through all the stages of preparation, the thought train has been chugging along. When, in writing Ellen's sketch, I noted that she was dominated by a *grande dame*-type mother, the explosive possibilities of a clash between this mother and Ned began to appear. Before I got back to Ellen, I had quite a collection of dynamite-laden speeches for Mama and Ned to throw at each other.

Later, the sketch was sidetracked again as I began to wonder how Mama's hatred for Ned would make her treat his (and Ellen's) son.

Before long I had a list of taunts and insinuations along the "like father, like son" line that later provides partial justification for the boy's windup in juvenile court.

That kind of seesawing—from formal note making to informal jotting—never stops. Ideas for exciting action, snatches of dialogue, emotional highlights, psychological twists—these will flow freely through your mind while you are making your various outlines and sketches. Get them on paper while they're hot, even if it means interrupting your more formal work a dozen times a day. The more interruptions, the better, for your goal is not a collection of outlines but a dramatic novel. And what a wonderful feeling, when you start the writing, to find the drama already there.

I began *The Missing Years* with a high stack of random notes. The major scenes were down in almost finished form, minor ones in summary. In addition there were hundreds of oddments—notes to myself, keys to character and motivation, an occasional word or phrase for which I hoped to find use. Among these briefer notes were such springboards as "in forgive, accent must be on give," "draw kaleidoscopic picture of children without a father—Ted and Cub Scouts, Tina and movie heroes," and "in desertion scene may use strange-interlude technique, pointing up difference between what they say and what they mean."

With all this material, I had primarily a job of sorting and assembling. Using a separate envelope for every chapter, I put into each the appropriate scenes and scraps. The final stage bears a strong resemblance to the making of a jigsaw puzzle. Gradually you use up all your pieces and have a completed picture. The most important part is to make sure the cracks don't show—in other words, to make your transitions logical, your continuity smooth. The hardest writing, it's often said, makes the easiest reading. Comparably, the main object of these elaborate preparations is to make it seem to the reader that the novel wrote itself.

How to Break Up a Conversation

Allis McKay

May 1954

I f you turned your characters loose to talk "the way people really do," what a field day you could have! But in fiction, conversation must be a skillful shorthand which suggests, but seldom fully states, the ups and downs, the hems and haws of spoken language.

An hour must pass, in the lives of your characters, between the time that John drops by the house to see Mary and the time he takes his leave. To reproduce everything that is spoken during this hour would be terribly tedious—for you and your readers. It is up to you to give the essence of what is said; but it is also necessary to give the feeling of the elapsed hour, the pace-sense that you have actually been with these people for the full sixty minutes.

So we come to what I call the technique of "interruptive dialogue": your characters go on talking while the reader's attention is momentarily distracted by something else. What John says to Mary while she glances at the cookbook, measures out the sugar and dumps it into the bowl is undefined and extensible; like a good china cement, it flows into the cracks between the actual speeches.

Break up your dialogue into extremely short sections. Sustained conversation, where question and answer come thick and fast, must be saved for the high spots, for the climaxes where every spoken word is important. The rest of the time, action and speech (and description, in small doses) must be judiciously mixed so that each supports the pace of the other. Old Maestro John Galsworthy understood this perfectly in *In Chancery*:

> He heard (her) latchkey in the lock, and reached her side just as she turned round, startled, in the open doorway.
> "Don't be alarmed," he said, breathless. "I happened to see you. Let me come in a minute."

She had put her hand up to her breast, her face was colorless, her eyes widened by alarm. Then seeming to master herself, she inclined her head and said: "Very well."

Soames closed the door . . . . He heard her voice, uncomfortably, pathetically soft:

"Why have you come again? Didn't you understand that I would rather you did not?"

He noticed her clothes — a dark brown velvet corduroy, a sable boa, a small round toque of the same. They suited her admirably. She had money to spare for dress, evidently! He said abruptly:

"It's your birthday. I brought you this," and he held out to her the green morocco case.

"Oh! No-no!"

Soames pressed the clasp; the seven stones gleamed out on the pale gray velvet.

"Why not?" he said. "Just as a sign that you don't bear me ill-feeling any longer."

"I couldn't."

Soames took it out of the case.

"Let me just see how it looks."

She shrank back.

He followed, thrusting his hand with the brooch in it against the front of her dress. She shrank again.

Soames dropped his hand.

"Irene," he said, "let bygones be bygones. If I can, surely you might. Let's begin again, as if nothing had been. Won't you?" His voice was wistful, and his eyes, resting on her face, had in them a sort of supplication.

Note that there are *never* more than two speeches actually juxtaposed — even when they are short! The action goes on between and around them, so that one is aware of the total flow of time, made up of sights, sounds and movement.

This interlacing of the essential parts of a narrative is governed by your own personal style. It can be terse like Hemingway in *Men Without Women*:

Manuel was facing the bull again, the muleta held low and to the left. The bull's head was down as he watched the muleta.

"If it was Belmonte doing that stuff, they'd go crazy," Retana's man said.

Zurito said nothing. He was watching Manuel out in the center of the arena.

"Where did the boss dig this fellow up?" Retana's man asked.

"Out of the hospital," Zurito said.

"That's where he's going damn quick," Retana's man said.

In addition to interruptive dialogue, two other devices for aiding the passage-of-time effect are retroactive sentences and sentences which emphasize progress of time or the time of day.

1. Retroactive sentences:
   The gentle sound of the rain had finally stopped.
   The frowning look had gradually left his face.
2. Sentences emphasizing progress of time or the time of day:
   Walking slowly, they had left the lighted corner behind.
   She looked around for a comfortable chair. If he was bent on telling his troubles, she might as well listen relaxed.
   It was noon now; the buzzer sounded faintly down at the school-house and she could hear the shouts of the children.

I had, in my last book, *Goodbye, Summer*, an unusual technical problem. The boy and the girl have been only casual friends. Time and again, Steve has tried to get to know Enid better; his overtures have been not so much rebuffed as unnoticed. It is not until Enid's last night in the city, when she indifferently asks him along for a walk, that in a scene lasting through an evening they become lovers.

The difficulties here were considerable. The time element was, by implication seven or eight hours, a long time to keep people talking in a story. The transition in mood, from casual to intense, took the most careful handling. The texture of the scene called for no violent action, nothing but a stroll through the streets, a glass of wine in a café. The talk starts *adagio molto*.

"Thank you for helping me with the play. I haven't had time to start another, but I mean to."

"Oh, that's all right." Enid was slightly piqued; she changed her mind about any further mention of her departure. "I'm certainly seeing this place for the last time in a typical mood. Just done raining, and so soft, and misty, and not too cold. As if it were sorry, and wouldn't do it again . . . . Not for a few hours anyway."

"It was like that when I first came to Seattle," Steve said, remem-

*bering the white collars of mist around the lampposts, and the muffled
sound of traffic.*

For a while they talk at cross-purposes. Enid is preoccupied with her
own plans, Steve has just had a disappointment in the work he is doing.
His curiosity finally leads him to ask her some questions about her past.
To her rather bitter answers he says:

> *"You sound as if men made all the trouble in the world. Women
> make trouble, too."*
> *"Ah, don't they!" Enid flashed a look at him. "Your woman been
> making you trouble?"*
> *"Well, as a matter of fact," Steve said stiffly, "she isn't exactly —
> that is, I'm — I'm not —"*
> *"I didn't think you were," Enid said.*

As the speeches intensify, the action picks up. They stop in a drugstore for coffee, inspect used cars in a lot, explore a viaduct from which
they get a view of the city. Enid decides that she wants to walk through
Chinatown.

> *"It's not very well lighted," Steve said, feeling responsible. His arm
> was trembling when she took it, and she did not think this was because
> he was afraid.*

In Chinatown they hear a thin sound of Oriental music coming from
one of the buildings, and Enid, her composure giving way, cries and
borrows his handkerchief. "Keep it," Steve says shortly. "It belonged
to one of those tiresome people you used to know out in Seattle." The
dialogue, now in its twelfth page in the book, has changed from small
talk to reminiscence (on the part of both) and then, on Steve's part, to
reproaches. To break the tension, Enid suggests a glass of wine.

Over the champagne Steve reminds her that they were at a party
together once before, where they drank champagne and listened to *Le
Sacre du Printemps*. The action is thinning out, to stress the speeches.

> *"And ever since then," Steve said recklessly, "I've been sort of
> following you around."*
> *"I don't believe you." But there was something in her eyes that
> was not wholly disbelief.*
> *"Why do you think I'm staying at this particular boarding house?"*
> *She drank thoughtfully. "Either you're a very foolish young man,*

or else you're telling an awful whopper. In either case I ought to send
you right home."

"I wouldn't go."

The corner of her mouth twitched ever so slightly. "No, I suppose
you wouldn't."

Then, having laid the groundwork, I did what you may do when the
values of a scene are fully established: I cut it off short, with a row of
asterisks. When it picks up again, it is becoming a love scene.

> *. . . "That's enough of that," Steve said. He took hold of her shoul-*
> *ders and kissed her on her rain-sweet lips.*
>
> *He had been trying to make up his mind all the way up the hill to*
> *do this, though he wasn't sure he could crowd his luck so far. Now*
> *he did not really think at all; it was simply that he had to stop her*
> *dear silly flow of words before she tore herself to pieces with them.*
>
> *Enid stared up at him. "You do that at your own risk," she said*
> *finally, in a little breathless voice.*
>
> *"That's what I figured." Steve put his arms around her, and this*
> *time it was the real thing.*

The "break" described above is a technical device that may be used,
along with interruptive dialogue and passage-of-time sentences, to make
a conversation seem longer than it is. Manipulation of dialogue—breaking it apart so that you may form it into a smoother whole—keeps the
speech of your characters from sharing the sad fate of *Oh, Katerina*—

> *I cannot love you;*
> *There's too much of you.*

Research in Reverse

Richard Deming

March 1956

One of the stock bits of advice hopeful writers get from professionals is: "Write about what you know." The usual meaning is that you should write only from your own intimate experience, and avoid backgrounds about which your knowledge is only vicarious. If you live in a small town, write only about small towns; if you're city bred, write only about cities; if your home is a ranch, write only westerns.

The pros themselves don't follow this advice, of course.

If they did, no one would ever write a historical novel, and certainly there wouldn't be any science fiction.

This advice should be turned around to read: "Know about what you write." Obviously your background must not only *sound* authentic, but *be* accurate, for otherwise dozens of gleeful readers will denounce you to your publisher because on page 104 your hero pulled a derringer from his sleeve and pumped a .44-caliber bullet into the villain, when any fool knows the derringer takes a .41.

But you don't have to grow up in a penitentiary to write a prison story. I won't go as far as to say you shouldn't at least make a visitor's tour through one, or talk to a warden or prison guard. But with only a sketchy knowledge of prison life you can write an authentic-sounding story, providing you know the techniques.

Vice versa, you could write a prison story completely lacking in realism, even after a lifetime in jail, if you don't know the techniques.

I used to have a cop friend, now dead, who on his retirement after twenty years of police work decided to try his hand at fiction. Rather understandably he chose crime fiction, feeling that with his background it would be a natural. He mailed his first cops-and-robbers yarn to one of those agents who take on novice writers on a reading-fee basis.

Except for personal letters my ex-cop friend hadn't written a word since the homework he reluctantly did for high school composition, so it wasn't surprising that the agent managed to find quite a few things wrong with the story. As a matter of fact the letter of criticism was nearly as long as the script.

My friend accepted most of the criticism humbly enough, but when he reached the point where the agent said his background lacked authenticity, he blew his top.

"Wait'll I write that jerk and tell him I was a cop for twenty years," he said.

"That's the only way he'll ever find it out," I told him. "It certainly doesn't show in your story."

And it didn't.

Of course, what the agent was criticizing in the story was not lack of knowledge on the author's part, but his inability to get across a *feeling* of authenticity. Any professional knows the distinction here, but it's a common mistake among tyros to think that detailed knowledge of a field of work or familiarity with a background will automatically give their scripts a ring of truth. Actually, what makes a story *sound* authentic is almost entirely a matter of technique. If you don't have that, you can be a walking encyclopedia on your subject and still not convince your reader.

SPRINKLE THE DETAILS

It's a simple enough technique to describe, though not quite as simple to put in practice. Basically it consists of sprinkling your script with realistic details, but in such a manner that they are unobtrusive. Too keep them unobtrusive, you use them only where they serve to advance the story. If you find yourself inserting odd bits of background simply to demonstrate to the reader that you know your subject, you are overdoing the technique.

To illustrate what I mean, here is a passage from *Hell Street* published a few years back. In this scene a woman has accused the head of the St. Louis Homicide Squad that he ignored her complaint that a death, the police closed as an accident case is actually a homicide. Irked at the woman for taking up his time, the lieutenant in charge gets off this statement:

> *"The Homicide Squad consists of me and ten other men, Miss Parker. All of them cops. We don't enjoy the luxury in Homicide of having police stenographers assigned to us. Not one of my men can*

take shorthand or type with more than two fingers, but they all have to type up their own cases. A city this size has lots of homicides. Besides that we go out on suicides, accidental deaths, attack cases and arson cases where somebody dies. Not a day passes but somebody comes in who knows Uncle Joe was pushed off that ladder while painting the eave troughs because they had a dream he was murdered, or knows Aunt Minnie never would have committed suicide because only last Christmas she said suicide was a coward's way out, or just plain has a theory after reading about a killing in the newspapers. You can't blame us for not putting the whole squad on an accident case because somebody tells us the guy never bathes on Tuesday.

In this passage a number of authentic facts about the St. Louis Homicide Squad are deliberately thrown at the reader, but in such a way that they will sink into his consciousness without his realizing that he is being educated. For every word the lieutenant says stems directly from his feeling of irritation at the woman who is bothering him, and therefore is important to the progress of the story. If I had the lieutenant state the same facts without an ample, or even a compelling motive, they would stand out as a deliberate attempt on the author's part to show off knowledge.

Incidentally this novel brought the following reaction from a publisher, in a letter to my agent: "I rather imagine Richard Deming is a St. Louis newspaperman and that he's written this story out of his experience as a police and crime reporter there. In any event to me it carries a sense of complete authenticity as far as police work goes."

I have never been in either police or newspaper work, and I live seven hundred miles from St. Louis.

SURE, BUT WHO'S GOT THE MONEY?

Sure, you say. But you did a lot of research. Who's got enough money for a seven-hundred-mile trip to do research?

I did do research, of course. Two weeks of it, which doesn't seem to me an unreasonable length of time to spend collecting background for a 78,000-word novel. Usually, collecting sufficient data for a short story takes me no more than a day.

The word *research* tends to create a mental image of exhaustive scholarly toil in the minds of many authors, with the result that they incline to write "off the top of their minds," either skirting around facts they aren't sure of by being deliberately vague, or plunging ahead armed with only half knowledge and risking being in error. But those who are scared off by the word usually visualize research as the sort of thing graduate students do before writing a thesis — poring over countless books and assimilating every known fact about the subject at hand.

You don't have to do that type of research for a piece of fiction. You aren't writing a treatise. You're writing a story. *All you need to know about your background is that part of it which appears in the story.*

Suppose you decide to write a tale with a canning-industry background. The scholarly approach would be to learn everything you could about the industry before setting a single word on paper. But you're not a scholar; you're a teller of yarns. You don't have to have an expert's knowledge of the whole field, because you're merely using the canning industry as background for a piece of fiction, not preparing a graduate thesis on the subject. The only knowledge you need is on the points which bear on the particular story you're writing.

The unobtrusive inclusion of a few authentic facts about the canning industry, plus a careful avoidance of factual errors, will give your script a ring of authenticity which would fool Mr. Heinz of the Fifty-Seven Varieties.

AFTER THE FIRST DRAFT

The time-saving device I use is to write my story first, then do my research and fill in my background after the first draft is completed. This has the advantage of fixing in my mind the specific data I need, so that I don't waste research time accumulating a lot of lore I have no use for.

For example, this is from the first draft of my next novel.

One of the fishing tugs, the Nancy Ree, appeared in the breakwall channel at that moment. We watched as it pulled into the dock. (Find out exact docking procedure.)

In the final draft, after I had done my research, the passage read like this:

One of the fishing tugs, the Nancy Ree, appeared in the breakwall channel at that moment. We watched as it bore directly toward the dock at full speed, swung around and reversed engine at the last moment, and smoothly settled its starboard side against the old automobile tires fixed to the dock to serve as bumpers.

The first drafts of my stories are full of such notes. When a first draft is finished, I make a list of the parenthetical entries, and know exactly what information I have to dig up. Often the realistic facts which appear in my yarns constitute *all* I know about the subject I've used as background. But that's all I have to know.

HELP FOR LAZY WRITERS

Being essentially lazy, I've evolved a time-saving method of doing research too. Instead of poring over books, I simply go to the people who are experts in the fields I want to know about.

For instance, in the book I just mentioned there is considerable background about the Lake Erie fishing industry, although that doesn't happen to be the central theme of the book. I got most of my data by talking to the captain and crew of a fishing tug, the rest by observation when I took a trip on the tug. Because I knew in advance the specific details I needed, my research took only one day.

If I had attempted to learn everything there was to know about the industry in advance of writing my story, with the idea that I'd sort out the data I needed as I wrote the script, a month wouldn't have been enough time for research. As is, practically all I know about commercial fishing could be condensed to two typewritten pages, and most of this scant knowledge appears in the book. Yet when I showed my tug-captain friend the sections of the book concerned with fishing, he said the story sounded as though an old-time tug captain had written it.

Nothing but the unobtrusive insertion of authentic detail, plus the careful avoidance of errors, accomplished this effect.

THE HARD WAY

I employed this same research technique in compiling data for the previous novel I mentioned concerning the St. Louis Homicide Squad. But as this was before I had learned the lazy device of writing my story before I did my research, I did it the hard way. I set out to learn everything on the subject I could.

I decided to do a crime novel with a St. Louis background more or less on the spur of the moment, mainly because I happened to be visiting St. Louis at the time. And since I knew nothing of St. Louis police and court procedure, I started calling on people who did.

During a two-week period I talked with the chief of police, the head of the Homicide Squad, the first assistant circuit attorney, the coroner and deputy coroner, the superintendent of the City Hospital (I wanted some dope on the hospital's prison ward), a private eye whose name I picked out of the phone book at random, and a couple of precinct cops.

To each person I explained I was gathering general background material for a novel and asked for a briefing on his particular field. Every one received me courteously and poured out information.

INVITATION TO AN AUTOPSY

To indicate how courteously I was received, not only did my informants answer all the questions I could think of, but I was invited to watch an autopsy, attend an inquest and observe a couple of homicide suspects being questioned.

I mention this courteous reception because I suspect that some readers at this point are mumbling, "Sure, that's fine procedure for an established writer, but would any of those guys give five minutes to *me?*"

The best answer to that is that, while I have since published five books and have two more coming up, and have now appeared in some high-paying magazines, this all happened five years ago. At the time I had never appeared anywhere except in pulp magazines and now a single person I approached had ever before heard of me. Believe me, all you have to say is that you're a writer doing research, and your welcome is assured.

You will find that nearly everyone is flattered to be asked for information by a writer, and no matter how important or busy he is, he'll usually spread the welcome mat at the magic words, "I'm a writer doing research."

If you want to specialize in historical novels or in exotic locales you haven't the transportation fare to visit, you're in for a lot of book research. But if you're content to write of contemporary people living in places you can get to, you can acquire all the background material you'll need simply and painlessly. Just walk up to the experts and ask for information.

Then when you have all the information you need, use it sparingly. Keep in mind that while readers like stories to have authentic flavor, they don't like to feel that they're being educated. Facts for facts' sake will only irritate the reader, but if your realistic details serve to advance the story instead of attempting to stand on their own isolated merit, your script will ring true and add immeasurably to its salability.

An Article Is Like a Sideshow

Helen Doss

November 1958

A well-constructed article is like a sideshow. Let's stroll down a typical circus midway, and take a look at one of the ballyhooed attractions.

First you see a teaser from the show, right smack in front of you, to catch your eye. Then a sideshow barker belts out a short spiel, telling you why you should plunk down your money and come in, and why you'll be glad if you do and sorry if you don't. If the teaser appeals to you, and the barker persuades you that this is something you don't want to miss, you go in and catch the tent show. The show works up to a rousing conclusion in the finale, and that's it. If the teaser was truly a foretaste of even better things to come, and if the barker was right when he told you that this was something you would not want to miss, you leave the show with good feelings about it.

The same is true of an article. Let's examine the elements, one by one.

THE TEASER

In sideshow business, this is a provocative act, or intriguing sample, taken from the show and displayed "out front," to catch the eye of the indifferent passersby. It not only calls attention to the fact that a show is going on inside, but also suggests something of its scope or its nature.

In writing, this trick of showmanship is called the narrative hook. It aims to catch the eye of the indifferent reader who is thumbing through a magazine.

The narrative hook must be more than merely interesting in itself; it should bear a definite relationship to the main point of the article. Like the sideshow teaser, it should suggest the scope, or the nature, of the article as a whole.

An anecdote or a dramatized incident makes an excellent narrative hook. A striking quotation from someone well known, or an authority in the field, is good. Startling facts or statistics can be eye-catching.

My own method is this: Having chosen a subject of general interest, I begin to gather material. The library is combed on the subject, with special attention to articles referred to in the ever-useful *Reader's Guide to Periodical Literature*. I hope to glean my freshest and most pertinent material from one or more interviews, and to do this I want to know all this background material before I go. It not only will save valuable interview time, but will also prepare me to ask the most intelligent and provocative questions.

When I have collected not only the bare facts and ideas, but also a wealth of good anecdotes, facts, quotes and figures, I am ready to organize my article. I pick out the very best anecdote (or fact, quote or figure) and save it for my finale; it should never be used for the narrative hook. If it actually was the best of the lot, everything coming after would be an anticlimax.

Among those which are left, I ask myself, which is the most arresting, the one most likely to make people sit up and take notice? Does it promise an opening into a subject of interest to the average reader? If the article is to entertain, does your chosen anecdote suggest fun to follow? If the article is educational, does the opening suggest something worth knowing about? If it is an article of challenge, does it begin by striking the reader where it hurts?

Let's suppose that an editor has shown some interest in an article you want to do on highway accidents. You have a great deal of choice in the kind of material you use in your opening. You might begin with some startling facts or figures about the number of highway accidents while the reader scans your own opening paragraph. A dramatized incident is always good; capture attention with a capsuled story of a specific, tragic car crash (actual or typical) in which you use detail and emotion to make the incident real and moving.

Your narrative hook is a bid for attention.

THE BALLYHOO

It is not always enough to have a teaser out front. Sometimes a barker needs to be there, too, pointing out that if you like the sample, there is much, much more in store for those who go inside the tent.

It is not always enough that a writer begins with a good narrative hook. Unless it is a subject of immediate and universal interest to all, like how to gain good health or how to make or save money, the reader may mutter, "This is all most interesting, but *so what*?" In such cases, the author must be a spieler at this point. It may be necessary to briefly and persuasively, and sometimes subtly, advance reasons why the reader should want to read about Horatio P. Bumbershoot, or the fascinations of button-collecting, or the incidence of pyorrhea in Samoa.

What will the reader stand to gain by reading on? A sense of adventure? A tickling of his funny bone? A chance to satisfy curiosity? Just good, solid entertainment? A chance to add to his collection of useful or curious knowledge? Or insight into some of his own personal problems or desires?

Check through some articles in issues of *Reader's Digest*, or some of the magazines for which you hope to write. Notice that in some articles, the reason why the reader should want to read that article is clearly spelled out. This gives the article purpose, significance, meaning.

In writing your article on highway accidents, you could follow the dramatized incident of the car crash with the warning thought that there is one chance in four that the *reader* will be killed or injured in a highway accident within a certain length of time. This brings the opening story right home in such a way that the reader will be prodded to read on, to see what he can do about it.

GIVING IT SIGNIFICANCE

The money you receive for an article—and the "play" the editor gives it—depends on its significance; the special meaning *you* give it.

Let's say that you have prepared an article on the basic difference between the agricultural policies of Secretary Ezra Taft Benson and those of former Secretary Charles Brannon. Your research shows that one favors modest government subsidies, while the other goes for broad government controls and direct bonus payments to all farmers. You compare their farm programs and the net profits of farmers under each system. You get quotes from leading farmers and economists.

That's the solid center of any national magazine "ag" article. Now, *how do we give it significance*? There are many excellent ways. One way is to project what will happen as a result of the Secretary's policies and to advise the reader how to prepare for it to the greatest advantage. Another way is to create ideas on how to improve the national "ag" program. Then get quotes on these ideas from the Secretary, himself, as well as from his political opponents.

These are the routine, normally successful methods of giving significance. But there is one other.

For this, you require intellectual prying plus a historical understanding of the subject. It is the road to originality in creating significance.

Specifically, in the "Case of the Two Secretaries," both men start on the same ground floor. They share the same intellectual base. Both are religious men, both believe in democracy. From that point, their roads part. One believes that God intervened personally when our Founding Fathers established this Nation, and any attempt to dissolve the spirit of private enterprise robs each American of his essential heritage.

The other believes that democracy is essential to freedom, and the only way to maintain a free, strong America is through a solid, numerically large farm population, even at the expense of government controls and large subsidies.

The end result is an article that shows the significance of the quarrel between the two Secretaries and is not a matter of technique, but actually is an Intellectual Divide.

THE MAIN SHOW

This is the real meat of your article; if this part isn't worth the reader's time, the editor won't want it no matter how tastefully you dress the whole thing up with an intriguing narrative hook and a coaxing spiel.

You'll note that articles in the better markets plug an idea, make a point, *have something to say*. There must be a thought-provoking idea to fit the size of the article. It cannot be too small and padded out to fit the space; it cannot be a skimming over the surface of a huge, sprawling book-length idea.

If you are doing an informational fact piece, organize those facts so that they guide the reader, with mounting drama, to an understanding of the overall picture. Or perhaps you might plan to begin with a familiar overall picture and break it down into the significant components.

If you are doing an idea piece, state your general idea, then break it down into the reasons which support it, in a rising order of importance. This can be done in reverse, too: Begin the body of the article with a related series of observations which lead inevitably to your conclusion.

In any case, no matter what kind of article you want to write, it should be worked out in *a logical progression of related ideas, in outline form. Build them toward a climax of interest. And illustrate, illustrate, illustrate!*

The illustrations in an article give it life, movement and human interest. You state an idea or a fact and then you say, in effect, "For instance —" Another idea or fact and another for instance. Another statement, then another illustration.

A lively or humorous anecdote, one which points up exactly what you are trying to say, makes an excellent illustration. So does a dramatized true incident. Anecdotes or incidents take the broad, generalized narrative statement from away up there in the clouds and bring the idea right down to earth.

Apt, well-put quotations can be effective illustrations. To show how a point can be strengthened by quotation from an authority, I'll quote a sample; this is from my book, *If You Adopt a Child*:

> *Is a divorce in the background of husband or wife bad? The statement of the Los Angeles County Bureau of Adoptions is typical of most agencies: "We believe . . . . "*

Facts and statistics can make either very dull illustrations or very good ones, depending on their pertinence and the way you handle them. Early in the adoption book I combined facts and figures with this quote:

> *In most places in the United States, especially metropolitan areas, the waiting period is likely to average one to three years. In a few areas, the wait may seem to be interminable, even fruitless. . . . A bulletin issued by the Wyoming Department of Public Welfare states: "As you may know, children who are available for adoption are scarce. Nationally there are approximately twenty-five families desiring to adopt children for every available child. Where our agency is concerned, the picture is even darker — nearer fifty families for every available child. . . ."*

Be careful that your facts and statistics are not too dull nor too long. Sometimes breaking them down into personal-sized figures will bring them home more vividly to the reader. If you are writing that article on highway safety, quoting the total number of traffic accidents in a year will not bring the statistics quite so shatteringly close to home as to quote the odds that the reader himself will be involved in a traffic accident during the next year. Or, even the odds of involving any normal American family group of five persons.

In gathering illustrations, I try to collect far more than I can use. After putting aside the best one for my ending, and the next best for my beginning, I still have a wide choice to illustrate the body of my article. Only the best need be used.

THE GRAND FINALE

It would be a pretty poor sideshow if it began with something of great interest and then gradually petered out.

It is also a pretty poor article if it begins with a bang and then peters out. When you have finished the body of your story, wind up neat and fast. *Cut it off; don't dangle to a close.*

One of the best ways to end is to use a top-notch illustration, which has been saved for that purpose. If it is to be a humorous, entertainment piece, leave the reader with the biggest chuckle of the whole thing. If it is biography, end with an anecdote, or dramatized incident, or perhaps a quote about, or by, your subject — one which beautifully sums up the point you have made about him.

If it's an idea piece, especially if it is a crusade article aimed to get the reader to act, sum up the reasons why he should act, or exactly what he *should* do about the situation. Do you want him to report to a clinic for a checkup? Write his senators? Adopt safer rules of driving? Become a whirling dervish? Let your parting words be specific.

If it is a fact article, stop when you have laid out your facts, when you have said what you wanted to say.

How I Write

Seventy-Five Years of Writing Advice

Throughout its seventy-five years, *Writer's Digest* has served as a link between those at the top of the writing profession and those who would join them at the summit. Through original articles, interviews and profiles, *Writer's Digest* introduces readers to the top writers of the day and—most important—reveals and explains those elements of craft that make the authors' work notable and successful.

In this chapter, you'll find a treasury of comments excerpted from our conversations with more than eighty of the authors who have shared their expertise with *Writer's Digest* readers. Only space kept us from including more writers—and additional comments from the authors already represented.

> I don't think a college degree is necessary to become a good writer. I'm not even certain it's an advantage. College probably won't *hurt* you—if you don't take it too seriously. But far more important, I believe, is broad general experience: living as active a life as possible, meeting all ranks of people, plenty of travel, trying your hand at various kinds of work, keeping your eyes, ears, and mind open, remembering what you observe, reading plenty of good books, and writing every day—simply writing.
> —Edward Abbey
> October 1988

> Life is terrible and is lived in the streets and in the fields and the place for the writer-to-be, therefore, is in the fields and in the streets. He doesn't explore anything by staying inside, safe from the beetles and the rain. His real subject matter is in the streets and in the courtrooms, in wards, in charity hospitals—in all the

places where people are in trouble. I think the writer must serve the inarticulate. I think it's wrong to believe that literature begins at the top with the most articulate and that our best writers should be the most educated and should write of the people who are most articulate and most socially important. It's always unpleasant to think that there's more vitality in the gutters than in the penthouse, and yet it's true. Nothing is commoner than for a man to write a play or a book or a short story, which is excellent and true, and then on the strength of that just do a fade-out so that you never hear anything more of him except in little pieces on suburban life in Westchester in the *New Yorker*.

—**Nelson Algren**
The Writer's 1960 Yearbook

A writer's style should not place obstacles between his ideas and the minds of his readers. Also I doubt that a writer can consciously create a style in the sense that a singer might be able to. Either you've got a certain style or you haven't. What you say is much more important than how you say it. Eugene O'Neill, judged sentence by sentence or page by page, could not be said to have an especially powerful style; his impact lies in the power of his ideas and the vigor with which they are expressed in toto.

—**Steve Allen**
February 1957

The contemporary playing area for comedy has moved. In the days of Buster Keaton and Charlie Chaplin, it was a more physical world. Keaton was running a locomotive and Chaplin was screwing nuts and bolts on things.

Now, if you work in a factory, everything is automatic and everyone's conflicts are psychological imbalance, loneliness and inability to relate. None of this stuff is very visual, and it is hard to find a vocabulary to express those conflicts.

—**Woody Allen**
The Writer's 1978 Yearbook

Regarding characters, my feeling is this: Get [the reader] to accept one thing, one weirdness, and then the rest of it must follow realistically. I try not to lie about psychology. I don't think I'm mawkish in my writing, I don't think I'm overly sentimental. I try to be emotionally honest within a framework which has one thing askew.

So in *Weaveworld*, the thing that's askew is the fact that out there is a world of magic hidden in that carpet. Once I've established that world of magic, the human response to it on the part of the characters must be emotionally true. Thereafter I've got to be as honest as I possibly can about the processes that take these characters to this place, that involve them in that story. Because as a fiction writer, the last thing you want to be is a liar.

— **Clive Barker**
March 1991

I think for a long time before I start a new book. It's got to be in my head a very long time before I start it. I know something about my main character. I know where I am starting and where I think I am going. I don't know some of the stuff that is going to happen in between. I think best with paper and pencil and make a million little notes to myself. I sometimes write on Kleenex boxes and then throw them away and get very upset. I try now to do all that scribbling in a notebook so I know where it is when I go back to it. Then I sit down at a typewriter and work in a very haphazard fashion. My first drafts are very rough. I think what I really start with is a basic situation. I don't know the characters. All of my characters develop on paper. The characters come as I am working every day. They surprise me.

— **Judy Blume**
February 1979

If you write a hundred short stories and they're all bad, that doesn't mean you've failed. You fail only if you stop writing. I've written about two thousand short stories; I've only published about three hundred and I feel I'm still learning. Any man who keeps working is not a failure. He may not be a great writer, but if he applies the old-fashioned virtues of hard, constant labor, he'll eventually make some kind of career for himself as a writer.

— **Ray Bradbury**
March 1967

You can't spread your ego *over more than one book*. No one on earth can keep pouring himself into every character. Even the greatest novelists, like Dickens and Tolstoy, had one autobio-graphical novel apiece in them. There was a writer, now editor of a country paper, whose work ranked as "literature" a few years back, but who made the mistake of putting himself into every character. If a scrubwoman spoke in a story of his, it was not a scrubwoman speaking; it was himself. Keep this up and suddenly you'll run dry; there just won't be any more. Remain an extrovert; look at your characters, take the reader inside their skins, but don't *be* those characters.

—**Louis Bromfield**
The Writer's 1935 Yearbook

The human brain is the laziest apparatus in the world. If you start to revise before you've reached the end, you're likely to begin dawdling with the revisions and putting off the difficult task of writing. Unless I find I've made some drastic mistake in character-ization or basic structure, I never go back until I've written the last page.

—**Pearl Buck**
The Writer's 1963 Yearbook

What I often do nowadays when I have to, say, describe a room, is take a page of a dictionary, any page at all, and see if with the words suggested by that one page in the dictionary I can build up a room, build up a scene. This is the kind of puzzle that interests me, keeps me going, and it will even suggest how to describe a girl's hair, at least some of it will come, but I must keep to that page. I even did it in the novel I wrote called *MF*. There's a descrip-tion of a hotel vestibule whose properties are derived from page 167 in W.J. Wilkinson's *Malay English Dictionary*. Nobody has no-ticed this. The thing you see, it suggests what pictures are on the wall, what color somebody's wearing, and as most things in life are arbitrary anyway, you're not doing anything naughty, you're really normally doing what nature does, you're just making an entity out of the elements. I do recommend it to young writers.

—**Anthony Burgess**
August 1975

I have been successful probably because I have always realized that I knew nothing about writing and have merely tried to tell an interesting story entertainingly. But there is another reason: From the beginning I have adhered to a policy of ordinary business honesty that was instilled into me by my father. My first stories were the best stories that I could write, and every story that I have written since has been the very best story that I could write. I have felt that it was a duty to those people who bought my books that I should give them the very best within me. I have no illusions as to the literary value of what I did give them, but I have the satisfaction of knowing that I gave them the best that my ability permitted.

— **Edgar Rice Burroughs**
June 1930

I decided a long time ago that writers should not be encouraged. They should be discouraged. That's more helpful to a writer than encouragement, because I think he's going to learn a lot more that way. If you are going to be a writer, you will be, encouraged or not.

— **Erskine Caldwell**
The Writer's 1960 Yearbook

A writer has got to be a cynic. You've got to look at life clearly. No rose-colored glasses. The human race is not very admirable. It was a big mistake of God's. . . . I think I appeal to readers because there's nothing false or hypocritical in what I write. And they recognize themselves, they recognize their fears. And they know what bastards they are.

— **Taylor Caldwell**
The Writer's 1980 Yearbook

I never specifically describe the sex act because it's such a bore laid bare. My readers wonder if they're normal if they don't have sex upside-down, swinging from a chandelier. So I'm their escape, their fairy tale. I give them the glamour and the beautiful clothes and the marvelous attentive men they are starved of.

— **Barbara Cartland**
June 1979

Aim at writing humor. Here is a country that loves to laugh, and there is virtually no one able to supply laughter for it. You can count the humorists on the fingers of two hands. Now that Thurber is dead, E.B. White is in a class by himself. There are one or two others, but the remainder are, for the most part, has-beens. I would say the writer who can turn out humor has ten times as good a chance of getting a first work published as those who continue to wallow in the sordid side of life.

—**Bennett Cerf**
The Writer's 1962 Yearbook

Every person you meet—and everything you do in life—is an opportunity to learn something. That's important to all of us, but most of all to a writer because as a writer you can use *anything*. There is not a person in the world who does not love to talk about himself and his job; who does not deem himself fascinating; who cannot tell you hours' worth of stories about the exciting life of an insurance agent, real-estate broker, garbage collector or preschool teacher. And they are all right. All people *are* interesting, and this is particularly true if *you* are writing a story about insurance, real estate, trash or a day-care center. From those people you will get information, and from their information you get verisimilitude, and verisimilitude is what makes fiction work. I never even got aboard a nuclear sub until *Red October* was in final editing. On the other hand, I *have* talked with a lot of people who are or were in this line of work.

—**Tom Clancy**
October 1987

When a man says his work is perfect, it's a sure sign that it is not. When he says his work is awfully good, it's not so good. When he says it's the best he could do, he is taking the right attitude. If he adds that he'll do better the next time, he has the proper spirit. If he says it's not as good as it might be, but he hopes to do better, he'll likely do better. At any rate, he should at least be satisfied with his effort, if not with his result. But I'll say that a man who doesn't believe in himself will get no one else to believe in him. The incurable egotist is the one who thinks the other fellow's work is not worth a hoop.

—**Irvin S. Cobb**
November 1925

I have learned something about working with editors, and that is to ask for their reactions to what they find wrong, and not for their suggestion for how to fix it. I always say, give me the symptoms, not the diagnosis or the treatment. I find it much more useful to hear "I got confused in this chapter" or "I don't know, I was bored here" than to be told to cut that scene, change this character.

Even the best editors don't know your book as well as you do, and their ideas for repair may not really answer their own objections. I think this is frequently the underlying problem when a writer makes the changes the editor requests, and the editor responds with, "Well, that doesn't fix it after all." In most cases the writer should blame himself, not the editor, because he has abdicated his own responsibility as a writer.

However, sometimes my editor can't exactly identify his objections to some part of the book. He has a problem, but I'm not clear what it is. At that point, I often say, "What sort of thing might fix it?" and then he'll respond, "Well, maybe if the character were a girl" or "Well, maybe if a bomb went off unexpectedly, something out of the ordinary." But now I am listening not to his specific suggestion but to what it implies. He's telling me he thinks the character needs to be softer, or he's telling me he thinks the plot needs something jarring and startling. So I try to satisfy his problems with the book, and not just do what he tells me to do.

Of course, sometimes he tells me what to do and he's right and I do it, and I'm very grateful. But you can't count on that.
— **Michael Crichton**
September 1986

Somebody who's starting out can save a lot of time by copying successful authors. You don't steal their concept or their story. What you steal is their style of writing . . . the way they structure their books. If you're writing adventure, see how someone like Alistair Maclean wrote adventure. How did his pace flow? How did he end the chapters?

It's like football. When the team comes back at the beginning of the year, the coach doesn't care if you're a big star or not. You start right in with the blocking and tackling . . . going back to basics. That's structure. Very simple stuff. For example: Are you going to write first person? Third person? How are you going to divide it up? Are you going to have a prologue? An epilogue? How

are you going to switch chapters back and forth? How will you start the next chapter? And how does it all tie in?
— **Clive Cussler**
April 1988

To me, the most important and difficult thing about writing fiction is to find the plot. Good original plots are very hard to come by. You never know when a lovely idea is going to flit suddenly into your mind, but by golly, when it does come along, you grab it with both hands and hang on to it tight. The trick is to write it down at once, otherwise you'll forget it. A good plot is like a dream. If you don't write down your dream on paper the moment you wake up, the chances are you'll forget it, and it'll be gone forever.
— **Roald Dahl**
August 1980

I believe that the entity of chance is very strong in any poet's writing. Even a mistake of some sort will lead to something that's maybe not a mistake, or at least not as much of a mistake.

I will not let a subject go until I have gotten it as close to what I think it ought to be as is humanly possible. I work by successive drafts. You never finish a poem; you abandon it. You should work hard to get as close as you can, not to some idea of pérfection you had before the poem was begun, but an idea of perfection that develops as you work and work on the poem. It's different and usually better than what you had originally conceived.

I use the same approach on all works, whether poetry or prose: I tacitly assume that the first fifty ways I try it are going to be wrong. Yet, the essential thing is to make it seem inevitable, to take all the sense of labor out of it. I very much believe in the principle of super-abundance and the attendant principle of cutting back. You can always take out or change, but you cannot always put in.
— **James Dickey**
The Writer's 1981 Yearbook

The idea for a short story will stay at the back of my mind for quite a time, and the same for a novel. Then, when I suddenly feel that I want to do them, I'll bring the idea out. Suppose I'm going to start writing a book in January. Well, about December, I'll get

a notebook, think it out in my head and just jot down what the chapters are likely to be and what events will be included in them: Chapter I—so-and-so meets so-and-so. That helps when you come to do the Chapter I. You look at what you've put down, "Ah, that's right," and then start—and type straight away nowadays. Have done for years . . . rather badly, on two fingers.
—**Daphne du Maurier**
The Writer's 1978 Yearbook

It is not enough merely to love literature, if one wishes to spend one's life as a writer. It is a dangerous undertaking on the most primitive level. For, it seems to me, the act of writing with serious intent involves enormous personal risk. It entails the ongoing courage for self-discovery. It means one will walk forever on the tightrope, with each new step presenting the possibility of learning a truth about oneself that is too terrible to bear.
—**Harlan Ellison**
The Writer's 1981 Yearbook

Concentrate on what you want to say to yourself and your friends. Follow your inner moonlight; don't hide the madness. You say what you want to say when you don't care who's listening. If you're grasping to get your own voice, you're making a strained attempt to talk, so it's a matter of just listening to yourself as you sound when you're talking about something that's intensely important to you.
—**Allen Ginsberg**
May 1984

Learn to listen when you're talking to people. Listen to how people say things, to what they really mean, because people frequently say one thing and mean another. Learn to separate the wheat from the chaff and look at your own poetry in the same way.

You must have a built-in shit detector. For example, if you've meant to be ironic or sarcastic, make sure you're not being just plain silly. Without becoming too down on yourself, learn to be your own worst critic.
—**Nikki Giovanni**
February 1989

What makes me happy is rewriting. In the first draft you get your ideas and your theme clear, if you're using some kind of metaphor you get that established, and certainly you have to know where you're coming out. But the next time through it's like cleaning house, getting rid of all the junk, getting things in the right order, tightening things up. I like the process of making writing neat. When I read my column in the paper and I find I've used the same word twice close together or if I've got something dangling, I can't stand it.
— **Ellen Goodman**
The Writer's 1981 Yearbook

Every author visualizes life from a different angle. I write of the features and scenic grandeurs that appeal to me, arranging my material in such a way to entertain my readers. Being a true lover of the West, the wild cañons, giant pines, silver-leaved aspens, wind-worn rocks, spear-pointed crags, saw-toothed mountains, purple sage and golden sunsets, I see much therein to write. The country haunts me — yet it thrills me. My mood is strange and melancholy, still I must thrill with my characters, else my novels would be lifeless. To produce something of real merit, the author must inject enthusiasm proper to the occasion, describe his characters vividly and powerfully, delineate his scenery in an appealing, artistic manner and pay particular attention to plot, suspense, characterization and all the other elements that go forward in the construction of a strong, realistic production.
— **Zane Grey**
October 1926

I had no time to write — zero time. But I figured I could *make* time if I could carve out little segments. I knew it would be a slow process, but I didn't care because I was in no hurry. I learned two very valuable lessons in doing that. One, you can't get in a hurry. Two, write every day if you want to see your novel completed. My goal was to write a page a day. Some days I could only find thirty minutes, some days two hours. Sometimes I would write five or six pages, sometimes just one. But writing every single day is of utmost importance. Especially if

like most beginning writers, you have another full-time job.
—**John Grisham**
July 1993

I never just sit and think; I do it by making notes because you doodle naturally. The first ideas are always very naive, and I always destroy them because I never want anyone to read them. Gradually, they develop and then I do several outlines. An outline is probably thirty to forty pages of single-spaced typing; writing that never sees the light of day as far as readers are concerned. I show that to my publisher, my agent and my wife to get their reactions, and I get a few reactions of people who, in the course of research, I came to know and whose judgment looks pretty good to me and perhaps a specialist in that area. Then I'll do another one and usually a third, and I'll more often than not go after the third outline.
—**Arthur Hailey**
August 1972

Ornately framed on my wall are two cans of sardines and eighteen cents. In 1960, I was living in a one-room apartment in Greenwich Village, New York. I was literally hanging on by my fingernails, trying to make it as a magazine writer. I was selling just enough to keep going from week to week, sometimes from day to day. In my little cupboard, I had those two cans of sardines that were all I had to eat in the world. And I had eighteen cents in my pocket. That's not the same eighteen cents by the way. I spent the original eighteen cents on a cabbage for dinner that night. I remember thinking at the time, there's nowhere to go but up. And I put the two cans of sardines in a sack and put it away. Whenever I would move because I didn't have the rent money, I would always take that sack with me. Six or seven years later I sold my first motion picture rights. That's when I had those two cans of sardines and that eighteen cents framed. No matter where I go, it will always be displayed as a reminder of the most significant lesson in the world—that when you're pursuing a creative goal, you must hang in there. You must have faith. You must believe.
—**Alex Haley**
August 1980

When I read a story and it gives me a wallop and I don't know how the hell the writer did it, I go back and look at it and try to figure out how. Sometimes it's really hard to figure out, if the guy is a deft magician. You're not going to see it right away. How did he do it? How did he saw that woman in half? When that happens you cheer, and then the craftsman takes over and asks how it was done.

You're looking both for what the thing is telling you—the content—and then how it is being told, which is the style. And I think there are lessons in both for everybody.
—**Pete Hamill**
September 1993

Despite the vast amount of outlining and thinking I do, when it comes to writing there's always new inspiration. My method of work is to get a very good idea of what I want to cover and assign a time percentage to it. I will rewrite each page, and then each few pages, moving ahead very slowly with the handwritten page. When I finish a whole section, I go back and type what I've rewritten. That is an extensive rewriting process—largely with language. Usually it will be taking out much and then getting new ideas to put in. Then I'll read it again, pencil it, and give it to a typist to type. It's not necessary to do much in the way of rewriting [after that]—it's largely a matter of cutting, changing words, catching an inconsistency.
—**Joseph Heller**
October 1977

My stories just reflect the sort of activities that country vets are doing all over Britain. There are animals and there are people, and I'm just putting down the interactions between the two in what I think is a readable form.

When I first started writing I tried to create beautiful, balanced sentences like something out of *Macaulay's Essays*. But I soon realized that was no good. So I got rid of most of my adjectives and high-blown prose and thought how I would tell the story if I were in a country pub.
—**James Herriot**
The Writer's 1979 Yearbook

What your readers expect of you, whether as reporter or as

columnist, is something exciting, something inviting, something for everyone, a comedy, tonight.

A cop told me, a long time ago, that there's no substitute for knowing what you're doing. Most of us scribblers do not. The ones that're any good are aware of this. The rest write silly stuff. The trouble is this: The readers know it.
—**George V. Higgins**
June 1978

The more you repeat your key word, the more successful your impact will be at the climax. Your words have to work *for* you. Don't use a word that means approximately the same thing. Be exact.
—**Shirley Jackson**
May 1966

There is too little humor in contemporary fiction. The number of women who have written funny books about the conditions of women can be counted on the fingers of one hand. I feel that almost anyone can write a droopy, depressing novel, but I am one of the few women who can write a truly funny book about my own sex. I think that the humorous vision of life gives you a philosophy that the wimpy, whiney outlook doesn't permit.
—**Erica Jong**
June 1981

When the question is therefore asked, "Are writers made or born?" one should first ask, "Do you mean writers with talent or writers with originality?" Because anybody can write but not everybody invents new forms of writing. Gertrude Stein invented a new form of writing and her imitators are just "talents." Hemingway later invented his own form also. The criterion for judging talent or genius is ephemeral, speaking rationally in this world of graphs, but one gets the feeling definitely when a writer of genius amazes him by stroke of force never seen before and yet hauntingly familiar (Wilson's famous "shock of recognition"). I got that feeling from *Swann's Way* as well as from *Sons and Lovers*. I do not get it from Colette, but I do get it from Dickinson. I get it from Céline, but I do not get it from Camus. I get it from Hemingway, but not from Raymond Chandler, except when he's dead serious.

I get it from the Balzac of *Cousin Bette,* but not from Pierre Loti. And so on.
—**Jack Kerouac**
    January 1962

To succeed as a writer one must have at least a tiny spark of that God-given flame which we call talent; a flexible and extensive vocabulary; a natural sense of word values and phrase forms; an aptitude for facile and rapid observation and the ability to record observations clearly and convincingly; a knowledge of human nature and an attitude of sympathetic understanding toward it; a sincerity which is so complete that, since it never permits self-deception, never fails to leave its imprint on others; a vivid imagination, a retentive memory and an unpoisoned sense of humor. It should be self-evident—but unfortunately does not always seem to be—that a would-be author also should be able to either spell by instinct or work with a dictionary within constant and convenient reach; should know and observe the rudimentary rules of syntax and punctuation; should attempt to describe only conditions and circumstances which are familiar, and should spare no pains to become more familiar with conditions and circumstances which it is desirable to attempt to describe; should regard a long novitiate as not only inevitable but desirable; should approach the preparation for authorship with at least as much patience, intelligence, zeal and earnestness as the average mechanic approaches the period of apprenticeship; and should furthermore remember that writing is not only a trade but a trust—a tremendous responsibility, for an author is answerable to every one of his readers for his statements—and that if it is to be successful in the highest sense of the word, it must, like matrimony, be approached not "unadvisedly or lightly, but reverently, discreetly, soberly, and in the fear of God."
—**Frances Parkinson Keyes**
    The Writer's 1931 Yearbook

Choosing a topic is really an important issue because you're going to be spending so much time and energy on a book. It's just guesswork, and it's a dicey question, but what I have finally come down to guide myself with is that the general subject had better be something I'm interested in. Sometimes things go wrong. I mean, I

wasted a year on two different projects that just didn't pan out.
— **Tracy Kidder**
November 1990

The best work that I've ever done always has a feeling of having been excavated. I don't feel like a novelist or a creative writer as much as I feel like an archaeologist who is digging things up and brushing them off and looking at the carvings on them. Sometimes you get a little pot out of the ground, and that's a short story. Sometimes you get a bigger pot, which is a novella. Sometimes you get a building which is like a novel. When I feel like I'm "creating," I'm usually doing bad work.

The thing is for me, I never get all that stuff out unbroken. The trick and the game and the fun of it is to see how much of it you can get. Usually you can get quite a lot.
— **Stephen King**
March 1992

As a young writer, I tried to stuff my mind with as much literary landscape as I could, which I supplemented with real lampposts and real people. When you're starting out, it's inevitable that you spit back out what you're absorbing. The trick is to spit out your own landscapes, to use the visions of others to give you a sense of what a mental landscape is in the first place, and then find your own.

The young writer must understand that he'll never pass this way again. He should extract from life its *real* essence, which is uniquely his, but that understanding is like an insect sleeping in winter: It's numb and it needs something to wake it. The best substance for waking up is the wisdom of those who have gone before. That's the best.
— **William Kotzwinkle**
July 1992

In science fiction and fantasy, a careful balance should be maintained between the science — or pseudo-science — and the story interest. Formulas and abstruse jargon won't make a yarn convincing; just the opposite. The vital factor in writing pseudo-scientific tales is to keep your feet on the ground. Remember that you're writing about human beings, and that men and women, whether

on Mars or in the fourth dimension, will act like men and women —
will have problems, desires, motives similar to present-day ones.
The old ogre of characterization pops up; in no type of pulp fiction
is strong character work as vital as in this.
— **Henry Kuttner**
March 1938

It takes practice, practice, practice. Lots of hours hunched over
the typewriter learning how to put all these impressions down on
paper. Many people can write one story, but writing many stories is
a different thing. I often think the worst thing to happen to a writer
is to have a big success with his first book. Unless the writer has
done a lot of writing before, he will never have learned his trade
properly.

There are techniques and skills to be learned for writing as in
any profession or trade. All the stories fall into certain patterns of
behavior which we call plots. Plots are nothing but a constantly
recurring human situation, patterns of behavior. It's my belief that
90 percent of all fiction is based on just twelve to eighteen plots,
and you can find them in any metropolitan newspaper in any given
week.

The same plots used by the ancient Greek dramatists were also
used by Chaucer, Shakespeare and Dickens. Nobody "invents" a
plot.
— **Louis L'Amour**
December 1980

Start to write, and let one thing lead to another. Whatever you
do, don't start to be funny. As for myself, I start my stories with
no given destination in my mind. I simply let the stories write
themselves. It seems that each paragraph leads to the next.
— **Ring W. Lardner**
February 1926

Watch children at play. They are terribly serious about it —
even running into a jump rope. You're very serious as you get
in, to be sure the rhythm is there; as you're jumping, it gets
less serious and more play. The same thing is true with writing.
The first fifteen to twenty minutes, half hour, is getting into
that rhythm. Then once you're in it, you get caught up in the

rhythm. That's when it really gets to be complete play.
—**Madeleine L'Engle**
March 1982

I start with a concept that outrages me, something that bothers the hell out of me. I think arresting fiction is written out of a sense of outrage. I try to find something with an underpinning of reality. I generally go back over recent history looking for a situation where the events have a conceivable official explanation but where the solution might be other than it is purported to be.
—**Robert Ludlum**
September 1977

Most beginners think that writing is a quick ticket to some kind of celebrity status, to broads and talk shows. Those with that shallow motivation can forget it. Here's how it goes. Take a person twenty-five years old. If that person has not read a *minimum* of three books a week since he or she was ten years old, or 2,340 books—comic books not counted—and if he or she is not still reading at that pace, then forget it. If he or she is not willing to commit one million words to paper—ten medium long novels— without much hope of ever selling one word, in the process of learning this trade, then forget it. And if he or she can be discouraged by anyone in this world from continuing to write, write, write—then forget it.
—**John D. MacDonald**
The Writer's 1979 Yearbook

I never miss an opportunity to try to point out that poetry is made of words, yes, that it is made of words and sound, yes. But above all, in structural elements, poetry is made of lines. Unless the line is working, the rhythm is gone, and the power of poetry over the unsayable has disappeared with it.
—**Archibald MacLeish**
The Writer's 1982 Yearbook

The poet, if he or she wants to be read and understood, should write in the language of today. While I've had no formal training in psychology, I find it easy to identify with the average human being. A great many of us have common hopes, desires and needs.

I write about what I know, but I'm not afraid to explore the unknown. Human nature is complicated, but each of us sets up a number of those complications. The trick is to reduce each of them to basics. There are roots from which the complications and appendages in everything stem. It isn't difficult to find those roots or initial premises once you've set up certain rules for your own thinking and writing. For instance, no matter how smart you think you are, how gifted or intellectual, never write over, under or around people. Write straight ahead. The only way to protect the language is to use it simply and straightforwardly. Writers are only communicators. We are not some lofty breed meant to speak only to other writers. If we are given the gift to communicate, we should not abuse it.

— **Rod McKuen**
  February 1984

For me the criterion for a good novel is that the author has created a total world in which his people move credibly. And the books that do this I prize. *The Idiot*, for example, and Thackeray's *Vanity Fair*, Twain's *Huck Finn*, which I like very much; these are fine examples. The novel is just a little cosmos and we're prepared to accept it, it's just a real world. This is a great accomplishment. I'm not good at plotting, it doesn't interest me at all, and I'm not good at writing the well-rounded English novel. I don't care about that. I get around it by spending so much time creating that world that I get thousands of letters from people who say how totally immersed they were in the world and how sorry they were to have it end. That works for me.

— **James Michener**
  May 1972

There's no harm in lying a bit. In a sense, art is a lie. It's one great lie. It isn't a replica of life, it's what life ought to be in the mind of the artist, or what it could be. [Writers] write about life as it is, but that's not what we want in art, as it is, I don't think. [Writers should write about life] as it might be or could be, even as it ought to be.

— **Henry Miller**
  November 1980

The most important influence on my writing technically has been ethical—as my brother once said of a florid piece of description, "Starve it down and make it run." My mother who first instructed us—my brother and me—in French and music (the piano) when we were very small, had a passion for books—finding gems amid the debris of booksellers. She advantaged me more than by exciting tests, when she remarked under crushing disappointment, "Sursum corda; I will rejoice evermore."
—Marianne Moore
October 1963

I revise endlessly—chapters, scenes, paragraphs. . . . I don't like to push forward with a story or novel unless it seems to me that the prose is strong enough to be permanent, even though I know very well that once the work is finished I will want to rewrite it. The pleasure *is* the rewriting. The first sentence can't be written until the final sentence is written. This is a koan-like statement, and I don't mean to sound needlessly obscure or mysterious, but it's simply true. The completion of any work automatically necessitates its revisioning.
—Joyce Carol Oates
April 1986

It is details, sprinkled through the narrative, that give a historical novel the feeling of actuality, the verisimilitude that is especially important in this kind of writing. They cannot, of course, be forced into the story merely to impress the reader; they must come naturally and, if possible, they should contribute to narrative interest and character development as well as background. Thus it is one thing to make the statement: "The Chippewa, unable to pronounce Ls, enunciated them as Ns." It is quite another to say: "The traders were amused to hear the Chippewa girls say Michinimackinac instead of Michilimackinac." Above all, the historical novel must never smell of the lamp.
—Walter O'Meara
June 1964

Horror and sensuality have always been linked. Good horror writing is almost always sensuous writing because the threat posed in horror fiction is usually a veiled erotic threat. If you go back to your earliest horror stories in English, there's always a tremendous emphasis on mood, and atmosphere, and the response of the physical body to the menace. Horror writers are almost always dealing in atmosphere and suggestion. Confusion of the senses, confusion of the mind to overwhelming physical responses. That's part and parcel of the genre.

With me, there's no method. Writing to me *is* sensuality. It is talking about the assault on the senses and the effect on the individual. The main thing is to immerse yourself in the material, and reach for the intensity. Again, go where the intensity is, to where the pleasure is, go where the pain is. Go for the passion. Do that honestly, and the rest will fall into place.

—**Anne Rice**
November 1988

You should spend thirty minutes a day looking at dirty pictures. Or thinking about sex. The purpose of this is to get yourself sexually excited, which builds tremendous amounts of energy, and then carry that into your work. Get yourself in that extreme state of being next to madness. Keep yourself in, not necessarily a frenzied state, but in a state of great intensity. The kind of state you would be in before going to bed with your partner. That heightened state when you're in a carnal embrace: Time stops and nothing else matters. You should always write with an erection. Even if you're a woman.

—**Tom Robbins**
March 1988

There must always be give-and-take in the creation of a musical. A book writer must realize that his best dialogue would be useless if the scene could be done in song more effectively. Conversely, the writers of the score must realize that their most beautiful song would be completely wasted if it did not fit smoothly into a specific situation in the plot. One of the great rules to remember in writing for the musical stage is never to love any single thing too dearly: The overall effect of the play is what should be uppermost in the minds of the writers.

—**Richard Rodgers**
The Writer's 1965 Yearbook

Without pressure, the work sometimes doesn't get done at all. You abandon most readily those works that have no destination other than your own wishes; that is, no editor or producer standing waiting for them. I often do this, although I don't like to. I prefer a pattern of seeing a job through. In fact not having such a pattern is what holds many young writers back. Their high standards, the demands they make of themselves, are so great they get a novel about a third done and then give up because they think it's not good enough. I've told every young writer I know to do the job all the way through even if he thinks it's no good. Then he'll have the precedent of having finished a work. It isn't unlikely that he's been mistaken anyway. All writers are discontented with their work as it's being made. That's because they're aware of a potential and believe they're not reaching it. But the reader is not aware of the potential, so it makes no difference to him.

—**William Saroyan**
The Writer's 1962 Yearbook

I think a lot of [success in Hollywood] is luck and continues to be. That in no way discounts the terrible urgency that you have talent. It's always who you know, what marvelous moment in time that you find him or meet him. I think one of the problems sometimes with the writer is the personality of the writer, because it becomes a very personal medium. Selling yourself is sometimes almost half the problem. The producer doesn't like you, consequently he reads the script with a very negative view. But I wouldn't preoccupy myself with that, I don't give a damn. You can be a hunchback and a dwarf and what all. If you write beautifully, you write beautifully, that's all.

—**Rod Serling**
The Writer's 1976 Yearbook

I wish I could tell you that in our great land of occasional prosperity, the vital writer can always find an immediate market. But I cannot tell you that. I cannot say anything different from what I would have said in Grub Street two hundred years ago. The man who has a real ideal of great writing, and has to live by it, will have to tighten up his belt and move into a garret or perhaps into a tent in the wilderness. But I can promise you the old, enduring satisfaction of being able to keep your own self-respect and integ-

rity of spirit; also the affection of the few readers who will be gathered to you little by little.
—**Upton Sinclair**
The Writer's 1931 Yearbook

Any sportswriter who thinks the world is no bigger than the outfield fence is not only a bad citizen of the world but also a lousy sportswriter, because he has no sense of proportion. He should be involved in the world in which he lives.
—**Red Smith**
June 1982

If not forced by considerations of nuance and meaning, I do not seek variety. Stay with the core of your poem, I say. Smart is OK, but lucky is better. Find the language that leads you easily onward in so natural a way that you do not have to be smart.

The needs of the developing poem will suggest what words fit right, and those phrases that emerge will enhance, or can enhance, any shabby beginning you had the nerve to start with.
—**William Stafford**
February 1992

If there is a magic in story writing, and I am convinced that there is, no one has ever been able to reduce it to a recipe that can be passed from one person to another. The formula seems to lie solely in the aching urge of the writer to convey something he feels important to the reader. If the writer has that urge, he may sometimes, but by no means always, find the way to do it. You must perceive the excellence that makes a good story good or the errors that make a bad story. For a bad story is only an ineffective story.

It is not so very hard to judge a story after it is written, but, after many years, to start a story still scares me to death. I will go so far as to say that the writer who is not scared is happily unaware of the remote and tantalizing majesty of the medium.
—**John Steinbeck**
The Writer's 1963 Yearbook

If one is convinced that he can really write, he should cast around for the sort of thing that he can do best and try to develop

that one thing. I can't pass out any rules for success because I don't know of any. As I said before, it was just luck with me; I wrote something that I thought was funny and the editor thought so too and so did the people who read it. Chance directed me to the parody theme and I worked it for all it was worth.
— **Donald Ogden Stewart**
   July 1931

To determine whether a subject will make a biographical novel, I first have to determine whether or not I can understand this person, grasp him, whether I can realize his values, whether I can live through his adventures, experiences, his failures, weaknesses, his faults, his errors, his collapses, as well as his successes, his ecstasies, accomplishments, realizations. It is imperative that I identify that closely, because in my way of writing, the reader must identify with the main character by the end of page 1 or 2 or the book is dead. I must feel that I can identify and become that person and that this story is well worth having lived and it is meaningful; that this life accomplished something, this life went through all the drama and against all of the obstacles and the stone walls that any human being can ever face and yet climbed the wall and emerged on the other side. There has to be some kind of triumph along with the corollary defeats. Once I think that this is a biographical novel and I can handle it, then all the elements come together.
— **Irving Stone**
   The Writer's 1968 Yearbook

I don't like first-person reporting. I believe that some of the density, some of the depth is lost if you do it first person. You see, if you start writing first person, you're going to have to stay with it. That means you yourself become the focal point of the piece, and everything reacts to your writing about yourself as a person who is going out and having things happen to him.

What I do is this: I go from person to person. I'm like a director, and I shift my own particular focus, my own cameras, from one to the other to the other; eventually I have a whole gallery of people I'm writing about. And you can only do this with the third person. I find that I can then get into the people that I am writing about and I just shift. That's where my own subjectivity, or creativity, as you will, comes into play. I make the choice of where the camera is going to go. I decide who I will focus on, and the order of the focusing too.

This gives me a lot of options. It allows me to be creative and yet factual. That's what I think is exciting about nonfiction these days. You can do all the novelist can do—you just have to do a *hell* of a lot of research. You have to know your people very, very well. And you have to be able to work within their words, and work within the framework of their lives. But if you dig deeply enough into their lives, you come up with so much that it gives a lot to work with, and you can still be creative and selective in what you choose to work with.
— **Gay Talese**
   February 1973

I have learned, as has many another better writer, to summon inspiration to my call as soon as I begin my day's stint, and not to hang around waiting for it. "Inspiration" is merely a pretty phrase for "the zest to work." And it can be cultivated by anyone who has the patience to try. Inspiration which will not come at its possessor's summons is like a dog that cannot be trained to obey. The sooner both are gotten rid of, the better.
— **Albert Payson Terhune**
   June 1930

I'm always trying to vary my routine. So I keep the poet in me going. I keep an element of tossing and turning in my job. The result is a real sense of satisfaction when a work is finally done.
— **John Updike**
   September 1977

Talent isn't enough. You need motivation—and persistence, too: what Steinbeck called a blend of faith and arrogance. When you're young, plain old poverty can be enough, along with an insatiable hunger for recognition. You have to have that feeling of "I'll show them." If you don't have it, don't become a writer. It's part of the animal, it's primitive, but if you don't want to rise above the crowd, forget it.

You have to evolve a permanent set of values to serve that function [of motivation]. For me, fighting the scourge of anti-

Semitism—an apparently incurable cancer—became my ultimate motivation. As a writer, you've got a shot at making an impact on the world until your dying day, and even beyond. And that allows me to keep saying, as I have before, that wise old writers never die. They don't even fade away. They just snarl forever.
—Leon Uris
August 1987

To keep a journal is a very good thing if you want to be a journalist. The novelist is always imagining. The novelist starts with a sentence: "I am Myra Breckinridge, who no man can possess." Well, that's all I needed. I didn't know where that book was going. I hadn't even made up my mind about the sex-change at that point. I heard this voice in my head. Absolutely like Joan of Arc, telling me to liberate my native land. And so, from one sentence came the next sentence. Then you weave the sentences together, and the sentences have their own kinetic energy. It's like Baron Frankenstein's electrical machine; suddenly the clay monster of language gets filled with life and sits up, and perhaps murders the little girl.
—Gore Vidal
March 1975

Writing a novel is like making a movie: All sorts of accidental things will happen after you've set up the cameras. So you get lucky. Something will happen at the edge of the set and perhaps you start to go with that. You come into it accidentally. You set the story in motion, and as you're watching this thing begin, all these opportunities will show up. So in order to exploit one thing or another, you may have to do research. You may have to find out more about Chinese immigrants, or you may have to find out about Halley's Comet, or whatever, where you didn't realize that you were going to have Chinese or Halley's Comet in the story. So you do research on that, and it implies more, and the deeper you get into the story, the more it implies, the more suggestions it makes on the plot. Toward the end, the ending becomes inevitable.
—Kurt Vonnegut
November 1985

I start out with an outline, but then I always abandon the game plan when the characters take over the story. I just let them do their thing and see what happens. Sometimes it works out—*usually* it works out. Sometimes it doesn't, but usually if I just let the characters take over I do better than if I sit down and calculate and try to plot the thing. I just write and it works out for me.

—**Joseph Wambaugh**
December 1973

Institutions and standards that seemed to be established altogether and completely unchallengeable in the novel of fifty years ago are now challenged and changing; and the discussion of such changes, which was once unthinkable for ordinary people, is now a determining factor in their lives.

Some people complain that in my novels, instead of picturing life, I discuss it. I certainly have it discussed. It is impossible to picture contemporary life without discussing it. People who are not discussing now are not alive. No doubt, it is hard to report people thinking in character as well as acting in character, and I admit that I do it at times atrociously, but it has to be done. I plead the pioneer's right to be clumsy. Better be clumsy than shirk the way we have to go.

—**H.G. Wells**
February 1932

The writing of a novel is taking life as it already exists, not to report it but to make an object, toward the end that the finished work might contain this life inside it, and offer it to the reader. The essence will not be, of course, the same thing as the raw material; it is not even of the same family of things. The novel is something that never was before and will not be again. For the mind of one person, its writer, is in it too. What distinguishes it above all from the raw material, and what distinguishes it from journalism, is that inherent in the novel is the possibility of a shared act of the imagination between its writer and its reader.

—**Eudora Welty**
February 1970

The whole secret in this business is overkill. I figure that an interview with a man, whether you print it or not, is an investment in the future. You interview everyone you can talk to and then

you use what is necessary to make the story. It's like being blind-folded while you go through a basket of black and red peas trying to pick one color. If I knew at the beginning of any presidential campaign what was going to happen, I could interview only twenty people to get my whole story. But I have to interview 150, 200 or 300 people during the campaign in order to get the proper stuff.
—**Theodore H. White**
  July 1975

Life is made up of such a conglomerate concoction of everything that nothing really good or nothing really bad comes the way of most of us. Consequently, it is up to the average person (the author) to make for himself a life out of life.
—**Thornton Wilder**
  November 1929

I don't like poems that seem to say, "Guess what I mean." This is not to say that I think everything in a poem should be on the surface. Not at all. It's simply to say that there should be a surface, a place for the reader to stand. Young journalists used to be taught to answer the questions *who, what, where, when* and *why* in the first compressed paragraph of a story. I would go so far as to say that the first four of these ought to be answered in a single reading of most poems.
—**Miller Williams**
  April 1993

A playwright goes through three phases. First, he is submissive. He is a nobody. He is afraid to assert himself. Everybody cuts his play. Or orders him to build up a part for himself. He yields.

In his second stage he has become a purist. Everything is a threat to his integrity. He throws his weight around.

And in the third he is a veteran. He has learned to accept the collaboration of other creative minds.
—**Tennessee Williams**
  The Writer's 1959 Yearbook

I don't actually compose in longhand. I lie back in a long chair and make notes, you know, bits of dialogue and then another bit of description. You see, I don't try to make it continuous. Then I work at the typewriter.

I find one system that works very well with me is to sit at the typewriter and have a pad on my desk, you see, on which I write out the next bit of the story, maybe a bit of dialogue or description, by hand, and then transfer it to the machine. But I make several drafts. The stuff I do on the typewriter isn't the final version. I mess it about a lot with ink, and put in bits and alter adjectives and things, and then make a fair copy of it. The great thing is, I like working on the typewriter. It rather inspires me.

—P.G. Wodehouse
October 1971

Success, reputation, audience are earned by some striking quality, not always admirable—it can be profundity, poetic brilliance, narrative power; it can be mere imaginative pornography, or a knack for crude sensation, or a skill at self-promotion. Fine authors are neglected. Critics make errors in guessing about the ultimate value of authors. But that has always been true of the literary life. Balzac, Twain and Maugham were dismissed as hacks in their day. This gives a permanent franchise to vulgar writers to consider themselves misunderstood abused failures; this encourages damned geniuses. Melville and Stendhal were authors to persevere and endure. In the long run justice is done. In the short run, geniuses, minor writers and mountebanks alike must just take their chances. Imaginative writing is a wonderful way of life, and no man who can live by it should ask for more.

—Herman Wouk
September 1966

1960s

What Way I Write!

Allen Ginsberg

October 1960

Once, chancing to read Blake, & dwelling on the words of the *Sunflower*, I heard his voice and looked out of the window, realizing that *this* universe was the Sunflower seeking Eternity. The experience led me to know Art as a time-machine to carry the secret revelation and transmit it unbroken from mind to mind.

Cézanne speaks of his "petit sensation," a feeling he derived from the observation of Nature, and at the end of his life refers to it in his letters as none other than "Pater Omnipotens Aeterna Deus." His Art became an attempt to "reconstitute" on canvas an abstract (by means of planes, cubes, etc.) of the spacetime data fed to his senses by Mt. St. Victoire.

Pound turned to the Chinese Written Character as a Medium for Poetry seeing that data can be juxtaposed (like planes, cubes, etc.) in clear word-pictures (visual images) on the page. Elliptical flashes of "sensation" in the reader's mind connect these polar images.

With this as the basic form of the poem, certain practical effects develop. There can be no interruption of the poem for mechanical measure, outside of the data presented. The images by their very nature are the design of the poem as in W.C. Williams or the later American School of Haiku. The purest shape of the image on the page is the true measure.

This seems to work in practice, since, when the natural-tongue words that compose these images are pronounced aloud, many curious rhythms are heard. These are rhythms heard in day-to-day speech, hitherto unnoticed. Practically speaking, classical systems of prosody are not workable in dealing with these natural rhythms.

It's premature to expect classification of sounds only recently noticed, but as they become familiar they will become subject to stereotype & classification perhaps.

Some methods of handling these rhythms consciously have become evident in the practice of various poets. Short lines in W.C. Williams are balanced mainly by relative weight of phrasing—speech-size, special emphasis, weight as mental imagery, silences indicated, etc. In Olson[1], the lines may be said to bear equal weight in that each is a unitary particle of energy in spontaneous composition. In Creeley[2], discrete short rhythmic entities are separated by breathstop to form new type couplets.

However, the mind is more than the tongue, as many writers have noticed recently. We are aware of events in other parts of the psyche besides that part which thinks in words. At certain times all diverse simultaneous impressions and events focus together to make a new, almost a mutant, consciousness.

It is necessary to resort to some very crude & rapid method of notation to sketch some fleeting sensory detail of this process of myriad sensations running thru the Being.

I have adapted, for myself, the single breath-unit as the measure of how much material I can handle-notate-compose at one continuous stroke. I learned much from Kerouac.[3]

The rhythm of this transcription becomes in this case the guiding rhythm of the poem when read aloud.

This means that I generally compose in long lines, depending on how falls my attempt to become conscious of my thought, look aside and notate it. I focus on the verbal transaction level, then my mind goes blank & I'm left only with words. So I must go on with the next thought. I do not know what I do. On what multitudes of levels do I operate? I get lost. I tell lies. I follow what comes in my mind next. Often short lines come in because I'm afraid I'll miss notating some particularly striking recurrent realization flashed thru the mind. The tricks of notation are many and varied. Just how do we think? and how can we watch ourselves think & notate that? I'm not sure what happens; generally I pause at the beginning of a new line, having short circuited my visual processes by the constant stop to notate. Unless the impulse-rhythm

[1]Charles Olson—See Selection in D. Allen's *The New American Poetry*, Grove, N.Y., 1960.

[2]Robert Creeley—*A Form of Women*, Jargon-Corinth Books, N.Y., 1959.

[3]Jack Kerouac—See some of the long sentences in *Visions of Cody*, New Directions, 1960 or *Doctor Sex*, Grove Press, 1959.

of the last speeds me forward; then I may stop in midline to invent a continuation of what I had forgotten after I began writing it down — or move on with a dash. I get some very strangely unexpected verbal & imagual connections this way, illogical recognitions that I cry as they are Poetry. In the course of this notation I finally get out beyond what I'd anticipated and discover what it is that's underlying my whole mind and soul at the moment — and find the course of that discovery now transcribed in the composition just finished. So that it is good to be able to say that I never in advance really know what I'm going to write, if the writing is to become anywhere near sublime. That's that.

The Short Story From a Purely Impersonal View

Hallie Burnett

The Writer's 1961 Yearbook

For a number of years I have been writing, teaching and editing the short story, yet panic overtakes me when I am faced with telling how to write one. I think I know; I think there are some (minor) rules to observe in writing a story; but on the great snow-covered plains of literature one cannot be sure if those mounds to the left and to the right are solid rock or simply drifts to be swept away by the next strong wind.

This is to say that the requirements of the short story, while substantially constant, change in manner and technique from season to season, and from generation to generation. Reread stories appearing in American magazines twenty or thirty years ago and see how they not only deal with different attitudes and environments, but are written in a style which now seems florid, overexplicit, or, at best—as in the early and so-called "typical" *New Yorker* stories—pedestrianly realistic. Go back to another generation, when a writer such as O. Henry—whose name identifies one of the annual "best" short story collections—wrote in a style which now one imitates at risk of appearing ridiculous; and before that, consider a literary masterpiece such as Leo Tolstoy's "The Death of Ivan Illyich," which, unhappily, shows us more about how not to write the short story of today than how one should be written. Yet all these stories have that requirement set forth by Robert Gorham Davis in his *Ten Modern Masters*, in that a story asks a question: "What is it like to be that kind of a person going through that kind of an experience?" and then answers it. And here is the rock on which your story may stand.

It is important to begin any article on the short story by speaking of other writers, for if one does not read deeply, it is likely one will not write deeply or even very successfully, in a commercial sense or any other. Actually the first rule for a beginning writer is simple, painless and even fun: Read before you write—fiction, that is, both short and long. Read to the point of intoxication, if you will, so that your blood-stream is changed by the alcohol of fiction, and then believe in the visions that fill your head.

The sober and important fact about deep and wide reading of other short story writers is that one begins thinking in fictional terms, and does not lapse into propaganda writing, or merely expository writing, or any other kind that does not contribute to that single, intense and limited effect that is the short story. A parallel here could be the practice of photography, where one's eye becomes so conditioned to the limitation of the lens that all subject matter must be framed in the mind, even before snapping the shutter. The short story writer must know there are bounds beyond which he cannot go—a limitation which does not apply to the novel writer—and the best way to know this, apart from actually writing a story, is to become familiar with the stories of the good writers and so challenged and excited by what can be accomplished *within* a limited scope, that one does not think of putting his subject matter into any other form. The length may run from 1,000 to 8,000 words, but the effect must have intensity, narrowness and focus on a single problem and its solution and on a single character—or on a few so linked that the effect is as of one. Too often an editor or a teacher finds the beginning writer has no interest in how other writers have achieved success—if indeed he has read them at all—and patiently must advise: Read Chekhov, de Maupassant, Katherine Mansfield, Sherwood Anderson, D.H. Lawrence—there are so many—as well as the good contemporary short story writers of today, the Malamuds, the Roths, the Capotes, the McCullers, the Peter Taylors—and here I cannot resist putting in: Read *Story* magazine where you will find the good stories of tomorrow as well as of today.

QUANTITY AND QUALITY

The second thing to learn is the necessity of writing as much as you read. Quantity may not make quality, but it is doubtful if quality will become the polished thing it can be without a very great amount of practical work. But there is an intermediate consideration here, too, that of finding out, first, if writing is the thing one really wants to do. Are you a word-oriented person, or do you express yourself, perhaps even more happily, in music, painting, the dance, or even in social conversation? The thing that has sustained many writers through the early discouraging days of learning their craft is, simply, that they find writing more exciting than any other occupation they can think of. Robert Frost has said he writes poetry because he does not find the same satisfaction in anything else. Writing should be so important to the writer that, even if he has failed in other ways to communicate—or even if he has succeeded—the typewriter is the friend to whom he always returns, not to the stretched canvas, the piano or the music for the dance. These tastes may also be part of the extracurricular equipment of a writer, but they are not his release; they are not so deeply loved. There are, in my observation, writers and nonwriters; and even though the nonwriter may write brilliantly and even sell successfully, he will give it all up when it gets hard, or when another and equally interesting form of expression suggests itself.

So, know that you want to write, that you believe from what you have read and observed and thought that you are ready to try, through characters, event and mood, to work out a story, relating it to the essential drama around you.

How do you know you have a story to tell? Where do you settle first, your wandering and rather anxious imagination.

HAVE YOU A STORY TO TELL?

The prime test of whether you have a story or not is that you find in every contemplated story an *explosion* —muted, perhaps, delayed, sometimes, or completely shattering—but something which explodes and thus changes the status quo. Somewhere, either at the beginning, middle or end, there is an explosion in which all parts of the whole are expelled from an existing pattern—the lives of the characters are jolted from their rhythm, chaos is produced in their universe, and out of this upheaval, "that kind of person going through that kind of experience," the creative skill of the author must find or imply some sort of solution. Thus the writer, before he begins to write, must anticipate and comprehend this explosion, and then, without being guided by anything but his own inner logic, create—or suggest—new order from the old.

An explosion can be many things, make use of any subject matter. The breakup of a marriage, the beginning of love, the death of an old man, each can create its own chaos, provide its own solution. Explosion may be used in three ways. One can commence with the explosion—in other words the gun goes off at once, and the universe seems shattered at the point the story begins. It is then up to the author to reassemble the characters, lead on to some final acceptance or solution in their lives, as in Mary McCarthy's "Cruel and Barbarous Treatment" where the marriage breaks up, and the story works out from there.

It may begin with calm and existing order, proceed with rising intensity to an explosion at the center, working back to a new order at the end — which, of course, is never quite the same as the old, such as in "The Man," by Mel Dinelli, both a story and a play. Or one can withhold one's ammunition to the very end, as in Shirley Jackson's story "The Lottery," when the stoning begins and the full meaning of the preceding pages bursts upon the reader, who is then left to reassemble the parts himself.

Any story, I think, will fall into one of these three patterns, and the author, by approaching the problem in his own mind before he starts to write, will know the moment in his story when it is most effective to light the fuse, how far back to stand from the subject at the time of the explosion, and whether he is going to set it off at the beginning, the middle or the end. An author can take his choice, and begin his story accordingly.

FINISH YOUR STORY

Once you start to write your story, the next important thing is to finish it. Writing is as simple and as difficult as that. An incomplete story is no story at all, while a piece of writing with all the faults in English grammar can be a story if brought to some related end. There is no substitute stage in one's development as a writer for finishing what you have begun. I, myself, can clearly remember the day I became a writer: It was the day I stopped dreaming up ideas without developing them, and forced myself through to the bitter end. Even though that story was never published and has been lost long since, it was an important milestone in my writing. Then, for several months after that I worked as fast as ideas came, and, miraculously, the more I completed, the greater the profusion of stories I thought to tell.

Then came the next stage, when a feeling of uneasiness came over me as I realized I was not yet succeeding, even though I knew then that someday I would. As I went back and reread all I had written, I saw that these stories would have to be rewritten, and maybe even rewritten again. This was the third stage of my becoming a writer; and one that has never ended.

How, though, does a writer get far enough back from his own work so that somehow he becomes no longer the author, but the reader and critic; how does he work to some point where it is as though the story had not been written by himself at all? Here, unfortunately for a writer's personal contacts, begins the notorious bad memory of a writer: At one point, consciously and deliberately, he learns forgetfulness — not memory — and even though he is in danger forever after of being late for dinner and dentist appointments, this brainwashing must take place in order to reach the next stage of self-criticism. For the words an author writes can form a groove in the mind which soon hardens and becomes unerasable. The trick here is to put the story away and practice loss of memory so intensively that — as I found a few months ago — I could pick up my own first novel and read on with curiosity to see what actually happened in the end!

THE CRITICAL STAGE

In this most critical stage of judging your own work, what errors do you look for? First, spots in which you have not succeeded in saying what you wanted to say, either because of writing too little or writing too much. In other words, the balance of its parts is the first thing to worry about; and this, properly achieved, will often eliminate any possible moments of lagging, or letdown, in holding the reader's attention. Generally speaking, the beginning takes too long in the novice writer's work; and frequently the explosion, the big scene, is passed over too quickly, written too sketchily. Savor this big scene, wherever it comes. Make sure it is perfectly realized, clearly visualized and properly understood; even though your technique is to write subtly and not *tell* all, the logic must be exact enough for those who will read it to find the key for themselves.

The second thing to look for is the credibility and sharpness of your character creations. This is a thing a novelist learns, but it is equally important for the short story writer. In a novel, a reader will want to know some things you have not told; if you cannot say you do know, cannot satisfy the reader's curiosity when he writes to ask what-the-hell —, then you are not close enough to that character to pretend to know how he acts or will act in any given situation. The same thing is obviously true in the theatre. In Lillian Hellman's play, *Toys in the Attic*, a foolish sister of the hero stands aside during a scene when the hero's wife telephones the man who will want to kill him; and although the foolish sister has no obvious part in this and answers only when asked a question as though she were not thinking at all, in the end, one knows, because of the author's skill, that the girl's phone call is the very thing the sister has schemed to have happen. In other words, the logic of character development, the consistency of actions and words, must be reconstructed as exactly as in a psychological laboratory.

Next, speak and challenge the things your characters say. Read their words aloud, even to yourself; hear if they speak stiffly, unnaturally, pretentiously—and ask yourself if the rhythm of their speeches suits the kinds of characters you have created. I like to say that dialogue should be thought of in terms of a chromatic and not a whole-tone scale. Use both black and white keys even if your speech is spoken in fifths or even octaves. The power of Hemingway's dialogue is that, even though he skips from C to C, he hears all the halftones that could be spoken between characters and suggests these in the careful selection of their words. Write dialogue as a singer sings, by holding your breath until you reach the end of a thought; and always "sing through your rests," for once you start a story, you must see that your attention does not wander for an instant, and that your reins are never slackened.

This seems to be about all I can say, except that someone else, whose name I wish I knew, has said, "If a story doesn't bore you to write, it won't bore the reader to read." When I begin to feel bored with any part of my writing, I skip to the next point that interests me, intending to come back and fill in—but often I find this unnecessary, and the words I have not written are never missed.

The writer's obligation is to the reader, not out of kindness or weakness, but as the only way to hold his reluctant attention. We must interest him, not by writing what he thinks he wants to read, but, by our own skill and passion, so dominate his interest with what we want to write so that he will go where we lead and believe what we want him to know. And the deeper our own involvement, the deeper can be the reader's gain and our own.

The Importance of Plot in the Novel

Taylor Caldwell

December 1965

I t was Shakespeare who said, "The plot's the thing." The ancient writers who survive, like Homer and Virgil and Ovid, were notable for their exciting and absorbing plots. Writers who followed: Tolstoy, Dickens, Thackeray, and before them the medieval meistersingers, knew that without a plot nothing was "told," and therefore nothing really happened, nothing *was*.

The plot—the framework of a story, the skeleton most vital, the reason for being at all—is one of the hardest things to form in literature. Many writers (though not myself) even make draughtsman-like outlines of the plot on paper, and then "fill" it up with chapters, dialogue and narrative. But the hard skeleton remains, either worked on objectively or kept subjectively in the writer's mind. No matter what is written— that is, written with authority and with interest—whether a novel or a short story or a poem or a journalistic account—it must have a rounded plot, a beginning, a middle and a strong ending. Without the skeleton-plot, on which everything grows, develops and ends, the result is what I call *nouvelle numb*, a piece of writing which is only "mood" or a vague impression and not a story at all. Something without a story shows a vast lack of true writing talent on the part of the author. It reveals lack of discipline, no grasp of the material, lack of adequate training, and worst of all, laziness and absence of imagination.

The plot is still the "thing."

A book has often become popular when it has a strong plot, even if the narrative, descriptive and dialogue passages are weak. It was Tolstoy who said that if a writer is not popular, widely bought and read, he has failed, and Tolstoy was a master-plotter. (He is also the perfect writer, for plot, dialogue and narrative are all perfectly balanced in his books.) So I have read books with marvelous plotting when the other parts were not as perfect, and have enjoyed them immensely. But who can truthfully enjoy the Nouvelle Numb, the plotless, rambling, lazy, inchoate mishmash of mere words which now pass, in some effete circles, as writing?

I am not an admirer of Norman Mailer, but he is a master-plotter. Someone has said that his book, *The Deer Park*, is a perfect novel. So it is, for the plot is strong and dominates the book; the dialogue is excellent, too, and the narrative and descriptive parts. The book is workmanlike; it is a product of a man who grasps his material.

The grasp of material, in short, the grasp of plot and its direction, is the sign of the real writer. The fine strong skeleton must reveal itself even through the "muscular" coat of mood, subplot, description, characterization and dialogue. These are the nerves, the muscles, the organs — but they are orderly and living only because they are upheld by the skeleton, the framework, the joints which keep them all in place and functioning efficiently. Without the skeleton all is chaos and formless.

No writer can tell another writer how to plot his novel. What is the best way for one is not the best way for someone else. I know of a novelist, now dead, who made a blueprint of every novel he wrote. It was a "project" to him, meticulously designed and outlined and filled in, long before he actually wrote the book at all. The first pages had all his characters written out, their ages, their appearance, their personalities, the way they talked and spoke, the clothes they wore, their likes and dislikes, the sports they favored or did not flavor, what they liked to eat, what they did not like to eat, their education, their immediate background of parentage, their occupations, the sound of their voices, their prejudices, their tolerances, their objects in living or their lack of objective, their religion if any, their politics, the houses they lived in or the apartments — with a minute description of the furniture and the pictures and the musical instruments — and whether or not their smiles were attractive or repellent. He had dozens of other details.

Then each chapter was headed something like this: "Charlotte comes in. She tells John what she has been thinking. He reacts. He moves — (have him move). She is wearing such and such (consult previous description). He is wearing such and such. The day is early spring. Describe it: hard and cold or warm and golden, etc. They are affected by it (or perhaps Charlotte is the only one affected; describe how). Try to write this chapter in the spring, if possible. Consult encyclopedia about native flowers suitable to be described for this time of year and in this climate (Connecticut). Trees? River? Yes."

Every chapter was like this. Sometimes the subject of a discussion was fully briefed, or a series of actions, one by one. This is making a hard skeleton with a vengeance! The novelist died when the novel was two-thirds finished, but so exact were chapters outlined, even to the last "mood," that one of his relatives was able to complete the book. I can't see how the original writer, however, got any enjoyment or sense of creation out of such a blueprint. And if a writer doesn't enjoy what he is doing, I don't believe he is a writer.

A novel starts with a sudden idea, a sudden sense of excitement and revelation. (Though nothing is really new under the sun, and there are supposed to be only about seven plots for a novel, there is a new way of writing a novel with new characters and novel situations, all in the framework of the old plots.) Without this sudden sense of creative fire, this excitement, the novel will not "live," and however careful the plotting and excellent the description, the whole thing will be lifeless. At least it would be so with me, if not for others. There are some writers, I've heard, who will set out deliberately to find a plot, and then will write within it. Again, that is not for me.

But the world is full of ideas. As one moviemaker told me, ideas are a dime a dozen. They are the match, only. The logs have to be gathered one by one, and the kindling laid, and there is the labor. The fire does not start and glow and give out heat and sound even with the match, until all the labor has been done, such as research, study, background. All this can fill notebooks, and I always have many notebooks. This is somewhat tedious, but a novel must have solidity and nothing is more solid than notebooks.

Many hundreds of would-be writers have written me enthusiastic letters telling of a "wonderful" idea they have, or what a marvelous and unusual life they have led, or an outline of the life of a dead relative or ancestor. "It would make such a glorious story," they write. "But I don't know how to write, myself. So, would you collaborate with me? I'll be glad to give you ten percent of the royalties, and with your name _____."

I patiently explain to them that I have scores of wonderful "ideas" of my own, and that ideas are quite worthless without a plot, and an ability to write well is not something one can acquire. You are born with it, or you are not. However, you do have to have an idea to begin with, and one feels somewhat euphoric when it blazes into the mind like a comet. But that is only the first step. The next, and very prolonged steps, are not so easy. A lot of careful drudgery enters on the scene and must be done.

Let us suppose you have an idea about what the world would seem like after a nuclear holocaust. You are fired by the thought; all sorts of great images and people pour into your mind. You can see it all, and hear it! (But, can you make your readers see and hear it?) You are absolutely sure it will be the most exciting book ever written. Then you think about it. You are suddenly aware of the fact that you aren't "up" on nuclear physics at all; you have only the vaguest idea of what such an explosion would be like. So, you start to study—and fill notebooks. You clip things from newspapers and magazines and scientific journals, especially the scientific journals. You cull remarks of men who are terrified of the blast, and you cull remarks of men who aren't terrified in the least. You go to libraries and read up on science—and fill your notebooks. You study the background of the first atomic bomb, what it did, where it was tested, who was there and why, who protested it and who advised it. You particularly study descriptions of it, and later explosions. You write down the number of deaths that occurred in those unfortunate Japanese cities, and you describe the lingering deaths of those afflicted by radiation. You cull doctors' descriptions meticulously—and write them down. You find photographs, color preferably. You get at least some sketchy idea of the very mechanics of the bomb. All this will probably take many weeks or months or even years. You want to be accurate, don't you?

Now, for your plot. Who are the people? Write it down in your notebooks. Describe them, if that will help you. Names, ages, characteristics, family trees. Where do they live, and in what circumstances? Poor, rich, middle-class, professional? What *kind* of people are they, thoughtful, heedless, all-for-the-day, active or passive? What concern do they have for humanity in general? Are they religious or not? Write it down.

As you write it down the people will take form before your inner eye. You will get acquainted with them, and knowing your characters is almost the most important thing, if they are to live—unless you are going to write a treatise or an article. But at this point you will suddenly want to know exactly what kind of people your characters were before the holocaust, and this will fill at least another notebook. It could all start like a pleasant overture. But suddenly you are aware you must have a locale. New York? Chicago? Cincinnati, Cleveland or where? You must know your city very well, or if you don't know any particular city, invent one. Give it a history. More notebooks. Describe your invented streets; you will need a mayor, a city council, the chief of police, the leading families, just for a starter. Of course, if you lay your scene in your home city you've got it made! But what writer, except a New Yorker, perhaps, or a person living in San Francisco or some other glamorous spot, wants to write about his own city! (Some do and like it. I don't.) It is better, perhaps, unless you want a real smashing scene of the tumbling of the towers of New York, to invent your locale. Small town? Big town? Village? Countryside? The locale is all yours, but you'd better make it authentic. I've found that inventing cities is the best, except when I write a historical novel. Then you can "move" around it easily and, strangely enough, an invented city is realer than a real one—for a novelist. Imagination is not curtailed to actual streets and scenes and buildings.

But the real plot comes now. You may like to write an outline of it, or a number of outlines, all in your little black notebooks. Or you may, like myself, just want to keep it in mind, where it will grow steadily and not be confined inside a rigid structure. After all, a novel is a living organism and it changes day by day. You will enjoy it more, too, if you only have it in mind, where it will be fresh every time you attack it. You will have to decide which of your characters are doomed to survive or doomed to die. Let them decide it for themselves! Now you have your plot, firmly nested in your mind or in your notebooks. But keep in view the fact that the plot may change here and there, and leave room for the changes, though the basic structure, the skeleton, must remain.

I've found it helpful, in the first flush of an idea, to tack a title onto it immediately. The title alone is almost a plot, for it is the polar star of it and must guide to something significant. You could call your novel about the nuclear war *Days of the Fools*, for instance, keeping in mind that it would be exactly that. But wait! Who is going to start the war and under what circumstances? Make it Russia? China? My God, you've got to fill more notebooks with quick histories of either of those countries, and you've got to invent the malign leading characters at once! With characteristics, backgrounds, why they'd want to do such a thing, whether or not they are hysterical, fearful, terrible, frightened, vengeful, suspicious or whatever. You must, of course, write down the general personalities of the people of your selected country, and now the newspapers and the magazines and the books must be gotten out at once, and lots and lots and lots of notes taken, and studied and authenticated with encyclopedias and whatnot. Not to mention months of careful reading until the inhabitants of your selected country are as familiar to you as the inhabitants of your own.

Now comes the first chapter, or worse, the first sentence. Not long ago I read a suggested first sentence, which, however, you will not want to use: "After Margaret had shot the doctor she wondered why she had done it." Do you get the general idea? The first sentence, the first paragraph, must absolutely strike at the browsing reader and intrigue him. It must break through his immediate preoccupations. Why in hell had Margaret shot the doctor? The reader pants to find out. At least you hope he does. But seriously, the first paragraph must capture your reader. If it does not, then all your subsequent labor is in vain unless critics have solemnly assured your reader that he must, he *absolutely must*, read this book, for his own sake. This is not too encouraging, however. Most readers carefully avoid books they have been told they must read for their own sakes. I know I do. Just as children avoid foods they have been assured are all for their own good. They expect, and usually with justice, that they will dislike the foods—or the book. I've rarely found it to fail.

So now all those months have gone by, and you have your plot and your characters, your locale, your background and your history and your fine blazing title, and your first significant paragraph—which you will rewrite at least twenty times.

Now despair will seize you. All this preliminary work, and there is no book except that one first paragraph, or even chapter, which seems to you to be positively terrible. Faith will—or should—run to your assistance. You will probably ask your husband or your wife or your best friend or your parents for reassurance. (But don't "talk" your book. I've heard more thrilling plots for books than I like to remember go quietly to their death after an exciting evening talking about them—on the part of the would-be authors. After all, when a novel is *expressed*, either by writing it or by talking it, it is finished. It has had its reason for being—communication. The reason is gone now.)

Don't even talk it over with an editor. Give him the barest idea of what you are going to write; don't ever be lured into writing a synopsis of it, unless you are the kind who works best with a synopsis and a blueprint. Keep the freshness and the life to yourself. I've heard many editors sorrowfully say that so-and-so had such a wonderful idea for a novel and such a marvelous plot—and somehow he never got around to doing it. The synopsis, or the long talk about the book, had done it to death. If you really keep it to yourself, except for the title which will give your editor the general idea, and a mere sketch of it, your editor may discover later that what you had told him doesn't exactly meet what he thought it would. But he may be pleasantly pleased at finding out that your completed work is far better than your original brief outline to him.

But in the meantime all you have is the title, the plot in your mind or very casually written down, your characters, your locale, your history, and those heaps of little black notebooks we have been talking about. The real work starts, the real intense drudgery. Day after day, night after night, week after week, month after month, year after year. Now despair will become your constant companion. You will reread what you have already written, and you will rewrite. You will cut, rewrite, cut and rewrite, endlessly. And in the midst of all this you will be writing. And thinking. You will never really stop thinking about your book. If you can go days without thinking about it, then your book isn't worth doing at all. If *you* have no real abiding interest in it, who will?

Every once in a while you will think about your original plot, or read the sketchy outline you did for it. Don't be surprised to discover that your characters have run away with it and that they obstinately insist on living their own lives. Be delighted, in fact. Your book is living. However, if you are going to write about a nuclear holocaust you can't end up writing *Peyton Place*, can you, or a pastoral complete with cows? Is your villain showing some indications of human nature and is not all black? Be happy; human nature is quite villainous, even in the best of men. Is your hero showing the jerky side of his character here and there? Be happy. Even the noblest men have their jerky aspects. Your book is living. Your characters are not one-dimensional. They are growing, and so is your novel.

If you are straining eagerly to put "finish" on your book then it probably is no good at all. A real writer of a real book is loathe to end his associations with his characters. They have become part of his life, part of the texture of his moods, part of his dreams — and nightmares. They have an existence apart from his, and what the devil they are doing in the dimness of the night is something you personally want to find out during the day when you are sitting, more or less reluctantly, at your typewriter, waiting to start. (The first ten minutes before a blank page is enough to discourage everyone but the born writer, and even he gets discouraged — though not for more than half an hour, say.)

Maybe you've decided at this point not to write the story of the nuclear holocaust at all, considering all it will entail. (You really have no idea how terrible the struggle is going to be, until you get beyond the third chapter.) You'll do something simple, out of your own "backyard," as some of the textbooks on writing advise. But what do you know about your own "backyard?" You'll be crushed to discover how little you know. Take your neighbor, whose backyard adjoins yours. Do you actually know her or him? Better invent a new neighbor. Do you get the general idea?

Flaubert wrote about his own "backyard," notably, in *Madame Bovary*. One wonders what huge epic he had first in mind, and then abandoned it when he found out how little he knew about anything, and it was too much trouble anyway. The world is filled with Madame Bovary and Mrs. Smiths. As every human being is fascinating and a wonder and a mystery, as you explore his mind and look into his eyes, it really doesn't matter whom you write about. Your finished character won't resemble Madame Bovary or Mrs. Smith, either. It will be someone infinitely more interesting to you—and, you hope, to your reader. For no one, you see, ever knew anyone else, not even his nearest and dearest.

Now, after all this, you may decide that writing is not your cup of tea. No writer utters a shout of joy when he discovers his offspring is considering a writer's career. He emphatically says, "Don't!" It is not only too precarious, it is hideously lonely. Worse, even the seasoned writer can never know if his opus is truly good or bad, and the critics are no help. If they praise his book for what he thinks are the wrong reasons, he is disgusted. If they criticize his finest chapters, he is outraged. If they don't like him at all, he dreams of criticizing one of *their* books, and the dreams are usually not kind. In any event, he will never honestly know, objectively, whether he has written a masterpiece or a stinker, just as he can never know what he truly looks like and whether or not the mirror-image resembles him. This is not conducive to a happy or contented life.

I have discovered that writers are the most miserable of people, including myself. They never know from year to year what their income will be, if any. After all, no matter how long it takes you to write a book your income is treated, for tax purposes, as a daily wage, without fringe benefits or any kind of security. Fame? Come on, now!

After considering all these matters, you will think, perhaps, that you ought to join the Nouvelle Numb school, where no plot and no real characters are necessary, but only a "mood." You may join the ranks of the nonwriters, the nonplotters. I hope not, because the rewards for both readers and writer are much greater on the other side!

Organizing Your Material

Allan W. Eckert

March 1966

Hold it!

Don't read the title of this piece and prepare to skip past it with an involuntary shudder—not if you're one of that abundant clan for whom rejection slips are far more common than acceptance checks. Because what follows here just might clarify where your articles are going wrong.

Sure, the term "organizing" has a sort of hard-labor connotation to it, but if that's the way you feel about it, odds are you've (1) been misusing it (which is a misdemeanor) or (2) abusing it (which is a felony) or (3) ignoring it (which is a capital offense). Kidding, am I? Not a bit; at least not insofar as article sales are concerned. Misuse of the technique of organizing is a writing misdemeanor that'll cut your chances of sales to ribbons. Abuse of the technique is a crime that editors can't forgive, and they'll sentence your manuscript to life imprisonment in your filing cabinet. Ignore the basics of organizing and your chances of sales are dead. It's that simple.

Organizing does not have to be tedious. Contrarily, in that period between initial idea and ultimate sale, it can be one of the most fascinating steps in turning out a fine manuscript. It can, in fact, be likened to putting together a complex jigsaw puzzle in which many of the pieces, if you force them, can be stuck in where they don't belong. With a job done carefully, the resultant "picture" has all the ingredients of a good salable piece: an overall value and pleasant "feeling" to it; a sense of fitting together perfectly; a smoothness and continuity not only admirable but downright essential.

Your research—library work, interviews, digging into records, correspondence and the like—should be finished *before* you sit down to actually begin writing your article. Between the processes of researching and actually writing must come organizing.

Assuming, then, that your research has been completed, where does organizing start? If you've researched well, regardless of subject matter, you will find yourself with roughly five to twenty times more material than you can possibly fit into the article's wordage limitation. (If you *don't* have this abundance of material, your research has been faulty.)

The very first step is to sit back and *think*. Seriously. Consider everything you've discovered about your subject. Do this in a quiet place where you'll be neither distracted nor interrupted. Consider well all the bits and pieces of information you've gathered and then — and *only* then — consider the theme, the peg, the basic idea you had in mind when you first considered doing such a piece. Consider this initial theme now in the light of what you've learned on the subject. Does it still hold up? Or, as is very frequently the case, has your research unearthed facts that make tackling the subject from another angle more advantageous or desirable? Settle this question beyond doubt in your mind before going any further.

WHAT'S YOUR ANGLE?

Theme established? Fine. Now start checking through every single bit of material you've collected and weigh each item carefully as to its value to this theme. Ask yourself: Is this piece of information absolutely essential to the development of the theme in this article? You'll be amazed at how often it will *not* be.

Example: Assume you're going to do a piece on donating bodies to science. In the course of researching you've picked up a wealth of material, including many pages of interviews with doctors, morticians and beneficiaries, bales of public relations literature, numerous excerpts from previous magazine pieces that may have touched on the subject, and voluminous notes of your own. Your theme is: Should the reader of your article donate *his* body to science? Here are ten random facts your research has turned up:

1. To adequately train medical students, bodies are extremely important, but they're hard to get.
2. There are over two hundred bones in the human skeleton.
3. In many states an individual cannot legally will his body to science.
4. Grave-robbing to get study bodies was once common.
5. Some religions forbid donation of the body.
6. Funeral practices in the U.S. are often barbaric.
7. Animals make poor substitute for human anatomy study.

8. There are currently seventy-four medical students to each cadaver available for study purposes.
9. Bodies can be stored for long periods of time.
10. College students have often played practical jokes using human cadavers.

Every one of these points bears directly on the subject of human bodies used for study by science. But remember the theme: Should the reader donate his body? With this in mind we find that only numbers 1, 3, 5 and 8 are *pertinent* to the development of our theme. The others are of tangential importance; that is, they are valuable for the writer of this piece to know and will provide a better foundation and understanding for him to develop this piece, but they need not be used *directly* in the article and, in most cases, should not be.

Thus, it becomes necessary for you, the writer, to carefully sift through your collected material and weigh each piece of datum individually for pertinence or tangentiality. By the time you've gone through all your material you'll find that the tangential pile, despite specifically pointed research, is by far the larger. Put this pile to one side for now. It has already served an important function in that it has strengthened considerably your knowledge of the subject. (Besides which, it often becomes the basis for more articles which suggest themselves as you go along.)

You are now ready to organize your relevant material for the article. First, thoroughly reread and study all of it. Depending on the length and scope of the article, this may take an hour or six hours or several days, but it should be done.

What comes first in the article depends in large measure on what specific publication you're planning it for (and you should always have a specific publication in mind before beginning). You should study and be guided by the style the magazine uses. The body-donation idea suggested above was one I actually wrote for *The American Weekly* which, though now defunct, was much like numerous other magazines in that it preferred an anecdotal approach to its pieces, yet without loss of the basic importance of the theme. Therefore, it was crucial to find one of the most important elements in my notes and weave it into a strong lead which would reach out and "hook" the reader. Just such a lead came from the first statistic mentioned above, coupled with an anecdote picked up during an interview. Here's how it turned out:

Wanted: Human bodies.

There's a critical shortage of them for research and education in America and the supply diminishes annually. The sources in this country that have provided human bodies for study, for research, for transplantable parts are rapidly drying up. In Cleveland, for example, a renowned ear surgeon is forced to import human tissues from a Hong Kong charity hospital. It seems incredible when one considers that nearly two million deaths are recorded in America annually.

Help is needed. You can provide this help . . . but should *you?*

Note how such a lead uses not only an extremely important datum of the article, but also gives an interesting anecdote, states a pertinent statistic and establishes the entire theme for the article—all in less than 90 words.

So, with the lead established in your own mind (not necessarily written out already) the next step in organizing is to consider not what immediately follows this, but rather how you will close the article. While the conclusion is not so essential as the lead in holding the reader, it is most important in leaving him in a good state of mind. If you disappoint him with a weak ending or leave him hanging with a mind full of unanswered questions, he'll turn against the article despite a good lead and body copy.

Where body copy is concerned, it is often helpful to outline. We speak not of a formal by-the-numbers type of outline, but just a casual jotting down of the principal points to be covered in the article and where best they should come in. The outline, once you've sketched it out, should help you organize your material, but you should be guided by it, *never led*. Do not follow this outline to the letter if, as you write, a better organization or presentation of your material suggests itself. The outline, in organizing, is a tool which should work for you, not vice versa.

General rules for organizing body copy without knowing the specific subject must, at best, be nebulous. However, once you've established lead and ending in your own mind, consider your remaining material in an overall light; i.e., how best could this be told so that the ultimate effect is a smoothly running commentary without redundancies, without hopping from one point to another and back again, without making the reader feel that these are merely collected facts tossed into the word machine and allowed to come out in any order.

Aim at all times for a cohesiveness in your presentation, and try to maintain a pitch of interest throughout. Above all, don't make the mistake many novices do of trying to tell everything there is to know about the subject. The piece is destined for failure if you do.

Themes in the
Traditional Novel

Robert C. Meredith and John D. Fitzgerald

May 1966

All traditional novels demonstrate that certain people had certain experiences, and these experiences comment upon life, leaving the reader with some nonfictional conclusion about life. This nonfictional conclusion, or significance, is the theme of the novel.

After reading *The Grapes of Wrath* by John Steinbeck, the reader cannot help but come to the nonfictional conclusion that both migrant workers and fruit growers during the 1930s were victims of the profit system, which is the theme of the novel. After reading *The Ugly American* by Lederer and Burdick, the reader cannot help but come to the nonfictional conclusion that if our government doesn't staff our Asian embassies with competent, dedicated, self-sacrificing and well-trained men, we will lose all of Asia to the Communists, which is the theme of the novel. After reading *The Lord of the Flies* by Golding, the reader cannot help but come to the nonfictional conclusion that if people were left to themselves, they would revert to the primitive forms of society, which is the theme of the novel.

It will help the would-be novelist to better understand the meaning of theme in the novel if he writes down what nonfictional conclusions about life he has arrived at after reading several of his favorite novels. And if the reader has written a novel which has proven to be unsalable, he would do well to ask himself if his novel would leave a reader with some such conclusion about life. If not, he will know that his novel lacks a strong theme.

All traditional novelists wish the novels they write to have thematic significance. Too often we find the would-be novelist believing that the way to achieve this is to begin with theme. This is the worst mistake he can make. To begin with, theme hampers creativity and makes author and characters prisoners of theme. The author will find himself editorializing and moralizing so much to prove his theme that his novel will lose all entertainment value.

Successful novelists begin a novel with a statement of purpose, knowing that *their* interpretation of *their* purpose in writing the novel will result in the theme. This permits them greater freedom in creativity and allows the characters to say and do what they want to say and do. A novelist begins with an idea, then an intention, then an attitude; and from this he arrives at a statement of purpose which gives him the direction he must take in writing the novel. We are sure Steinbeck will not mind our using his powerful novel as an example to clarify this:

Idea — The sight of a jalopy filled with Okies during the 1930s.

Intention — To write a novel about these people.

Attitude — A great deal of sympathy for these people.

Purpose — To expose the terrible, poverty-stricken and hopeless conditions under which these migrant workers are forced to live.

John Steinbeck knew before beginning *The Grapes of Wrath* that *his* interpretation of his *purpose* would result in the strong theme of this novel.

How, then, do successful novelists give their novels thematic significance if they do not begin with theme? The answer lies in viewpoint, embodiment and exaggeration.

THE CHOICE OF VIEWPOINT

Let us first look at viewpoint as a means of giving a novel thematic significance. The choice of the right viewpoint brings the writer closer to understanding the meaning of his work. No better examples for study can be found than two of Mark Twain's novels. *Tom Sawyer*, with Tom as the viewpoint character, is a lighthearted boy's adventure story without thematic significance. *Huckleberry Finn*, with Huck as the viewpoint character, is one of the most significant works in American literature; the dark elements that were minor details in the idyllic scenes of Hannibal began to emerge in the view of the outcast Huck Finn, to assert their significance, to compel reappraisal, and to give the novel great thematic significance. The would-be novelist should weigh very carefully which of the eight possible points of view is best for narrating his novel to give it thematic significance.

In choosing the viewpoint or viewpoints of a novel the writer must decide which one or ones will make the novel most interesting, realistic, believable and significant. A novelist may choose from eight possible viewpoints:

1. First Person Protagonist Narrator. (*Anatomy of a Murder* by Traver.)
2. Third Person Protagonist Narrator. (*The Ambassadors* by James.)
3. First Person Supporting Character Narrator. (*The Great Gatsby* by Fitzgerald.)
4. Third Person Supporting Character Narrator. (*Lord Jim* by Conrad. A very difficult viewpoint to handle.)
5. First Person Minor Character Narrator. (*Life with Father* by Day.)
6. Third Person Minor Character Narrator. (*The Razor's Edge* by Maugham. A very difficult viewpoint to handle.)
7. First Person Shifting Viewpoint Narrators. (*Wuthering Heights* by Bronte, or *Company K* by William March. A very difficult viewpoint.)
8. Third Person Shifting Viewpoint Narrators. (The most popular of all viewpoints with novelists. *The Man in the Gray Flannel Suit* by Wilson; *Another Country* by Baldwin; *Giant* by Ferber.)

In selecting any of these viewpoints, the novelist has to consider whether his novel will gain the most in thematic significance from his use of a restricted viewpoint, a restricted viewpoint with limited omniscient powers or a viewpoint using full omniscient powers.

EMBODIMENT AND EXAGGERATION

Embodiment is the next technique for giving a novel thematic significance. Embodiment is giving characters flesh and blood and making them realistic and believable to the reader by revealing their weaknesses as well as their strengths and showing all sides of their character:

1. General Traits. (These are the nationalistic, regional and group traits of a character formed by heredity, environment, life's work, social role and so on.)
2. Physical Traits. (These are the physical traits expressed in the bodily makeup of a person.)
3. Personal Traits. (These are traits found in the social or ethical aspect of character: stinginess, greed, pity, etc.)
4. Emotional Traits. (These are traits of the mental or psychological makeup of character: optimistic, sardonic, gay, etc.)

Thematic significance is the result of the conflict between good and evil, or the result of the conflict between motivating forces. Embodiment, therefore, is not only in-depth characterization but also conflict; giving substance and meaning to all the minor complications within the framework of the major complication. But embodiment means nothing without exaggeration which brings us to the most important principle of all for giving a novel thematic significance.

Thematic significance in the traditional novel arises from an exaggerated impression of life.

Here is a statement that is bound to cause controversy, but we believe that the schoolroom myth that a novel must be true to life, should be laid to rest once and for all. If the myth were true, novelists would simply turn reporters and record the exact truth about life, and what dull reading that would be. The novelist, like the short story writer, must make his characters and the things that happen to them more interesting than in real life, in order to hold the reader's interest, and to make one central significance emerge. He does this by exaggerating characterization, complications and situations. He brings into focus dominant exaggerated impressions about people, motivations, environment, and concepts. And from this exaggerated impression of life, he achieves thematic significance.

To prove this, let us look at the central themes of several novels derived from an exaggerated impression of life and ask ourselves if they are true to life or exaggerated.

Could Flem Snopes take over the whole of Yoknapatawpha County as he does in *The Hamlet* by Faulkner? Were all migrant workers during the 1930s and the fruit growers victims of the profit system as they were in *The Grapes of Wrath* by Steinbeck? Must all young men suffer degradation through military service as Robert E. Lee Prewitt does in *From Here to Eternity* by Jones? Are *all* our embassies in Asia filled by incompetents as in *The Ugly American* by Lederer and Burdick? Did romanticism really commit suicide because it could not live among nineteenth-century apostles of dull progress as in *Madame Bovary* by Flaubert? Is it true to life that men cannot act in idealistic terms because dehumanizing sensual and commercial interests have the greater power as in *The Time of Difference* by Moravia? Would a poor revolutionary commit suicide for the sake of art rather than carry out his pledge to strike for social progress as in *The Princess Casamassima* by James? Would people, if left to themselves on an island, revert to the most primitive forms of society as in *The Lord of the Flies* by Golding? Is satisfactory sexual experience the fundamental guarantee of a full life as in *Lady Chatterley's Lover* by Lawrence?

We think our readers will agree these central themes are all derived from an exaggerated impression of life just as the cartoons one sees on the editorial pages of newspapers exaggerate current events to drive home their thematic significance. The novelist, like the editorial cartoonist, must exaggerate to capture interest. How then, is it possible for a reader to arrive at some nonfictional conclusion about life after reading a novel? In the same way one arrives at some factual conclusion about current events by studying a cartoon on the editorial page of a newspaper. Behind the cartoon is the cartoonist's insight into the truth about a current event. Behind the novelist's exaggerated impression of life is the novelist's insight into the truth about character and life, but he knows he must exaggerate to call attention to it and hold a reader's interest. He knows if he simply says a character was stingy, the reader couldn't care less. So he exaggerates and portrays a character such as Old Grandet (in Balzac's *Eugenie Grandet*), a rich and avaricious man, on his deathbed who is almost brought back to life by the crucifix advanced toward him by the priest — not because the crucifix is a symbol of life eternal, but because it is made of gold. He knows the minor complications in his novel and the major complication must be exaggerated to make them more interesting than life. It is through the fictional existence of the novel with its exaggerted impression of life that the reader comes to some kind of nonfictional conclusion about life.

Of the embodiments and exaggerations available to the novelist to give his novel thematic significance — character, environment, motivating forces, the conflict between good and evil — none is more important than the last. The theme of any novel is chiefly derived from the struggle between good and evil. If the would-be novelist doesn't know what constitutes "good"and what constitutes "evil" in his novel, he will say nothing worthwhile. It is necessary in the traditional novel that good and evil be the conditions of the conflict, however subtle the novelist is in his depiction of the two opposed forces. The route toward thematic significance lies in the conflict of probably exaggerated incarnations of good and evil. Theme is the end product of this conflict.

Because the popular novelist always employs motivating forces with tangible objectives which are readily understood by the reader, the struggle between good and evil is clearly defined. As a result theme is less of a discovery to the popular novelist than to the literary novelist. The theme may begin to emerge with the first chapter and become full-blown before he is half way through the novel. Because the literary novelist frequently adds *intangible objectives* to the motivating force of his hero or heroine, he frequently puts such conventional stress on definitions of good and evil as to make it impossible always to know in advance the ultimate tendency of his protagonist's motivation. Consequently the literary novelist may only have a vague idea about the theme of his novel until it is finished. Cervantes started out to satirize "good" in Don Quixote but the "good" turned out to be precisely that idealistic, fanciful and impractical zeal of Don Quixote. The witty pride of Jane Austen's Elizabeth Bennet, so aware of false valuations, so contemptuous of snobbish narrow-mindedness, turns out exactly to be a cover for a neurotic withdrawal from the dangerously threatening masculine figure. The escape of Huck Finn from the Widow and from his Pap turns out to be a positive indictment of slavery, a dedication to brotherhood beyond "sivilization." The motivation of Hyacinth Robinson to support the cause of suffering humanity turns out finally, in *The Princess Casamassima*, to have been misdirected into political agitation rather than into the support of old tyrannies and great art.

It is impossible to state a discovery before one makes it, and the only way the literary novelist can make this discovery about theme is through the incarnation of the conflict between good and evil that his original purpose has directed him to pursue. Until that conflict is resolved, the literary novelist may have only a vague idea of what the theme of his novel is to be. That is why, when a literary novelist begins a new novel and is asked what the theme of the novel is, he will refuse to answer. He knows if he states a theme it will make him and his characters prisoners, for one thing. But more important, he knows that he himself won't really know what the theme is until he interprets his purpose and the novel is finished.

A statement of purpose will point the direction a novelist must take in writing a novel, but to call such a purpose the theme is to overlook the distinction between a cause and its effect.

In order to round out the reader's knowledge about theme we must also investigate thematic patterns. Thematic patterns are discoverable in the conception of protagonist and his story, which may make two or more novels similar in thematic pattern to each other but different in thematic significance. Let us look at some examples of thematic patterns in novels.

1. The novel that deals with the Young Man from the Provinces, as Lionel Trilling calls him. It is the novel that presents the abrupt and fortuitous rise to high life of a young fellow of rustic or poverty-stricken

origins. *Great Expectations* by Dickens and *Old Goriot* by Balzac are classic examples. More modern examples are *The Princess Casamassima* by James, *The Red and the Black* by Stendahl and *Youngblood Hawke* by Herman Wouk.

2. The novel that presents the Journey to a Promised Land. This thematic pattern can be found in *Grapes of Wrath* by Steinbeck, *The Odyssey of Kostas Volakis* by Harry Mark Petrakis and *Giants in the Earth* by Rolvaag.

3. The novel that presents the Innocent Observer of a Corrupt Society. This pattern can be seen in *Huckleberry Finn* by Twain, *What Masie Knew* by James, *A Portrait of the Artist as a Young Man* by Joyce. (The artist is a special kind of innocent, as David Daiches remarks.)

4. The novel that deals with the Young Woman of Sensibilities Fallen on a Dull Age. *Madame Bovary* by Flaubert and *Tess of the d'Urbervilles* by Hardy are classic examples. A more modern example is *Lady Chatterley's Lover* by Lawrence.

Of the thematic patterns of current literary novels, the foremost is the Whimsical Flight toward Sincerity by the Underground Man. This thematic pattern operates in such widely differing novels as Céline's *Journey to the End of the Night*; Svevo's *Confessions of Zeno*, Greene's *The Man Within*; Peter Weiss's *The Leavetaking*; and Grass's *The Tin Drum*. In many ways these novels cast off traditional literary techniques.

There are many more thematic patterns found in novels but these five are among the most frequently used by novelists. They have been used in the past and will go on being used as long as novels are written. Although the thematic pattern is the same, the written novels are entirely different, and the thematic significance in each case is the author's very own. The would-be novelist must prepare himself in knowing his novel will fall into one of the established thematic patterns. His job is to create his own individual thematic significance. And it will help him to read the works of authors who have written novels using the same thematic pattern. He can learn a great deal as to why these thematic patterns endure.

Keep It Brief and Blend It In

Don James

July 1969

Description still may be essential to most fiction and nonfiction, but for some time the word has been out to keep it brief and blend it in.

Last year staff members of CBS television did a special hour on our language. Among other things they showed a printed page from Conrad and a page from a contemporary John O'Hara novel.

Conrad's page was almost solid typeset. O'Hara's was light and inviting. The commentator observed that the long, descriptive passages of yesterday have given way to dialogue, as demonstrated in O'Hara's piece.

This does not mean that O'Hara uses no description. He uses it with a master's skill. But it does suggest what most professionals in the business have known for some time: Busy readers in today's world of competitive communication usually look for "the action." They want the story—not lovely prose.

Actually a study of magazines and books published over the last half century indicates that it has been a good many years since many readers have been very interested in long passages of description, heavily larded with adjectives and adverbs, and dedicated to the art of colorful prose.

The trend has been to blend description with the action, both in fiction and nonfiction. This process of blending frequently seems to cause beginning writers considerable trouble.

When do I describe the setting? The characters? The period? Do I describe the setting of the scene first or begin the story? How much should I describe?

There are no set rules. At times all of us must play it by ear. But there are a few accepted practices that make good sense. Background, action and characters frequently can be described quickly and effectively in an opening paragraph.

An excellent example is the opening paragraph from the best-seller, *Valley of the Dolls*, by Jacqueline Susann:

> *The temperature hit ninety degrees the day she arrived. New York was steaming — an angry concrete animal caught unawares in an unseasonable hot spell. But she didn't mind the heat or the littered midway called Times Square. She thought New York was the most exciting city in the world.*

In less than fifty words the author skillfully sets the scene in New York during a heat wave, describes Times Square, and introduces a girl who believes that she has just arrived in the most exciting city in the world.

Let's look at another example.

Irwin Shaw skillfully blends description into the lead of a story called "Whispers in Bedlam."

> *He was a typical 235-pound married American boy, rosy-cheeked, broken-nosed, with an excellent five-tooth bridge across the front of his mouth and a sixty-three-stitch scar on his right knee, where the doctors had done some remarkable things with a floating cartilage. His father-in-law had a thriving insurance agency and there was a place open in it for him, the sooner, his father-in-law said, the better. He was growing progressively deafer in the left ear, due to something that had happened to him during the course of his work the year before on a cold Sunday afternoon out in Green Bay, Wisconsin. He was a professional football player. He played middle linebacker on defense and a certain amount of physical wear and tear was to be expected, especially in Green Bay.*

In one paragraph Shaw paints a powerful word picture of the lead character, gives us pertinent information about his family life, and lets us know that he has a problem with progressive deafness.

The opening paragraph of *Orchestra & Beginners*, a novel by Frederic Raphael, performs multiple tasks:

> *The little Daimler buzzed out of its garage between the rhododendrons and rolled across the raked pebbles in front of the house. The next Linda saw of it, Jeremy had turned up the gravel path past the tennis court and was heading for the gap in the rosy brick wall which squared the kitchen garden.*

In a continuing flow of movement the author describes a setting, creates a milieu and introduces two characters in fifty-five words. Note how description is blended in.

A quick research of newsstands and book racks will supply writers with dozens of similar examples. The technique is the accepted and not the exceptional. Blend description into the action.

Meanwhile nonfiction is taking on a refreshing new look that smacks of fictional openings. An example comes from an article by William Kloman called "My Mother Said I Should Give It a Try." It begins with description:

> *Resplendent in pink plastic curlers, forest green ski pants and white angora sweater, Juliet Goldman stood surrounded by luggage. A sudden rain had left New York awash, and Juliet's feet were wet. "As if I don't have enough problems already," Juliet said. She had just read in a sociology text that after an American girl passes twenty, her chances of getting married suddenly drop 50 percent. . . .*

Or we might look at the beginning of an article about John Lindsay written by Rasa Gustaitis. This description of a slice of New York living leads the reader into a well-written article about the city's mayor.

> *One of the lesser delights in a New Yorker's life is the subway at rush hour. You're trapped hip-to-belly with strangers, trying to keep your balance as the train rocks and jolts, squirming away from someone's breath or a creeping hand. And you tell yourself it's insane to live in this city. At such times, your eyes fasten on the ads above the grimy windows and beside the doors. Those pictures of elegant men and girls smoking, laughing, sipping drinks at elegant parties become icons. They remind you that somewhere above you is the most exciting city in the world.*
>
> *Nearly two years ago, in the dank heat of summer, there appeared in the subways a color photograph of a good-looking, lanky young man in shirtsleeves striding along a city street . . . .*

This, of course, also is an example of the freshness that Helen Gurley Brown has brought to the magazine. It may be a subtle signpost for budding nonfiction writers.

LETTING THE READER SEE THE CHARACTER
Beginning writers frequently ask, "When do I describe the characters?"

Again there is no rule. In fiction there appears to be a satisfactory trend to describe a character as soon as the character is introduced.

John D. MacDonald, an outstanding craftsman in his profession, deftly blends description, setting, dialogue and character introduction with story action in this example from one of his famous Travis McGee series, *Pale Gray for Guilt*:

> *"Don't you know where you are, boy?" he asked. "You're a good mile west of that county line. You are in Shawana County, Mister McGee. A garden spot. Go right over to Sunnydale, to the County Courthouse, and ever' one of those happy, smiling five commissioners will tell you a man couldn't pick a better spot to live and raise his kids and grow with the county." He astonished me. I had never thought of Tush as being capable of irony. He was a big, amiable, beefy man, with mild blue eyes and stubby pale lashes and brows, and a pink, peeling, permanent case of sunburn.*
>
> *I heard a car drive in. He went to the window on the road side and looked out and said, "Oh . . . no!"*
>
> *I followed him out. Janine had gotten out of the car, a very dusty pale blue sedan about two years old. At twenty paces she still had the gawky, leggy look and stance of a teenager. She stood in an attitude at once defiant and disconsolate, staring at the left rear corner of the car, which squatted expensively low. Their youngest, about two and a half, stood nearby, scowling, giving the intermittent snuffle of tears not long ended. Janine wore bleached khaki walking shorts and a yellow halter in a coarse fabric. The shorts were darkened with perspiration around her narrow waist. She had cropped her black hair very short. With her deep tan, and the length and strength and slender delicacy of her face, her dark eyes, she looked like a young man, Mediterranean, ready to guide you to the Roman ruins, pick your pocket, sell you fake heirlooms, send you out in a leaky gondola with his thieving cousin.*
>
> *But the shape of the ears was girl, and the corners of the mouth, and the elegance of the throat, and from there on down no doubt at all, even were she clad in a loose-fitting mattress cover, no doubt whatsoever. And I knew her maiden name was Sorrensen, and she was Wisconsin Swede, and she birthed towheaded Swede kids, and so she was one of the improbabilities of genetic mathematics, or maybe one of the Scandinavian raiders who brought home from a far country a swarthy boy to be a kitchen slave.*
>
> *Tush got down behind the car and rolled onto his back and wormed his way under it. She said, "It was just a half mile this side of the*

hard top. I guess the rains dug it out and then the dust drifted into
it, and I swear, honey, nobody could have seen it."
    He slid out. "Spring shackle."

In the first paragraph of the passage, the author sets some of the
background, lets a character tell something about the area and himself
through dialogue. He then gives us a quick description of Tush with an
inference to trouble.

A brief transition takes us into a description of Janine where MacDonald blends description, background and characterization through an
imaginative freshness that is typical of his writing.

Then, without fuss or bother, the story action continues.

The technique is quick, certain, and sets the characters in the
reader's mind. Used as it is here, the technique not only sets the physical
description of a character, but frequently gives the character a background and additional depths beyond the visual description. Almost always the description is blended into the story action.

Morris L. West sets his first scene in *The Tower of Babel* through the
eyes of a character:

> *The watcher on the hilltop settled himself against the gnarled bole*
> *of an olive tree, tested his radio, opened his map case on his knees,*
> *focused his field glasses and began a slow meticulous survey from the*
> *southern tip of the lake of Tiberias to the spur of Sha'ar Hagolan,*
> *where the Yarmuk River turned southwestward to join the Jordan. It*
> *was eleven o'clock in the morning. The sky was clear, the air crisp*
> *and dry after the first small rains of autumn.*
>   *He studied the eastern ridges first . . . .*

The author goes for almost two full pages of description and action
through the eyes of the watcher. With the first two words the reader is
into the action of the story and the description — background — is blended
into the story through the eyes of the watcher.

Leon Uris sets a scene through a character's viewpoint in the first
chapter of *Topaz*:

> *The day was balmy. That certain magic of Copenhagen and the*
> *Tivoli Gardens had Michael Nordstrom all but tranquilized. From*
> *his table on the terrace of the Wivex Restaurant he could see the onion*
> *dome of the Nimb, saturated with a million lightbulbs, and just across*
> *the path came a drift of laughter from the outdoor pantomime theater.*

The walks of the Tivoli were bordered with meticulous set-in flowers which gave a riot of color.

A character might walk to a window and through description of what he sees the mood of the character may be suggested, or pertinent facts about the setting described.

In two paragraphs, shortly after the beginning of *Airport*, Arthur Hailey describes a key character, dresses the stage and presents some of the problems with a succinct use of description.

> *Mel, airport general manager — lean, rangy, and a powerhouse of disciplined energy — was standing by the Snow Control Desk high in the control tower. He peered out into the darkness. Normally, from this glass-walled room, the entire airport complex — runways, taxi strips, terminals, traffic of the ground and air — was visible like neatly aligned building blocks and models, even at night their shapes and movements well defined by lights. Only one loftier view existed — that of Air Traffic Control which occupied the two floors above.*
>
> *But tonight only a faint blur of a few nearer lights penetrated the almost-opaque curtain of wind-driven snow that was piling up new drifts — at the same time that plows were clearing the old. Maintenance crews were nearing exhaustion.*

Because we know that Mel is conscious of these things, the descriptions help to define his problems and are part of the action. Hailey is expert in using the technique.

Description of persons through the eyes of the beholder is evident in nonfiction. These two examples delightfully avoid the tired clichés and overworked adjectives sometimes found in "profile" pieces.

The lead paragraph from "My Husband, the Clotheshorse" by Laurie Gaines Harrison:

> *Love isn't that blind. Not even utterly myopic passion could obscure the shabby reality. The man I married was a total slob. He was a warm, lovable, now-and-then-shaven hunk of shapeless tweed, droopy flannel, aging oxford cloth, clashing red stripes — all unfailingly mismatched.*

From "The Super Girl," an article about Vanessa Redgrave by Thomas Meehan:

> *With the added advantages of photographing like a latter-day Garbo and possessing considerable acting talent, Vanessa, at thirty-*

one, can be seen as a symbol of all that the complete Contemporary Girl should be — a natural for movie stardom.

I was somewhat disappointed, however, at my first sight of Vanessa offscreen. At five feet ten and one half, she is toweringly tall, beanstalky, and, like many beautiful women, she can sometimes look absolutely ordinary. Last year she made a Hollywood designer's list of the World's Ten Worst-Dressed Women, described as "a do-it-yourself kit on stilts that came unglued." Certainly, entering the Palace bar in a loose-fitting sweater, tangerine hip-huggers, and flats, wearing no makeup and a pair of blue-tinted grannie glasses, with her hair pulled severely back in a bun to reveal noticeably protruding ears, Vanessa reminded me not so much of Greta Garbo as of a spinster librarian. The grannie glasses were no help, but they were entirely necessary, for Vanessa is only slightly less farsighted than Mr. Magoo.

Today nonfiction sparkles with fresh, zestful writing and description keyed to contemporary times. The beginning writer should study issues of any magazine carefully before submitting any queries or manuscripts to it.

MAKE EVERY WORD WORK FOR YOU

When description is necessary, write it well. Use words that describe. "The 'wino' *slouched* away from us." "The horse *pranced* toward us." "The gale *threatened* . . . "

Avoid the passive voice. Instead of: "There was a great quantity of fallen timber on the mountain slope" try "Fallen timber covered the mountain slope." Instead of: "We were forced down by inclement weather" try "A storm forced us down."

Use words that invoke pictures: ". . . trapped hip-to-belly with strangers" or "Resplendent in pink plastic curlers."

Remember that good description observes *all* the senses. Not only do we see the forest setting, but we can *hear* the wind through tree tops, *smell* the frying bacon, *feel* the warm morning sun, *taste* the hot coffee.

Write with nouns and verbs. Shun adjectives and adverbs unless they strengthen your piece. Occasionally they do. Usually you get better emphasis, description and writing when you rely on nouns and verbs that do the job for you.

Beginning writers frequently become addicted to adverbs: he said *angrily*, she said *consolingly*, he replied *grudgingly*. Let the dialogue speak for itself. Let the man's words be angry. Let the woman's words console.

An overabundance of adjectives in any description weakens the material. Adjectives should be used with greatest care. Beware the trite. Learn to use a good figure of speech occasionally.

Check back through the examples above and discover the impressive absence of adverbs. While you're doing it, notice how sparingly adjectives are used.

Avoid qualifiers such as: "He was a *really* honest man." "It was a *truly* beautiful sunset." "It was a *rather* warm day." "The *honest* truth was that . . ."

Occasionally we can give inanimate things personification: "The mountain lifted angry crags to the sky" or "The tree spread its branches over the group."

Also remember that it's a shrinking world. Sometimes a short, identifying description is all we need to set a scene in New York, Italy, San Francisco or London. Almost everyone has become acquainted with almost everywhere through television, motion pictures, photographs.

Readers want to know the setting in relation to the story and the characters.

In other words, we're back where we started. Description may be essential to most fiction and nonfiction, but the word is out: Keep it brief and *blend it in*.

It goes better that way!

1970s

Eight Types of How-to Articles and How to Write Them

Hugh C. Sherwood

November 1970

Americans are among the most practical people on the face of the earth. They always have been. And I suppose they always will be.

To guide them in their various endeavors, they have rarely relied on theory. Instead, they have relied on knowledge gleaned from practical experience.

It's no accident, therefore, that various kinds of how-to writing have flourished in this country. Thus, we have how-to books, articles and pamphlets. They deal with subjects ranging from how to buy insurance and how to make a corporate acquisition to how to knit a sweater. Almost always, these books, articles and pamphlets contain specific, practical advice, drawn from everyday life, on how to cope with or solve a given problem.

Before discussing the various kinds of how-to articles, let's look at the how-to piece as a whole. It differs from other articles, such as news stories, feature articles and personal profiles, in one very important respect: It aims not only at describing something to the reader, but also at telling him what he should learn from the description. In fact, the very essence of the how-to article is that it contains advice as well as information.

At its simplest level, the how-to article is not very hard to write. If you had to write an article entitled "How to Build a Sandbox for Your Children," you could, at about the fourth or fifth sentence, start listing the steps a reader should follow in order to build a sandbox. Thus, the first rule might be: Get lumber of such and such size and such and such quality.

Writing a how-to article at this level is little different from writing a manual. The main attributes of the article must be thoroughness and clarity. The writer must cover all the points the reader needs to know in order to achieve the promise of the article's title or theme. And he must discuss these points clearly enough so that there is no confusion in the reader's mind as to what must be done.

It is when a writer attempts to write a how-to article on more complex subjects that problems often crop up.

The problems may arise from the nature of the subject matter itself. Thus, the subject may be so big and complex that it defies easy treatment in the confines of an article. Whole books have been written on "how to make a corporate acquisition or merger," yet fall far short of exhausting the subject. I have seen successful magazine articles on this very same topic, but, of course, the subject contains too many facets for the writer to treat all of them with any degree of thoroughness and authority.

The topic may present still another problem. The topic may be so subject to different approaches and different interpretations that it defies a simple, step-by-step, one-track approach. There may be a number of ways it can be approached and solved.

The difficulty with doing a how-to article may also lie with the writer or with the person or persons he interviews. Unless he is a news reporter who is usually given assignments for which there is little time to prepare, the wise writer prepares in advance for his interviews.

In the case of a how-to article, however, he must be more than ordinarily prepared. For I think it safe to say that a how-to article cannot usually be written unless the writer has gone into his interviews with that purpose in mind. His questions must be geared not only to obtain information but also advice from the people he interviews.

Unfortunately, these people may not be prepared to meet this need. They may be willing and able enough to describe what they or their companies or their organizations have done to solve a given problem. But they may have given little or no thought as to what lessons from their experience can be transmitted to others who may want to follow their lead.

When this happens, the whole burden of obtaining such advice is thrown back on the writer. He must probe and thrust to obtain those little insights, those little bits of experience, that can turn a descriptive article into a how-to article.

And this may be especially difficult if the person interviewed does not appreciate that even minor insights can be helpful. The things an organization failed to do in implementing an otherwise successful course of action, the minor mistakes it made, the matters it would handle differently if it had to do the whole thing over again—these are the stuff out of which much of the how-to in a how-to article is built. But if the person interviewed does not understand the importance of such information, it may have to be dragged out of him.

What questions are most helpful in this regard? For a business how-to, it would be questions like these:

1. In setting up the system you describe, were there any pitfalls you were careful to avoid?

2. Were there any musts? Did you decide your system demanded certain basic ingredients in money, manpower, materials or whatever?

3. Has experience with your system led you to make changes in it?

4. If you had to approach this problem again, would you handle anything differently than when you did it the first time?

5. Do the people who set up (implement, oversee) such a system require certain personal qualities or professional qualifications?

6. What other people or organizations would be most likely to profit from your system?

7. Are there any kinds of people or organizations that you think could not adapt or benefit from it?

Most of what I have written so far leads to two inescapable conclusions: First, many successful how-to articles do not cover—and do not try to cover—all the things a person should know or might like to know about solving a given problem. Rather, they cover some of the things. They give some insight into how a problem can be dealt with instead of trying to provide a complete how-to-do-it manual. Second, a how-to article can be written in a number of different ways, and the best way often depends on the circumstances in which a writer finds himself.

TYPES OF HOW-TO ARTICLES

Let's look at these ways. The names I have given them are my own and are not sacrosanct by any means. But I do think they are reasonably descriptive of the approaches that can be taken.

1. *The pure how-to article.*

This article is just what its name implies. Whatever the length of the introduction, the main body of the article is geared to support various points of advice. This copy may appear in the form of anecdotes, examples, quotations, statistics, plain expository writing or some combination of these things. Yet whatever form such commentary takes, it is always designed to elaborate on specific rules or points of advice.

"How to Build a Sandbox for Your Children" is a pure how-to article at its most elementary level. One can, of course, go on up the ladder. Thus, entire books have been written employing this approach, bearing such titles as *How to Make Money in Real Estate* or *How to Travel to Europe on $5 a Day*.

The potential danger in this approach lies in the possibility that you will be too glib and superficial. This danger is particularly acute if you are writing a magazine article rather than a book and if you are trying to cover a broad subject that may be open to several different methods of attack.

Nevertheless, the pure how-to article should always be considered before one tries some other kind of how-to article. It is the granddaddy of them all. And when well done, it is still the best because it comes closest to fulfilling the how-to promise of the title or theme.

2. *The narrative how-to article.*

The narrative how-to article is probably the easiest of all how-to articles to write. That's because it differs little from any other kind of expository writing.

The reason is that the main body of the article consists of a reportorial account of the matter at hand—perhaps of how a company instituted a cost control program or how an individual made money in the stock market. The article ends with the company's or the individual's advice on how other organizations or people can best adapt its system. It ends, in other words, with the how-to.

The narrative how-to is best employed when the nature of the subject is so complex that the reader will quickly become confused if you plunge into the how-to without first making perfectly clearly what you are talking about. To put the matter another way, the reader may have to grasp the *what* before he can understand the *how-to*.

I recall one article entitled "How to Measure Dealer Effectiveness," which appeared in *Business Management*. It reported on how one midwestern company checked on the efficiency of the sales dealers through whom it sold its products. The reader couldn't possibly have understood the company's advice about adapting its system without first understanding how the system operated.

If the narrative how-to article is the easiest to write, it is also the most dangerous. That's because the article may be strong on the narrative, yet weak on the how-to. When this happens, the writer has failed in his main purpose.

How can this be avoided?

First, list as many specific points of advice as possible. The more you can list, the better.

Second, include minor bits of advice as well as major ones. Not all the how-to has to deal with important matters. Readers may benefit from knowing about little shortcuts and improvements, too.

Third, flesh out each rule or word of advice to the fullest extent possible. Even two or three additional sentences may be helpful.

Does the advice need brief explanation? Would it be worthwhile to show, by examples, quotations or statistics, why it is important? These are the questions you should ask yourself in writing the how-to section of a narrative how-to article, although in point of fact, they should be helpful in preparing any article of this genre.

3. *The various ways how-to article.*

As I have already suggested, one of the difficulties with how-to articles is that there may be no one perfect way to handle a given problem. Or various organizations or individuals may have tackled different facets of the same problem and come up with equally good solutions to these different facets.

When either of these conditions prevails, the solution may lie in what I call *the various ways how-to article*. One such article appeared in *Reader's Digest*, under the title "20 Ways to Save Money at the Supermarket." It discussed a score of ways to save money, covering such matters as when to shop, how to shop and what to buy.

One of the main features of the various ways how-to article is that it does not go into any great detail in describing any one way. Instead, it discusses each way in perhaps a few paragraphs. In view of this, it is usually necessary to include a number of different ways of handling the problem under discussion—in most cases not fewer than ten or twelve.

The various ways to approach has two great advantages. It is not hard to handle. And it gives the impression—hopefully accurate—that the writer of the publication has done a great deal of research on the subject and dealt with it comprehensively.

4. *The questions-to-ask how-to article.*

This kind of how-to article lists various questions that should be asked about the problems posed in the article's title, then comments on these questions in some detail. Implicit in this approach is the thought that the problem the article deals with is so broad and complex, or the conditions that affect it vary so much from organization to organization or person to person, that the writer can't possibly tell the reader how to solve it. But he can relate some of the basic points the reader should consider and some of the questions he should ask.

I recall another *Business Management* article dealing with the pros and cons of corporate advertising—that is, institutional as opposed to product advertising. The article stressed that no company should undertake a corporate advertising campaign unless it had some problem to solve. Then, the article went on to raise and discuss ten questions about such a campaign. Among the questions: Does the company have something important and interesting to say? Does the advertisement bear some obvious relation to the company? Does it deal in corporate abstractions? Does it have the right tone of voice?

5. *The pitfalls-to-avoid how-to article.*

This kind of article resembles the questions-to-ask how-to article in two important respects. Again, the writer may be implicitly saying to the reader: The problem is too broad for me to tell you all the things you will have to do to solve it, but I can at least tell you some pitfalls to avoid. Also the development of this kind of article is apt to resemble the one listed immediately above.

Nonetheless, there is one important difference between the two. The pitfalls-to-avoid how-to article must rely far more heavily on anecdotes than the questions-to-ask how-to article. In other words, it is not enough to tell the reader about the pitfalls. It is important to show him, through real-life examples, how these pitfalls have ensnared individuals or organizations who have attempted to solve the problem in the past.

Obviously, then, this kind of article presents some research problems. The writer must come up with enough pitfalls to make it worthwhile to attempt this approach in the first place. In addition he must come up with good illustrations of the pitfalls. Presuming the research is adequate, however, the actual writing of the article should not be difficult.

An imaginative and witty variation on this approach appeared in *Family Circle*. It was called "Marriage—Unsafe at any Speed!" and it dealt with the mistakes married couples often make by saying the wrong things to each other. It did so in the form of a multiple choice questionnaire, with the various possible answers to the questions indicating the right and wrong ways to answer the kind of remarks husbands and wives commonly make to each other. In other words, the answers indicated both the pitfalls and the how-to, and the correct answers were always self-evident.

6. *The question-answer how-to article.*

This kind of article strongly resembles any other article based on an interview, the results of which are presented in question-and-answer form. It differs from the ordinary question-and-answer article, of course, in that most of the questions and answers are aimed at providing how-to rather than mere commentary or opinion.

This approach can be particularly appropriate if you are talking with an honest-to-goodness VIP, particularly if he is very colorful, very quotable or very articulate. It can also be effective when you are talking with a VIP who knows the broad nature of what his organization has done, but who is not able to provide you with all the statistics and other details that would enable you to write a pure how-to or narrative how-to article. In other words, you can get away with somewhat less detailed how-to in this kind of article than you can in most other kinds.

7. The don't-do-this how-to article.

This kind of article advises the reader not to do certain things in trying to solve a certain problem. But, in discussing the various points the article makes, the writer may also include some positive tips on how the problem can be dealt with.

Then why use this approach at all? Why not use the pure how-to approach if at all possible? For any one of several reasons.

The subject may already have been covered by other magazines or even by the magazine for which you are writing. In other words, a fresh how-to approach may stir more reader interest than a more conventional one.

Then too, the advice the interviewees have provided may lend itself more readily to this approach. As a result, the writer may be able to milk more out of the subject through this approach than through a more straightforward one.

Finally, for one reason or another, it may be difficult to provide the reader with a total solution to a problem. Yet it may be possible to tell him what mistakes to avoid.

Naturally, the don't-do-this how-to article may seem to resemble the pitfalls-to-avoid article. And in some respects, it does.

Yet it also differs. The points it makes are much more apt to be put in flat, rule-like form than in a pitfalls-to-avoid how-to article. The errors it advises against are apt to be much less serious. Finally, this kind of article is much less dependent on anecdotes to illustrate its points.

The don't-do-this approach can be highly effective, partly because it is not often used, partly because it appeals to people's innate desire to avoid errors. The very negativism of the approach, however, would suggest that it is an alternate choice that is most effective when used sparingly.

One good recent example of this approach was entitled "Don't Lose That Job Before You Get It." It appeared in *Changing Times* and dealt with ten mistakes people often make in job interviews.

8. *The checklist how-to article.*

As its name implies, this kind of how-to article consists primarily of a checklist of questions to ask about a problem — or of points to consider about it. The accompanying text is usually brief.

By its very nature, this kind of how-to story is the weakest of them all. That's because the checklist's points or questions are rarely elaborated on. They're just listed — without individual explanations.

This approach is most often employed when there are truly a great many points to be considered in approaching a given problem and when you want to be sure the reader does not overlook any of them. By "great many points," I mean 40, 50, even 100 or more.

In considering this approach, it's important to remember that it can only be used when the importance and meaning of the points are obvious. They will either have to be obvious in and of themselves or else made so through the accompanying brief text.

Occasionally, the checklist how-to appears in shorter form. The most prevalent example of its use in brief form is in a box accompanying an article of normal length. In such cases, the points in the checklist may be briefly discussed rather than merely listed.

Whether long, short or of intermediate length, this kind of how-to article does serve a purpose from time to time. But if you are writing a how-to article, the best general rule is to consider one of the other possibilities first. They simply make it possible to be more thorough — and hence more useful to the reader.

Whatever form you decide on in a given instance, remember that the production of a good how-to article rests almost entirely on your shoulders. You must not only ask those questions that will elicit the how-to, but you must also see the seeds of the how-to, even when the person you are interviewing is not aware that he is providing such. In short, you must not only garner facts, but also perceive the lessons to be learned from the facts.

Sensory Detail in Your Writing

Carl E. Johnson

May 1972

Editors — and readers — are demanding more and more feeling, more personal warmth, more color, more meaning in what we write. Yet much of what is written today does not answer these needs. Rather, the reader is presented more and more evidence that the fragmented, lonely, computer-dominated life is the norm, perhaps even his essential heritage. A renewal of sense-oriented writing, while not a magic elixir, can make our communication more vital.

How can we bring sharpness of sensory detail to our writing efforts? Three directives seem quite beneficial to all writers:

1. Try to capture first the sensory impact of a moment. To do this, consider underlining sensation with colored pencils in your rough draft. This will reveal emphasis and balance. When you're writing, try to get a child's viewpoint, then superimpose an adult's perspective. Recall the wonder of touch, of first viewing, of haunting sights and sounds.

An example of such wonder is my own experience as a small boy. While riding a streetcar in Kansas City, I noticed a young woman with fine clothes and wondrous silk-blond hair. When she left the streetcar in the gathering gloom of evening and bobbed off through the night I pressed my nose against the streetcar window and watched her until all I could see was her hair floating away as an apparition under the occasional light of swaying street lamps. It was the exact image I wanted just a few years ago when, in a short story, a boy watched his mother walk out of his life, leaving only the memory of her luminous hair as she floated away beyond the window glass.

Catch the universals. What sensory details will set every man's mind spinning backward in time to experiences which do not dissipate with age? By suggestive word choice, summon the reader's mind to flash detail.

Here's the opening paragraph in Bernard Malamud's *The Assistant*:

> *The early November street was dark though night had ended, but the wind, to the grocer's surprise, already clawed. It flung his apron into his face as he bent for the two milk cases at the curb. Morris Bober dragged the heavy boxes to the door, panting. A large brown bag of hard rolls stood in the doorway along with the sour-faced gray-haired Poilisheh huddled there, who wanted one.*

Malamud's choice of the word "clawed," and his use of the detail, "It flung his aprong into his face," graphically involve the reader, pulling him into the life of Morris Bober. In the opening paragraph the mood of the book is established.

Isolate personal implications. What affects you deeply may affect the reader deeply if you trigger the stimuli that exist within him.

Here's how Ernest Hemingway does it in a dispatch appearing in the *New York Times*. Cabling from Madrid, Hemingway writes of the Spanish Civil War:

> *The window of the hotel is open and, as you lie in bed, you hear the firing in the front line seventeen blocks away. There is rifle fire all night long. The rifles go "tacrong, carong, craang, tacrong," and then a machine gun opens up. It has a bigger caliber and is much louder— "rong, cararibg, rong, rong."*
>
> *Then there is the incoming boom of a trench-mortar shell and a burst of machine-gun fire. You lie and listen to it, and it is a great thing to be in a bed with your feet stretched out gradually warming the cold foot of the bed and not out there in University City or Carabanchel. A man is singing hard-voiced in the street below and three drunks are arguing when you fall asleep.*
>
> *In the morning, before your call comes from the desk, the roaring burst of a high-explosive shell wakes you. You go to the window and look out to see a man, his head down, his coat collar up, sprinting desperately across the paved square. There is the acrid smell of high explosive you hoped you'd never smell again . . . .*
>
> *On the corner, twenty yards away, is a heap of rubble, smashed cement, and thrown-up dirt, a single dead man, his torn clothes dusty, and a great hole in the sidewalk from which the gas from a broken main is rising, looking like a heat mirage in the cold morning air.*

Make the fragments suggest the whole. It is in the bits and pieces of reality that we catch our meaning in life, rarely in the great entirety. Find those fragments which cling to the memory with universal tenacity and set them in a contest that will accomplish the process most readily.

Such a fragment found its way into my daybook on a recent trip to Singapore:

> *A stroll in Singapore's heavy night air. I'm lonely, cut off as I walk in step with my Asian brothers. Horns and Hondas, cabs and careening caravans, bikes and buses, lorries and lurching vans. Singapore has wheels, and they're all spinning, going somewhere.*
>
> *The muggy air pushes at me. Heat lightning flashes. The night tightens. Singapore settles in the stomach, churning and straining. Why can't this city give in to description? It squirms out of control, careens off down Tanglin Lane. Small stores, run by aged, passive (only the eyes acknowledge activity) Chinese, stay open into the night.*

Later, when I was writing an eight-chapter series, "Instant Asia, a Journal of Sorts," for *Light and Life Evangel*, this fragment helped to recapture the sensory minutiae surrounding the Singapore moment.

2. Be selective with your images. One simple way to develop a repertoire of sensory detail is to keep a notebook (such as that suggested above) in which you daily record sensation. Such notebooks are what Vincent Sheean has called "stones thrown into the pool of memory."

According to Joseph Conrad, the aim of the artist is "to arrest, for the space of a breath, the hands busy about the work of the earth, and compel men entranced by the sight of distant goals to glance for a moment at the surrounding vision of form and color, of sunshine and shadows; to make them pause for a look, for a sigh, for a smile—such is the aim . . . and when it is accomplished—behold!—all the truth of life is there."

As a moment is isolated, it has unique properties calling for unique images. To ensure the uniqueness, write until it hurts then write some more. The exact image for a moment often does not come in a moment. Energetic forceful prose emerges from an energetic forceful mind. We need to think fiercely and write with great moderation.

If an image calls attention to itself, it has probably veered out of control and out of context. In England I heard an Anglican minister refer to young radicals in the church as "a different cup of tea." Two sentences later he saw them "laying the ax to the root of the tree." Now, he concluded, "We have a growing movement of radicalism within the church." The audience that can follow an image through such rapid changes in so short a time is nimble indeed. The senses are as basic as breathing and should work their way into print as naturally. Read your rough draft aloud then rely on your ear to ferret out crudity of form or overblown phrases—which leads us to the final consideration:

3. Delete ruthlessly to recapture a moment. Let some of the blue pencil ferocity of the newspaper copyeditor get into your manuscript. Writing is a skill but rewriting is a greater skill. Samuel Butler once said, "A young author is tempted to leave anything he has written through fear of not having enough to say if he goes cutting out too freely. But it is easier to be long than short." As you rewrite consider these four remaining directives:

Avoid mawkishness. The word *mawkish* connotes blandness of flavor, insipidness (literally, not savory), as well as flabbiness of emotion and lack of vivacity. Beware of sensory detail which *per se* evokes a stock response, choosing rather that detail which creates in the reader a fresh response, a new perspective on an old truth.

One way to portray an insignificant old man languishing through bad days might be to dwell on his suffering, to get the reader sympathizing with him rather than empathizing with him. But Bernard Malamud simply shows Old Morris Bober scanning yesterday's Jewish paper in his grocery, the store looking "like a long dark tunnel."

> *The grocer sighed and waited. Waiting he thought he did poorly.*
> *When times were bad time was bad. It died as he waited, stinking in*
> *his nose.*

Malamud clearly creates in the reader a fresh response as the reader empathizes with the protagonist. Morris is believable in his suffering and his honesty. He "could not escape his honesty, it was bedrock; to cheat would cause an explosion in him, yet he trusted cheaters—coveted nobody's nothing and always got poorer."

Avoid overwriting. To reach for effect is to call forth twenty words when five will do. We need to get more of Maxwell Perkins into our writing and less of Thomas Wolfe.

Prose writers can take a tip from playwrights who must make dialogue reveal a character's ideas and feelings in the briefest of space. In *Mary of Scotland*, Elizabeth says:

It's not what happens
That matters, no, not even what happens that's true.
But what men believe to have happened.

Avoid abstractions. Scout for picture-making words which concretely say what you want to say. Inexact qualifiers and vague generalities cause a manuscript to lose precision. Which is the better sentence:

When Ross scrutinized your manuscript he was thorough and highly skilled, not missing anything.

Having a manuscript under Ross's scrutiny was like putting your car in the hands of a skilled mechanic, not an automotive engineer with a bachelor of science degree, but a guy who knows what makes a motor go, and sputter, and wheeze, and sometimes come to a dead stop; a man with an ear for the faintest body squeak as well as the loudest engine rattle.

James Thurber comes through rather clearly in his reminiscences of *New Yorker* editor Harold Ross.

Finally, avoid a one-dimensional viewpoint. The successful writers of all time have employed sensory detail in such a way that more than one level of meaning was exposed. A surface narrative meaning is matched by a lower iron-rich complexity of meaning that lends itself to more than one reading.

As Judith Wheeler writes, "A writer can make a collection of random sights and sounds relevant to each of us. He separates us from the mass audience and makes us feel important. He even makes us feel wise. Television shows us what we do; writers tell us why. Television turns reality into news; writers make news into reality. As we probe farther into physical space, deeper into human awareness; as we devour our world, the only one left may be the one the writers make."

As the writer carefully catalogs sensation, selects exact images and deletes ruthlessly, he approaches the best writing that is in him.

Ten Rules for Suspense Fiction

Brian Garfield

February 1973

The English call them thrillers and in our clumsier way we call them novels of suspense.

They contain elements of mystery, romance and adventure but they don't fall into restrictive categories. And they're not circumscribed by artificial systems of rules like those that govern the whodunit or the Gothic romance.

The field is wide enough to include Alastair McLean, Allen Drury, Helen MacInnes, Robert Crichton, Graham Greene, Arthur Hailey and Donald E. Westlake. (Now *there's* a parlay.) The market is not limited by the stigmata of genre labels and therefore the potential for success of a novel in this field is unrestricted: *Day of the Jackal*, for instance, was a first novel.

Game's object: to perch the reader on edge, keep him flipping pages to find out what's going to happen next.

Game's rules are harder to define; they are few, and these are elastic: The seasoned professional learns the rules mainly in order to know how to break them to good effect.

But such as they are, the rules can be defined as follows.

1. *Start with action; explain it later.*

This is an extension of Raymond Chandler's famous dictum: When things slow down, bring in a man with a gun. To encourage the reader to turn to page 2, give him something on page 1: conflict, trouble, fear, violence. I realize you've got a lot of background that needs to be established, leading up to the first moments of overt conflict; but you can establish all that in chapter two. Flash back to it if you need to. But in chapter one get the show on the road.

2. *Make it tough for your protagonist.*

Give him a worthy antagonist and make things look hopeless. Don't drop convenient solutions in his lap. The tougher the opposition, the more everything is stacked against him, the better.

3. *Plant it early, pay it off later.*

Don't bring in new characters or facts at the end to help solve the protagonist's dilemma. He must work out his own solution based on a conflict which is established early in the story. No cavalry to the rescue, and no sudden unearthing of a revealing letter written before she died by a character who was dispatched 'way back in chapter three. (Unless, of course, you established in chapter four that such a letter exists, and followed that revelation with a race between the protagonist and his enemies to see who'll get the letter first.) No cavalry to the rescue.

4. *Give the protagonist the initiative.*

All good dramatic writing centers upon conflict: interior (alcoholism; oedipal conflicts) or exterior (a dangerous enemy; an alien secret police force). Only in *poor* Gothic fiction is the protagonist habitually and tearfully and hand-wringingly at the mercy of evil opposing forces which push him/her around at will. *The best story is usually that in which the protagonist takes active steps to achieve a goal against impossible odds, or to prevent opposing forces from overcoming him or his loved ones.* The protagonist may begin by reaching but in the end he must act from his own initiative.

5. *Give the protagonist a personal stake.*

No longer is it acceptable for the hero to solve a mystery just because it presents an interesting puzzle. The more intimate his involvement in the main conflict of the story, the better. He himself, or his aims, should be in jeopardy: His own life or his loved ones should be in danger, or his best friend has been murdered, or he is the kind of character whose values and principles won't let him sit by and allow injustice to destroy people around him. Whatever the conflict is, if he loses, it's going to cost him horribly; that's the essence.

6. *Give the protagonist a tight time limit, and then shorten it.*

This doesn't always work because the logic of many stories prohibits it; don't use it unless you can work it in believably. But when time is a factor, and when the brief span of time in which he must resolve the conflict is then shortened, you have gone a long way toward heightening the suspense.

7. *Choose your character according to your own capacities as well as his.*

Don't use as your protagonist an accomplished professional spy unless you are prepared to do the research and groundwork necessary to create such a character convincingly. It is better, particularly when approaching the early stages of your own professionalism, to stick to the familiar. Some of the most successful suspense-novel protagonists — many of Eric Ambler's for instance — are ordinary, innocent people caught up in dangerous webs. The indignant, honest idealist makes a good protagonist because his innocence makes the professional opposition all the more frightening. Yet a plot-structure for this character is often difficult to contrive because in spite of his naïveté he has to be clever and resourceful enough (*not* lucky) to prevail over his awesome enemies. The other face of this coin, of course, is the professional-crook-as-protagonist; he's easy to identify with because he's an outcast, an underdog, one man using his wits to survive against society's oppressive machinery; but the pitfalls of this genre are treacherous and unless you know criminal procedure and feel comfortable competing with Anthony Burgess and Richard Stark, it's better to avoid the crook-hero in the beginning.

8. *Know your destination before you set out.*

The prevailing weakness of many suspense stories which are otherwise successful is the letdown the reader experiences at the end: the illogical and disappointing anticlimax. It isn't enough to set up intriguing conflicts and obey all the other rules if you haven't got an ending that fulfills the promise of the preceding chapters. It becomes disgustingly obvious when a writer has confronted his hero with thrilling obstacles only to paint himself into a corner. Presented with his own unsolvable cliffhanger he is reduced to bringing in *deus ex machina* to solve the hero's problems for him. It is not necessary to tie up all loose ends but the climax should resolve the principal conflict one way or another. (In recent years, to avoid the traditional clichés of virtue-triumphant or ironic-downfall, several talented novelists have resorted to obscure endings which no reader can possibly decipher. I rather hope the fad is dying out; whatever the reasons behind it, it demonstrates lazy thinking and infuriates the reader.) The best key to a good ending is to know what the ending will be before you start writing the book. Whether you write a preliminary outline or not, you should know where the journey will end, and how.

9. *Don't rush in where angels fear to tread.*

I admit this one is a catchall. Essentially I mean that it is wise to observe not only what the pros do but also what they *avoid* doing. The best writers do not jump on bandwagons; they build new ones. The pro doesn't write a caper novel about the world's biggest heist unless he's convinced he can write an unusual story with a unique and important twist. Otherwise he risks unfavorable comparison with the classics in that sub-genre. "Why bother with it if it's not as taut as *Rififi* and not as funny as *The Hot Rock*?" Yet this should not be taken to mean every writer must obey faddish advice such as "Spy fiction is dead," or "Historical novels are *out* this season." There is no such thing as a "dead genre" because the human imagination is limitless and there is never a dearth of new ideas, new twists, new talents. The question is, is this idea strong enough and important enough to make this story sufficiently different from its predecessors to merit publication? If a novel is good enough it will find a publisher whether it is a hard-boiled detective story, a western, a spy novel, a historical adventure, or a novel about bug-eyed monsters from Mars. If it isn't good enough the publisher may reject it by saying that such novels are out of style, but this is merely a euphemism.

10. *Don't write anything you wouldn't want to read.*

This one sounds self-evident but I've met several young writers who decided they wanted to start out by hacking their way through Gothics or westerns just to learn the ropes, because those categories looked easy to imitate. Nuts. If you start out that way you'll end up a hack. Now if you like to read westerns, then write a western. But don't write into a genre for which you have contempt. If you don't like Gothics, but insist on writing one, your contempt will show; you can't hide it. You'll end up by "writing down" and the reader will resent your attitude. I don't say you can't sell books this way; God knows people do, all too often; but if you thoroughly enjoy sea stories — even if you don't know a thing about nautical life — you're better off attempting to write a sea story because you'll go into it with enthusiasm, you'll make it a point to learn the terminology and the life, and you'll write a far better book.

The Horror Market Writer and the Ten Bears

Stephen King

November 1973

A t parties, people usually approach the writer of horror fiction with a mixture of wonder and trepidation. They look carefully into your eyes to make sure there's no overt blood lust in them, and then ask the inevitable question: "I really liked your last story . . . where do you get your ideas?"

That question is common to any writer who works in a specialized genre, whether it's mystery, crime, western or science fiction. But it's delivered in different tones for different fields. It's directed to the mystery writer with real admiration, the way you'd ask a magician how he sawed the lady in half. It's directed to the science fiction writer with honest respect for a fellow who is so farseeing and visionary. But it is addressed to the horror writer with a sense of fascinated puzzlement — the way a lady reporter might ask mild-mannered Henri Landru how it feels to do away with all those wives. Most of us, you see, look and seem (and *are*) perfectly ordinary. We don't drown houseguests in the bathtub, torture the children or sacrifice the cat at midnight inside of a pentagram. There are no locked closets or screams from the cellar. Robert Bloch, author of *Psycho*, looks like a moderately successful used car salesman. Ray Bradbury bears an uncomfortable resemblance to Charles M. Schultz, creator of *Peanuts*. And the writer generally acknowledged to be the greatest master of the horror tale in the twentieth century, H.P. Lovecraft, looked like nothing so much as a slightly overworked accountant.

So where do the ideas — the *salable* ideas — come from? For myself, the answer is simple enough. They come from my nightmares. Not the nighttime variety, as a rule, but the ones that hide just beyond the doorway that separates the conscious from the unconscious. A good assumption to begin with is what scares you will scare someone else. A psychologist would call these nightmares phobias, but I think there's a better word for our purposes.

Joseph Stefano, who wrote the screenplay for *Psycho* and who produced a mid-sixties television series called *The Outer Limits*, calls these fears "bears." It's a good term for the aspiring writer of horror fiction to use, because it gets across the idea that general phobias have to be focused on concrete plot ideas before you can hope to scare the reader—and that's the name of the game. So before we go any further, let's take a few bears—ones we're all familiar with. You may want to rearrange some of the items on my list, or throw out a few and add some of the skeletons in your own closet. But for purposes of discussion, here is my own top ten.

1. Fear of the dark
2. Fear of squishy things
3. Fear of deformity
4. Fear of snakes
5. Fear of rats
6. Fear of closed-in places
7. Fear of insects (especially spiders, flies, beetles)
8. Fear of death
9. Fear of others (paranoia)
10. Fear *for* someone else

The bears can be combined, too. I took numbers 1 and 10 and wrote a story called "The Boogeyman," which sold to *Cavalier* magazine. For me, fear of the dark has always focused on a childhood fear: the awful Thing which hides in the closet when you're small, or sometimes curls up under the bed, waiting for you to stick a foot out under the covers. As an adult looking back on those feelings (not that we ever conquer them completely—all those of you out there who don't have a bedroom lamp within reach of your hand please stand up), it seemed to me that the most frightening thing about them was the fact that grown-ups don't understand it very well—they forget how it is. Mother comes in, turns on the light, smiles, opens the closet (the Thing is hiding behind your clothes, well out of sight—it's sly) and says, "See, dear? There's nothing to be afraid of." And as soon as she's gone, the Thing crawls back out of the closet and begins to leap and gibber in the shadows again. I wrote a story about a man who finds out that his three children, who have all died of seemingly natural causes, have been frightened to death by the boogeyman—who is a very real, very frightening monster. The story takes a childhood fear and saddles an adult with it; puts him back into that dream-like world of childhood where the monsters *don't* go away when you change the channel, but crawl out and hide under the bed.

About two years ago I decided that the scariest things going would be rats — great big number 5s, breeding in the darkness under a deserted textile mill. In this case, I began with the fear and built the plot (including the deserted mill) to fit it. The story climaxed with the main character being overwhelmed by these giant rats in the dark and enclosed subcellar of the mill (slyly hedging my main bet by working in a generous dose of numbers 1 and 6). I felt sorry for the poor guy — the thought of being overrun by giant rats frankly made my blood run cold — but I made $250 on the sale and managed to take one of my own pet fears for a walk in the sun at the same time. One of the nice things about working in this field is that, instead of paying a shrink to help you get rid of your fears, a magazine will pay you for doing the same thing.

George Langlahan, a Canadian author, wrote a novelette called *The Fly*, using number 7 bear, made a sale to *Playboy*, and has since seen his bear made into three movies — *The Fly*, *The Return of the Fly*, and *The Curse of the Fly*. The late John W. Campbell wrote a cracking good horror story in the early fifties called "Who Goes There?" using a number 2 bear which turns out to be a sort of walking vegetable from another planet. The story was turned into a classic horror movie called *The Thing*. Hollywood has always understood the principle of working from the bear out — surrounding a basic fear with a plot, rather than the other way around. Edgar Allan Poe wrote the same way, and suggested again and again in his literary essays that the only way to write a short story was to begin with the effect and then work your way out.

The would-be writer of horror stories may be tempted to stop right here and say: That's a lousy list of bears, fella. There isn't a werewolf or a vampire to be had. True enough. Not even an escaped mummy hunting for tanna leaves. My humble advice is to leave these bears to their well-deserved rest. They've been done to death. There are undoubtedly a few twists left in the Old Guard, but not many. Even the endlessly proliferating comics market is turning away from them in favor of more contemporary subjects — but more of that later.

Another caution is in order at this point: Don't think that because you have selected a scary bear, the rest of the story will be a snap. It won't be. Horror isn't a hack market now, and never was. The genre is one of the most delicate known to man, and it must be handled with great care and more than a little love. Some of the greatest authors of all time have tried their hands at things that go bump in the night, including Shakespeare, Chaucer, Hawthorne ("My Kinsman, Major Molinaux" is a particularly terrifying story, featuring a number 9 bear), Poe, Henry James, William Faulkner (*A Rose for Emily*) and a score of others.

So where is the market today? For straight fiction, it's mainly in the men's magazines. But the writer who can approach magazines with a 1930s style blood-pulp-and-sex meller is going to find the market has progressed beyond that to a reasonable point of sophistication — good for the professional who wants to work seriously in the genre, bad for the amateur who thinks he can mix a couple of sea monsters with an Atlantic City beauty contest and come up with a few hundred bucks. And so, before a listing of some possible markets, a few practical hints on selling horror to the men's magazines:

1. Don't feel obligated to add sex to your story if there isn't a sex angle there to begin with. We've both been to the corner drugstore and know that pinups are a stock in trade, along with articles that deal with the sex life of the American male. But a fair proportion of the fiction steers clear of women entirely, dealing with "escape" subjects instead: survival situations, science fiction, crime, suspense . . . and horror.

2. Read the market. To be perfectly blunt, your chances of selling a story to a men's magazine you haven't read is probably no more than 2 percent, even if your story is another "The Lottery." Get rid of the idea that all men's magazines are the same. Find out who is buying stories from 2,000 to 4,000 words, who is buying out-and-out fantasy, who has a penchant for psychological horror, who is publishing good stories by people you never heard of.

3. Take a hard, critical look at your own story and try to decide if it's better, worse or about equal to the fiction being published in the magazine you're considering. The realization that your brainchild may not be up to *Playboy*'s standards may be a bitter pill, but it's better than wasting postage in a lost cause — especially when you could be selling your story to another editor.

4. Throw away Poe and Lovecraft before you start. If you just screamed in agony, wait a minute and let me expand a little on this one. If you're interested in the horror story to begin with, you were (and possibly still are) an avid reader of Edgar Allan Poe and Howard Phillips Lovecraft. Both of these fine writers were rococo stylists, weaving words into almost Byzantine patterns. Both wrote some excellent short-short stories ("The Tell-Tale Heart" by Poe can be read in ten minutes,

and Lovecraft's "In the Tomb" is not much longer—yet the effect of both stories is never forgotten), but both did their finest work in longer form. *The men's magazines don't buy novelettes.* The average length of accepted fiction is 2,500 to 4,000 words. Neither will they buy much, if any, fiction written in the styles of Poe or Lovecraft. In spite of the antique charm both hold for modern readers, most editors regard the style as outdated and bankrupt. If you're still screaming and cradling your wounded manuscripts, I'm sorry. I'm only telling the truth. If it's Poe or Lovecraft, send it to a fanzine and be content with your contributor's copies.

A great many writers begin with the mistaken notion that "the Lovecraft style" is essential to success in the field. Those who feel this way no doubt pick up the idea by reading the numerous Lovecraft-oriented anthologies on sale. But anthologies are not magazines, and while the idea is no small tribute to H.P.L.'s influence in the field, it's simply not so. If you're looking for alternatives (ones that are adaptable to the men's magazine format), I'd recommend John Collier, Richard Matheson, Robert Bloch (who began as a Lovecraft imitator and has made a successful switch to a more modern style) and Harlan Ellison. All of those writers have short story anthologies on the market, and a volume of each makes a wonderful exercise book for the beginner.

5. When your story is ready for rewrite, cut it to the bone. Get rid of every ounce of excess fat. This is going to hurt; revising a story down to the bare essentials is always a little like murdering children, but it must be done. If the first draft runs 4,000 words, your second should go about 3,000. If the first is around 3,000, you can still probably get down to about 2,500 by tightening up the nuts and bolts. The object here isn't to shorten for the sake of shortening but to speed up the pace and make the story fly along.

Take Five:
The Most Common Mistakes Among Beginning Freelancers

M.L. Stein

February 1976

A fter teaching nonfiction writing to college and adult education students for more than ten years, I have a pretty good idea of why most beginning writers get their manuscripts back from magazines. But my impressions go beyond rejection slips. After all, who hasn't gotten turndowns? What really bugs me is that too many of these tyros won't come to grips with certain basics that mean the difference between success and failure in the marketplace.

The conclusions I offer here are based on my reading of hundreds of manuscripts from students ranging in age from nineteen to sixty-seven. A number have been intrigued by the thought of making a living as a freelancer. But few want to pay the dues. These are their—and perhaps your—five principal pitfalls:

1. YOU CAN'T BE A NONFICTION FREELANCER BY STAYING IN YOUR OWN BACKYARD.

My hardest job in some classes is to persuade students that they can't depend on personal experiences, family and friends for their ideas. Some cringe at the thought of contacting strangers for interviews, settling instead for the friendly and familiar. Usually this means adopting home-grown situations for articles and relying on personal connections for interviews.

Of course, a personal experience may be a dazzler that prompts *Reader's Digest* editors to jump for joy. And who is to say that an article obtained through intimate contacts won't bring a check in the mail? But what novice writers often don't realize is that these are sources that dry up quickly. What will they do for an encore? Freelance nonfiction writing demands the widest possible search for material. Once he has an idea, the writer must go wherever the facts are. This may mean interviewing a dozen total strangers in as many different places. "Try it," I urge students. "It isn't as tough as you think. Once you break the ice with a question or two, the rest often comes easily."

2. WRITE ABOUT A SUBJECT, NOT AN IDEA.

Recently, I asked my magazine article students to come to class with five ideas each for their next assignment. Their contributions included such "ideas" as "Environment," "Camping," "Vietnam Refugees," "The Food Crisis" and "Surfing."

"What about 'Environment'?" I asked one student. He shrugged and admitted that he hadn't really thought the idea through. Nor had the others given much thought to the shape their broad subjects would take. They were victims of the essay syndrome: Just grab any big topic and fill out enough pages to satisfy an instructor that they had visited the library at least once.

This approach and $1.50 will buy you a new typewriter ribbon, but it won't work at all in selling articles. Run through the contents of today's magazines. You will see that nonfiction pieces are narrowed down to *specific* themes. A recent *Reader's Digest* issue, for example, carried such titles as "Swindlers in the Sex 'Clinics,' " "Is the Presidency Too Powerful?" "Is Science Creating Dangerous New Bacteria?" and "The Jungle World of Juvenile Sports." All of these are spin-offs from vaster subjects. Specialized magazines, also, lean toward the sharp focus. *Travel & Leisure*'s table of contents revealed such headings as "The Small Hotels of Amsterdam," "Santa Barbara" (not "California") and "Climbing Kilimanjaro."

Professional writers look for ideas within the wide panorama. If you find a large subject that interests you, break it down. Sniff around your sources until you can drag out something concrete. If, for instance, you'd like to do an article on neighborhood action groups, hunt for a special situation in a particular neighborhood—a group that is doing something nobody else is. When you quiz sources, ask precise questions rather than vague, general ones: Who? What? When? Where? Why? Why not? These will get you where you want to go. Prodded long enough, a community leader may tip you off to a neighborhood unit that has developed a unique art project.

Newspaper stories also can provide you with leads to possible articles. Again, pinpoint angles not cosmic subjects. News about a raging forest fire should not trigger thoughts about devastation caused by such holocausts. Leave that to the editorial writers and the Department of the Interior. Instead, you ought to investigate the story for possible offshoots which can ripen into an article. There may be a special contingent of parachute firefighters who were credited with containing the blaze. Where is the unit from? How did it get started? How do the members regard their jobs? Is this the method of the future in battling timber fires?

Sometimes the newspapers furnish ready-made, detailed ideas. Follow them up. An account of a government crackdown on fake vitamin pills may need only a little more digging on your part to turn it into a salable article. How widespread is the sale of vitamins containing no vitamin power? How badly are consumers being ripped off? Can these faulty pills be found at the corner drugstore? If so, how did the manufacturers fool the Food and Drug Administration?

Finding the right angle for an article takes more time but is worth it if you want to see your byline in print. The soft, bulging subject is merely your starting point—not your bread-and-butter idea.

3. GET THE FACTS, MA'AM.

Not long ago, an evening student turned in an article about the revival of big band music. An interesting idea. But the writer apparently expected readers to believe this kind of music was enjoying a revival just on his say-so. He did go into some detail about the popularity of a local orchestra featuring the big band sound, but this was insufficient to support his claim. There were vague references to the sound catching on in other areas, but no examples. He obviously had not tried to document his thesis, a job which would not have been too difficult. Interest in thirties and forties swing, even among young people, is part of the current nostalgia kick. The Jimmy Dorsey Orchestra plays on cruise ships, and some radio stations broadcast Glenn Miller and Harry James records all day long. The author's failure to go after these facts fatally damaged his piece.

To me, it was a familiar experience of reading manuscripts long on words and short on data. Writing skill is essential, but it can't carry the article by itself. Editors want facts and more facts. Seldom is the author an authority on anything. Nor are his opinions in great demand. Professional article writing means getting facts through interviews, library research, handout materials and observation. In the article mentioned a moment ago, "The Small Hotels of Amsterdam," detailed information is given about thirteen hotels: architecture, ambiance, furnishings, number of rooms with and without bath, prices, food, services and any special qualities. The author, Robert S. Kane, a professional travel writer, went from hotel to hotel, checking them out and talking to the staffs. His purpose—to acquaint readers with a clutch of pleasant but inexpensive hotels in that city—was accomplished through a combination of good writing and solid facts.

When you've written your first draft, look for the weak spots. Mark the places where you skimmed over your topic by substituting poetic language for firm facts. Then go back to your sources for them. Better yet, collect the material the first time around. Nonfiction articles—and books—cannot float on the bubbles of your imagination.

4. ADD ANECDOTES.

Anecdotes can make the difference between a sale and a rejection slip. Some magazine pieces can survive without anecdotal leavening, but almost any article can benefit from the technique. Yet, new writers often submit manuscripts totally devoid of anecdotes. I find this even in profiles, a form which cries out for the personal touch.

Anecdotes are little stories revealing an individual's frailty, courage, character and humor. They are the human interest part of the article, the element that makes the person come alive for the reader. Anecdotes also add to the credibility of your article. It's one thing to describe a millionaire as frugal, but the description takes on much more meaning when you follow it with an incident in which he drove back home from his office because he had forgotten his brown-bag lunch.

How does one uncover such tidbits? By doggedly asking questions. It's rare when the writer is handed anecdotes by the interviewee. For one thing, most sources are unaware of the value of the anecdote to the article. For another, their memories must be nudged to produce the little events that lend color to the piece. In almost every interview are opportunities to glean anecdotes. Pursue a line of questioning until an incident pops out. Let's say that an actress tells you that her career was going nowhere until she met a certain agent. Don't let it go at that. Find out how she met the agent and what made him so influential. Probe long enough and you'll surely uncover an anecdote worth reporting.

In the profile, friends, enemies, lovers, husbands and wives of the main subject are frequently better sources for anecdotes than he is. They may recall happenings that he has forgotten or was reluctant to reveal. But again, the name of this game is asking questions.

5. WRITE WITH LIFE AND CLARITY.

For most of us, our first expository writing involved themes, essays and term papers. Unfortunately, a number of first-time magazine writers have trouble shucking the style of those efforts. They continue to write in a florid, long-winded manner ill-suited to today's periodicals. Other symptoms of the disease are extensive use of the passive voice, gilded euphemisms, runaway adjectives and a formal, academic tone.

Magazine editors deal mainly with professional writers whose styles are lively, interesting and, above all, contemporary. They look for articles that move — that delight, alarm, amuse, inform and even outrage readers. A plodding, pedantic style is about as welcome to an editor as a dismissal notice, because that's what he's likely to get if he fills his pages with term paper-type articles.

But you can determine this for yourself by reading the magazines sold on the newsstands. One of my discoveries as a teacher is that too many students in article-writing classes have not read articles. They may have glanced at magazines from time to time but they never really studied the content for style. This is a must for anyone seriously thinking of nonfiction writing. Even a bright, topical idea cannot save a piece presented in wooden, pretentious language. One of my students got a rejection notice from an editor who termed his writing "too official." "Heavy-handed" might have been a better assessment. The author actually thought such a style would impress the editor, he told me. I suggested that he thoroughly read fifteen or twenty general and special interest magazines, soaking up style until he could almost memorize the articles. Shortly after, he sold his first piece to *New York*.

There are other beginning mistakes. They include failing to slant for a specific market, shaky organization, a tendency to moralize and spout opinions, lack of attribution, and a weak grasp of grammar, syntax, spelling and punctuation. No one should try to write professionally with the latter handicaps. Nor should he sign up for an article class. His first step should be to seek remedial aid in an English class or through private tutoring.

Having laid out writers' starting faults as I've observed them, let me add the good news. A fair number of my students have displayed a high degree of talent, energy, creativity and curiosity. They also have one other thing going for them: commitment. They're willing to spend the time at the typewriter to make themselves writers. And that's what it's really all about.

Writing Science Fiction: Think Like an Alien, Write Like an Angel

Gardner Dozois

February 1976

F
or a number of years I worked as a "slush pile" reader, evaluating the endless flow of unsolicited manuscripts — sometimes as many as a hundred a day — that come into a magazine or publishing house and end up heaped in filing cabinets or cardboard boxes. I read thousands of manuscripts — from duds to instant classics to near misses to outright plagiarisms — and with the exception of those turned down because they were illiterate or indecipherable, most of the science fiction stories that came into the slush pile were rejected because they suffered from the 1950 Syndrome.

You can easily recognize such material. It's the year A.D. 2653, and yet people drive around in gasoline-fueled automobiles with internal combustion engines, live in suburbia, shop in supermarkets, subscribe to the Book-of-the-Month Club and mow the lawn every weekend. For amusement they go to the movies, dances and barbecues, or sit at home and watch television. Every man has a crewcut; usually he is a soldier and is called "Captain," "Major" or "Sarge," or a teacher called "Professor." Or he is a wealthy, self-employed scientist who whips together world-saving devices out of scrap metal and bailing wire in his basement workshop, and is called "Doc." More rarely is he a politician, referred to by his title — "World-master Jones" or "Coordinator Grey"; or he is a bigwig white-collared businessman called "Mister Andrews" by everyone, including his children and wife. No other professions exist. No women work except an occasional snappy, wise-cracking, gum-chewing girl reporter who quits the arena when she marries the hero at the end of the story. The only other women who exist are dumb younger sisters of the hero, or the shy and sheltered daughters of atomic physicists with basement workshops. There are no races: Everyone is white, middle-class, American, middle-of-the-road. No one has ever heard of homosexuality or drug addiction or pollution. Either they use twenty-year-old hipster slang ("cool," "you cats," "dig it") or they all say "gosh" and "darn" a lot. Everyone is unflaggingly and unquestionably patriotic. Everyone is smugly contented. They are all the most trusting of optimists.

FUTURE SCHLOCK

You recognize this world, don't you? In spite of the calendar that reads A.D. 2653, it's certainly not the future. No. It's 1950. Or rather, an oversimplified and prettied-up version of 1950, distilled by the popular imagination from years of *Ozzie and Harriet, Father Knows Best,* and *Leave It to Beaver.* In an age that has seen Watergate, Watts, My Lai, the energy crisis, *Deep Throat,* sex-change operations, moon flights and women's liberation, it's hardly credible as the Past, let alone the Future.

And yet, stories reeking of the Syndrome turn up over and over again in the slush pile.

Why?

Well, after all, science fiction is pretty easy to write, isn't it? It's just a matter of using fancy jawbreakers—just change the names, apply a thin layer of technologese and jargon, right? Say "helicar" instead of car, "helipad" instead of driveway, "tri-vid" instead of television, "feelies" (or "smellies," or "grabbies") instead of movies. Better still, use the word "space" as a prefix for everything: spacesuit, spacegun, spacehelmet, spacehouse, spacedog, spacecow . . . and so on. Right? Just change the names and you can take a confession, a cowboy story, or a Gothic or a nurse novel, and sell it as science fiction. Right?

Wrong.

There's no better way to ensure that your story will not sell. Stories deeply tainted by the 1950 Syndrome are not science fiction; they do not do what science fiction should do—they are swindles. They are thin and transparent frauds that are almost automatically rejected by nearly every sf editor in the business. Even the most routine of hack space opera demands and delivers more.

Why do people of intelligence and talent turn out Syndrome stories when they first try their hand at writing science fiction?

Because of tunnel vision. Because they know no better. Because they have not learned to unleash, discipline and control their imaginations. Because they simply have not been taught to look at a future society as *real, self-consistent and organic.*

NOTHING NEW AMONG THE SUNS

It works like this: A layman decides to write sf and immediately starts to grope for a science fictional idea. He reaches down into his subconscious, the well of creativity, and sinks into the vast harvest of concepts and assumptions and ideas he has gleaned over the years from all the bad comic books and horror movies and television shows that have been labeled *science fiction*. A moment's rational reflection should tell him that if the idea were floating about in the easily accessible part of his mind, probably it has been used to death in print years before—why else would it be such common property as to show up in the mind of someone with only the most casual contact with the genre? But he does not so reflect because he is mentally lazy, and off the story goes. Like General MacArthur, it will return.

But even the more habitual science fiction reader may fare no better. In fact, he is often more susceptible to the Syndrome, for in addition to comics and the visual media, he must cope with the sediment entrenched by years of reading bad pulp space opera. Twenty years or more after they've ceased to be salable, the same old stock sf gimmicks, cousins-germane to the 1950 Syndrome stories, march endlessly across editorial desks. . . . Stories wherein, in Harry Harrison's words, "Bright young things voyage out from Earth in miraculous ships that get anywhere in a flash, to alien planets with oxygen atmospheres where exotically shaped aliens talk colloquial English and think exactly like their American counterparts. . . ." Kurt Vonnegut's Eliot Rosewater complains that science fiction writers "write about Earthlings all the time, and they're all Americans. Practically nobody on Earth is an American." Damon Knight asks, "Where is the space hero who is an Indian from India, or a black African, or a Malay or a Chinese, or—all right, let's not ask too much—where is the hero who is Italian?"

Why aren't there different kinds of people and ways of thought among the stars? Why doesn't anything *new* happen in these stories? Because bad fiction perpetuates itself, and stifles the imagination that might otherwise revitalize it.

THE COSMIC CONNECTION

To write good sf today, you must go beyond all that. You must push further and harder, reach deeper into your own mind until you break through into the strange and terrible country wherein live your own dreams. You must attempt to make the future a real place, then visit and explore it.

The first step is a philosophical—almost a mystical—one; an act of faith and will. You must retool your mind. You must teach your eyes to see. One of the premier values of science fiction as literature is that it enables us to look at ourselves through alien eyes. It enables us, as do few other forms of art, to see not only what is, but, submerged in it, what has been and what will be: to perceive the connections, the web of cause-and-effect that holds the world together. The *interdependence* of things. Today this is sometimes called "thinking ecologically," but sf writers knew about it long before ecology became fashionable, knew that in the long run (and sometimes the short) everything affects everything else.

The mental retooling is the first and biggest step: Without it, one cannot proceed. For the central philosophical vision of good science fiction is that *everything* changes: If you cannot adjust to it, believe it, *feel* it, see it in everything around you and in yourself, then you're wasting your time trying to write the stuff.

Nothing is simple. Everything changes. Things connect.

You are what you eat.

And want, and do, and think, and fear, and dream.

NEARSIGHTED SF

Imagination is vital, but not enough. One must have the vision to see the connections, and the sense to make them consistent. Much science fiction has failed on these grounds. Jules Verne predicted much of our present technology, but described it as working within a Victorian economy and society; as a result, he is much less germane than Wells, who knew better. No social change, no technological innovation, takes place in isolation.

Fictionally, this means that one postulate will spawn a host of others.

Alfred Bester, in *The Stars My Destination*, postulates that teleportation is a common ability—and the social ramifications of that one fact are endless: If you can teleport, and you don't like it where you are, why stay? Why live in cities at all? Why suffer night when you can follow the sun around the world? Why endure cold when you can teleport to the tropics? Why work when you can teleport to the scene of a natural disaster and loot and get away before the police catch you? And if the police do catch you, how are they going to hang on to you if you can teleport out of prison? The factors must add up, and the books must be balanced.

If you are writing about a near-future society, you must be careful of what Arthur C. Clarke has called a "failure of nerves" in prediction. Often a writer will present as a daring innovation something that has already been developed and is in use; or worse, depict an advanced society that is less technologically sophisticated than the present. One example was the slush pile story wherein myopic women of the future had to choose between wearing "ugly eyeglasses" or "stumbling near-sighted through life"—it's the twenty-first century, and they haven't even heard of contact lenses!

BLUE SUNDAYS

To write good sf, then, you must learn to perceive the hidden relationships that most do not; to pinpoint the trends just emerging in the present which might become prominent in the future, and to extrapolate logically their results in fictional terms, in terms of what they mean to *people*.

For practice, examine our own society and try to see it as a time traveler might. It has come from somewhere; it is going somewhere else. There is a reason for everything, and a history behind every reason, right down to the design of your chair. Slums turn into high-society districts, then back into slums. A hundred years ago, the street where you live might have been a swamp; a hundred years from now, it might be a swamp again, or a radioactive crater, or the lowest level in a two-mile-high city, or preserved in lucite as a memorial to the quaint glories of the past.

And these are just the details of your physical environment. There are countless more, affecting the way you act and think and talk and dress and eat, who you think you are and how you feel about it. The world only seems static because we are too short-lived to see it change. If we could speed up time, condense eons into seconds, we would see mountains flow like water and fish learn to walk.

Probably you will use only a relatively small percentage of these details in any one story—after all, your characters will not come in contact with *everything*—but you must still work out the other details. They must still be present in potential; otherwise you will constantly stumble over contradictions and mistakes. Even if the reader never has occasion to learn in the course of a story that the city was overrun by the Vandarians two decades ago and that citizens paint themselves blue on Sunday as a consequence, still the *author* must know that they do, and *the characters in the story must know it, too.* Your society should be worked out in detail and in depth, both wonders and warts, monuments and pay toilets. If you thump it, it must ring sound, not hollow.

WILD CARD

Remember that science fiction depicts not only new technologies and societal trends and their effects, but also how people react *to each other* because of them.

Be careful with emotional emphasis, with how your characters *feel* about the things making up their lives. Even if their everyday appurtenances would be wondrous beyond belief to us, they would be mundane to them. This was often a mislaid detail in much sf of the thirties and forties, which tended to worship the wonders of future technology. We don't sit in awe of our television sets, after all, even though in some ways their impact on us has been much more profound than the early prognosticators ever imagined. Conversely, what is commonplace to us someday may seem remarkable and romantic to our remote descendants. Robert Heinlein, Larry Niven and others have postulated that the people of the future, used to spaceships and supersonic shuttles, will nevertheless be aghast to think of the ordinary commuter of today going to work in the family car—no radar, no ballistic computer, no gyrostabilizers, no regulated traffic pattern; everything done by muscle power and guesswork. Who would ever dare to trade places with him? James Tiptree, Jr., has a beautiful story bit in which a highly advanced alien is staggering around the rush-hour traffic in Washington, D.C., taking deep breaths of the smog and saying things like, "How primal. How unspoiled. Such peace!" It all depends on your context.

Be aware that wild factors can upset the most impeccable timetable. Hardly anyone foresaw the incredible acceleration of technological advance since WWII, or the mass cultural/psychological nervous breakdown of the late sixties. If your fictional scenario is exceedingly neat and tidy, perhaps you should throw in some wild factors, mess it up a little, make it more like our commonplace confusion.

Remember that our descendants won't be in chrome helmets and plastic tights. The people in the worlds of Jack Vance, Ursula K. Le Guin, Robert Silverberg, Samuel R. Delany, Gene Wolfe, Joanna Russ, Philip K. Dick, Brian Aldiss, Damon Knight, Kate Wilhelm, Frederik Pohl and many others are creatures of their own times, formed in thought and spirit and habit. Isaac Asimov's people in *The Caves of Steel*, who so suffer from agoraphobia that they never leave their enclosed cities or see the sun; the Urbmondwellers of Robert Silverberg's *The World Inside*, who have not only learned to live with extreme overcrowding, but have come to find it spiritually satisfying; Jack Vance's Sirenese, who hide their naked faces from birth to death, indicate their status by the type of mask they wear, and communicate with each other by playing appropriate passages on a bewildering variety of musical instruments. These are not people we know. Yet they are our kin, in earth or in heaven; and when we meet them we feel the shock of recognition, part fear, part amazement, part joy.

THE PROBLEM WITH POWERPACKS

Like all literature, science fiction should entertain as well as enlighten. The most profound Heavy Thinking is useless if you don't have a story to tell.

One of the major narrative problems is to transmit to the reader an enormous amount of background material without gumming up the story's flow. There are as many solutions to this problem as there are writers. Some prefer to explain little or nothing directly, to tell the story as if it had been written by someone in the future for his contemporaries. One of the best examples of this is *Murder in Millennium VI*, by Curme Gray, a book that actually fulfills an ideal most writers only give lip service: It explains *none* of the highly complicated far future background. The reader must figure out or intuit what is happening page by page, on the fly, or he's lost. James Tiptree, Jr., has said his preferred narrative technique is to "start from the end and preferably 5,000 feet underground on a dark day and then *don't tell them*." Many authors have achieved remarkably successful results and striking effects by this technique; but of course, the danger is that the reader will give up in bafflement. *Murder in Millennium VI*, for instance, is about as accessible and pellucid as a brick, and was not much of a commercial success.

One popular technique is to introduce an outsider into your society as an observer, who will then learn about the society—taking the reader with him—as the story progresses (Ursula K. Le Guin's *The Left Hand of Darkness*). Its major drawback is the plausiblity of the observer. Sometimes he tends to be a rabbit-out-of-a-hat, popping out of nowhere with only the most tenuous of justifications.

Or you can couch the story as a historical analysis from a viewpoint of a future *ahead* of the story's time; or, in a variant, write your story as an open-ended testament or memoir addressed to an unknown future audience, by an isolated survivor of an atomic war, for instance. Either of these approaches justifies your narrator's explanation of much *his* audience doesn't know (as well as *yours*), either directly in the narration or through "scholarly" footnotes, introductions, afterwards and appendices. The problem: Your story may become dry and talky, so encrusted with pseudoscholarly baggage that it has trouble moving.

Or the material can be conveyed through the omniscient author technique, or through interrelations of characters, or in any of a half-dozen other ways. You will learn in time which is best for you: how much to tell, how much to imply, how much to conceal. Perhaps you will make up a new technique.

It may be a technical bottleneck at first, but you must at all costs resist the temptation to break through it by having your characters explain at length to each other things they logically should know: "As you know, Frank, we are all androids, and must recharge our powerpacks every four hours or die...." *That's probably the most common beginner's mistake on the books.*

EASTER SMEERP

Be careful with language, both in dialogue and in narration. Alexei Panshin says, "The future equivalent of 'damn,' expressed in present terms, is 'damn.'" But it cannot be denied that many authors have been successful in working future slang and "alien" terminology believably into their stories. Clearly, however, this isn't a knack every writer has, and you must be ruthless in your self-appraisal. You can't afford to fool yourself, or you will wreck the mood and believability of your stories again and again with language which sounds wrong or even ludicrous. You may end up writing what the late James Blish labeled "call a rabbit a smeerp" stories: "They *look* like rabbits, but if you call them smeerps, that makes it science fiction."

Beware of the Star Trek Syndrome: Don't create stories that unabashedly duplicate the Roman Empire or Nazi Germany. Such societies are untenable on at least two grounds: One, in spite of the time-honored proverb, history does *not* cozily repeat itself; and two, such societies are drawn not from historically accurate sources, but from grossly distorted popular simplifications. The Roman Empire was vastly more complex, contradictory and surprising than the simplistic version we get from television, movies and bad historical novels.

Finally, remember that there is no such thing as The Future—only many possible futures.

SHAPE OF STORIES TO COME

Science fiction is not easy to write. It is often beyond the capabilities even of authors of talent and intelligence, because they also need imagination, perception and mental flexibility.

If, however, this is what you really want to write, take heart: The task is not as impossible as it may appear. The biggest hurdle is the already discussed psychological reorientation. After that it is mostly a straightforward matter of learning your craft. Like any craft, it becomes easier with practice.

There are a few things you can do to make it more likely that you will succeed: First, and perhaps most importantly, *read* sf. Learn the present state of the art, learn which magazines and anthologies are buying what. By reading sf, you'll learn in advance that such-and-such is a worn-out cliché. And most basic of all: *If you don't enjoy reading science fiction, you're wasting your time trying to write it.*

Have as many inputs and interests as possible: Most sf writers read copiously and catholically, and this greatly enriches their work. Anything and everything can be grist for your mill: science, anthropology, psychology, poetry, mythology. There are many good popular science books available—some written by sf writers like Isaac Asimov, Arthur C. Clarke and Ben Bova. Subscribe to some of the less technical scientific journals, like *Science News* and *Scientific American*.

And use your charms. Science fiction is a friendly field—established authors will frequently be willing to share their expertise with you, give you tips, point out pitfalls; and genre editors are often willing to work extensively with you to renovate your story, sometimes spending much more time on it than is commercially justifiable.

And if none of the above eases your trepidation, consider this: There is a joy to this business of creating worlds that almost becomes its own reward.

Professor J.B.S. Haldane once said: "The Universe is not only queerer than we imagine—it is queerer than we *can* imagine."

To write good science fiction, we must try to reason and intuit our way to a vision that is at least somewhat as complex as reality. We shall fail, inevitably, but perhaps we shall learn to fail less totally.

And meanwhile, it's fun to try.

Where Do You Get Your Ideas?

Lawrence Block

September 1976

I n the past fifteen years I have established two incontrovertible facts. One: Glass-topped coffee tables can really hurt your shins if you're not careful. Two: Admit you're a writer and someone will immediately ask you a foolish question. I avoid glass-topped coffee tables insofar as possible, and for a time I stopped admitting I was a writer, generally attempting to pass myself off as a gentleman jewel thief. I stopped this when I found that the questions they ask jewel thieves are even more unsettling than those they ask writers.

Questions, questions, questions! *Have I read anything you've written?* I wouldn't know, sir. I'm a writer, not a mentalist. *Have you had anything published?* Why, no, madam. As I've told you, I've been doing this for fifteen years, and have written somewhere in excess (oh, wretched excess!) of one hundred books. And not a one of them published, madam. I am a compulsive masochist, you see, and I live in the woods on roots and berries. *How long does it take to write a book?* Long enough to get from the beginning, sir, to the end. Like Mr. Lincoln's legs, don't you know.

Say, where do you get your ideas?

Indeed.

There, to be sure, is the rub. Because for all the banality of the question, it is one every writer asks himself often enough, one that ought to be answerable, and one that evidently is not. The writer clearly requires ideas. Precious little (and too much at that!) gets written without them. In many types of writing, once a certain level of professional competence is granted, the strength or weakness of the idea itself determines the success or failure of the finished piece. It is this absolute need for original ideas that makes the process of literary creation wholly incomprehensible to a great many people not engaged in it. The writer is not buying widgets from Mr. A and selling them to Mr. B. He is making something out of nothing, out of thin air. He is getting ideas, and it would seem to follow that he must be getting them somewhere.

But where?

Or, more important for our purposes, how?

Because every writer knows what it's like when the mind is as fertile as a field of Illinois bottomland, with ideas sprouting at every turn. And sooner or later every writer knows the other side of the metaphor, wherein he languishes in a vast dust bowl of the mind, barely able to type his name at the top of the page. "I've been rich and I've been poor," Sophie Tucker said, "and believe me, rich is better." I believe her, and you may believe me that ideas are better than mental stagnation.

Where does one get one's ideas? I had a friend once who told askers of this particular question that there was a semimonthly magazine called *The Idea Book* or some such. "It's loaded with excellent plot ideas," he said. "I have a subscription, of course, and as soon as I get my copy I select half a dozen ideas and get clearance on them, so that no other subscriber will go ahead and write them. Then I just work up stories around those ideas and Bob's your uncle."

An encouraging number of oafs wanted to subscribe to the magazine. "You have to be a professional writer," my friend said, dashing their hopes. "Have to be a member of Author's League and have a dozen sales to your credit. But keep plugging away by all means."

Enough. Let us address ourselves to fundamentals. Obviously, many ideas spring from the subconscious, lodged there by means of various phenomena from the trauma of birth onward (or back into the collective unconscious of the race, if your outlook is Jungian), and liberated there from and directed along creative lines by other processes impossible to understand.

I submit, though, that plenty of ideas turn up in less abstruse ways, and that a look at them might help us to encourage their development.

So where do I get mine?

• **Bits of fact can fit together.** Almost all of the successful fiction writers I know share a tendency to retain odd scraps of data to no apparent purpose. Sometimes these orts prove useful, sometimes they do not. I recall, for example, that in 1938 the state of Wyoming produced one-third of a pound of dry edible beans for every man, woman and child in the nation. I should be roundly surprised if I should ever build a story around this nugget.

But perhaps a dozen years ago I read an item in a news magazine about a handful of people in the world who seemed to exist without sleep. I digested this item, and went on to study a bit about sleep, and then I set it aside. Shortly thereafter I was reading about the British House of Stuart in the encyclopedia and learned that there was still a Stuart pretender to the English throne, though he certainly didn't work at it very hard. Happily enough, he seemed to be a Bavarian. I now had the notion of a permanent insomniac with a madcap scheme to restore the House of Stuart, and that didn't add up to a story either, so after some more speculation on the sort of life a sleepless man would lead, I found other things to think about.

Two years later I spent an evening doing some moderately serious drinking with a numismatic journalist who had recently returned from Turkey, where he'd spent a couple years earning a very precarious living smuggling ancient coins and antiquities out of the country. I found his conversation fascinating, especially when he spoke at length about a rumor he'd tracked down about a cache of gold coins in the front stoop of a house in Balikesir, where the Armenian community had hoarded its wealth at the time of the massacres in Smyrna. He and some associates actually located the house as described by a survivor, broke into the stoop in the dead of night, established that the gold had been there, but established, too, that someone else had beaten them to it.

Aha!

A couple of weeks later I began a book about a young man, his sleep center permanently destroyed by a shrapnel fragment, and a devotee of all lost causes, restoration of the House of Stuart just one among many, who goes to Turkey and damn well finds that Armenian gold. I called him Evan Tanner, I called the book *The Thief Who Couldn't Sleep*, and I wrote seven books about the chap before he quit on me and stretched out for forty winks.

If I'd tried writing about Tanner when I first got the idea of insomnia as a character trait, I'd have had no story for him, and my mind wouldn't have had time to keep him on the back burner while his character defined itself. If I'd forgotten him entirely, if I'd dropped the insomnia notion once I failed to find an immediate use for it and had let it stay permanently dropped, the item about the Armenian gold cache would have led at best to a routine foreign intrigue chase with stereotyped characters. But everything came together, and I had as much fun writing those seven Tanner books as I've ever had with my clothes on.

- **People give you ideas.** In the vast majority of cases, those who say they have great ideas for stories are quite wrong. The people who *do* provide good story ideas are almost invariably other writers or people in publishing.

What? Other writers give away good ideas? Are they crazy or something? Oh, yes, they'll give away ideas, and they're not crazy at all. Everybody does it. The fact that I might have an idea that ought to make a good novel or short story is not reason enough in and of itself for me to write it. It might be the foundation of a good story without being my kind of story. Either I wouldn't have fun with it or I wouldn't do a good job with it—or most likely both. So I'll give it to someone else.

Publishers are far more likely to give away book ideas. In a sense they're not giving anything away; they supply the author with the idea and contract to publish the book once he's written it. This happens rather more frequently than the reading public realizes. There are quite a few writers who spend most of their time working up novels from ideas supplied by publishers. I'm not just talking about lower-level writers knocking out formula paperback fiction to order, but carefully calculated and well-promoted best-selling novels the ideas of which, and sometimes a fair portion of plot and characterization, originate with the publisher.

There is a very real danger in working from an idea that is spoon-fed to you in this manner. When an idea is your own, the odds are that it's been kicking around in your subconscious for a long time, and as you work on it you'll be bringing all of that subconscious concentration to bear. When you're working with someone else's idea, *unless you like it a great deal right from the start*, you won't improve it as you go along. That's why so many books developed in this fashion, written by good writers and based on commercially sound ideas, turn out flat and mechanical.

I wrote one book that I stole—with permission—from another writer. He had a premise—a bride is raped on her wedding night and the groom hunts down the bad guys. And he had a title—*Deadly Honeymoon*. I stole them both.

I waited over a year to do it. Then when I couldn't get to work on anything else and couldn't get *Deadly Honeymoon* out of my mind, I called him up and asked if he was going to do anything with the idea—he wasn't—and did he mind if I did. He didn't. I had the bride and the groom join to hunt the villains, and Macmillan published it and Dell reprinted it and the movies kept optioning it, and dropping it and it was like an annuity for awhile there.

• **Writers get ideas the way oysters get pearls.** There are those who would hold that all creative ideas are spun out of one's neurotic defenses. They may be going a little far but sometimes the process is fairly obvious. Several years ago I was in state of depression that made Schopenhauer look positively giddy. Every day I got up a little after noon and played solitaire until it was time for dinner. Then I played solitaire for a few more hours and then I drank myself to sleep. I must have been sensational company.

I would try to write now and then but I couldn't seem to motivate a character. I couldn't think of a sound reason for anybody to do anything. Ever. I would get a plot notion and think, "Hell, why doesn't he just turn over and go back to sleep?" And I would do just that.

So I wrote a book about an ex-Green Beret, a burnt-out case turned down for employment by the CIA, who just can't get it together and can't think of a reason to do anything at all, who finally winds up all by himself on an island in the Florida Keys, fishing for his meals and living a rigidly controlled life. Then somebody from Central turns up and gets him involved in an operation, but by that time the character is set and the book virtually wrote itself. (It was published as *Such Men Are Dangerous*, by Paul Kavanagh.)

• **Ideas turn up on television.** I suspect television is a great source for story ideas. I'd use it more often if I could bear to watch it, but I generally can't.

I don't mean that you take what you see on television and write it down. That's called plagiarism, and it's a no-no. What you do—and you can't set out to do it, it just happens now and then—is rewrite what you see on the screen. You improve on it, which, given the state of the art, is not by any means a Herculean task.

I probably did this several times unconsciously, but I recall one time when I knew just what I was doing. (Which is rare for me in any area of human endeavor.) I was watching *Alfred Hitchcock Presents* and there was this man who was not getting along with his wife, and he seemed to be having episodes of madness.

"Ha!" said I to my future ex-wife, "I see how they're going to end it. He's pretending to be mad, establishing a pattern, and after he's got a mental history he'll kill that bitch he's married to, and he'll get off easily on a temporary insanity plea, while actually he's been planning it from the beginning."

Wrong. Dead wrong.

I don't remember how the silly thing ended, but I wasn't even in the ballpark. He wasn't pretending to be nuts. Maybe his wife was making him think he was nuts, or making other people think so, or something. I don't remember. Actually, I didn't pay too much attention to their ending. I was busy working out mine.

I didn't even wait for Hitch to come out at the end and explain that the criminal didn't really get away with it. I went straight to my typewriter and wrote the story my way, tagged it "If This Be Madness," and sold it first shot out of the box to *Alfred Hitchcock's Mystery Magazine*. I figured they deserved first crack at it.

That brings up a point. I wrote that story immediately on getting the idea. In that instance it worked out fairly well because I got the whole story in mind in the course of the program. But I've written a lot of stories that way, getting to the typewriter as soon as I had the idea, or shortly thereafter, and I've come lately to the conclusion that it's a great mistake.

One idea may carry a short story, but for the story to be at its best it should be played out in the right setting by a cast of well-realized characters. The sort of alchemy that gets place and background and characters to the right spot at the right time will occasionally take place while you're at the typewriter, and certainly *some* of the creativity that makes a story work will happen during the writing of it.

But I have found that if I take a couple of days to mull a plot notion over, other ideas will spring to mind to complement what I've started out with. I'll get characters, plot complexities, whole slabs of dialogue. I may not use all of this, but I can sift through it all while I'm actually writing.

My present routine lends itself to this practice admirably. I spend my time traveling from place to place, following the sun around and endeavoring to leave a town before I'm asked to. I get up in the morning, put in a couple of hours at the typewriter, then either drive a couple hundred miles or, if I'm going to stay in the spot another night, wander around looking at things, talking to people, and fishing. All that time with myself for company lets plots and situations develop so that they're well formed by the time I tackle them in my morning's stint. And all those new places and new people are productive of ideas.

• **Ideas come out of conversation.** I was in a gift shop on the North Carolina Outer Banks a couple weeks ago. The storekeeper and I got into a rap about recycled jeans, which she sells a great many of at six dollars a pair. I learned that she ordered a hundred pairs at a time from one of the nation's chief suppliers of this commodity. I learned, too, that all the jeans thus supplied were just at the broken-in stage.

Now where does the company get them from? Who on earth sells jeans that have just reached the comfy stage? And what can the company *pay* for them if they retail at six dollars? A buck a pair?

Curious.

So we talked, and I said maybe I'd write a story about an agent of the firm murdering young people for their jeans, and we laughed over that, and I went on my way. Now here's a good argument in favor of giving an idea time to develop. If I'd written the story right away, it would have been thin, and besides it's hardly worth murdering someone for jeans that will retail for six dollars. But by the time the story got written, the jeans-recycling operation was just a sideline for the company; their major business, you see, was the manufacture of dog food.

Well, I might not sell that one. It's a little grisly. But I *like* it.

When I lived in New Jersey, my neighbor's father ran the local animal shelter. They had an incinerator for disposal of dead animals, and my neighbor told me how a couple of local cops were eyeing the machine longingly. "That dope peddler we can never make anything stick on," one said. "Just pop him in there one night and there's nothing left but a little envelope of ashes, and nobody'd ever know, would they?"

And, said my friend, they were dead serious.

I almost turned that into a story but it was missing something so I forgot about it. Quite awhile later my friend's dad had to close the outdoor animal compound where he kept farm animals penned up for kids to feed and play with. For the nth time, vandals had come over the fence at night and slaughtered animals for the thrill of it. So he closed up.

And now I had a story. In my story, the operator of the shelter traps a kid who has slaughtered a sheep, gives him a tour of the place, then pops him in the incinerator and cooks him. Hitchcock's magazine published it as "The Gentle Way" and Al Hubin selected it for *Best Detective Stories of 1975*, and neither plot component would have been worth dust without the other.

Sometimes a writer can draw on the same idea source more than once. Awhile back I was trying to come up with a character with enough substance to be the hero of a series of detective novels. I read a copy of *On the Pad*, by Leonard Shecter and William Phillips. Phillips, a New York policeman who cooperated with a committee investigating police corruption, was himself a frankly corrupt cop who spent most of his time hustling a dishonest dollar but who happened to be a damned good cop when he put his mind to it.

I thought of basing a character on Phillips, but I couldn't make it work. My heroes just can't operate as organization men or insiders, and I couldn't come up with a character along these lines that I felt would interest me for more than a single book, if that long. But as I mulled and pondered, the character shifted and changed and gradually took form. My detective, Matthew Scudder, emerged as an ex-cop who accidentally killed a child with a stray shot some time ago. This launched him on what you might call an identity crisis; until then he'd been a reasonably corrupt cop and not a terribly introspective person, but after the girl's death he quit the police force, moved to a monastic hotel room in mid-Manhattan, became alcoholic and quirkily religious and now does occasional unofficial work as an unlicensed private detective. His character as it ultimately developed is a lot closer to a fusion of Ross Macdonald's Lew Archer and Graham Greene's *Burnt-Out Case* than to Phillips, but Shecter's book got the wheels turning and gave the old subconscious something to play with.

Ideas, ideas, ideas. An idea doesn't do you much good if it's not right for you, however good it may be in and of itself. The idea of a corrupt cop solving crimes while turning a dirty dollar might have worked out just fine in another pair of hands than mine, but I had to turn it six ways and backward before I got something right for me. The idea of casting Dashiell Hammett as the detective in a period mystery is nothing less than brilliant, but how many people besides Joe Gores, himself a San Franciscan and ex-private eye, could have begun to do the book justice? (And it doesn't hurt a bit that Joe writes like a dream.) Why, if I'd had the idea I'd have given it away — or more likely, I'd have simply forgotten about it.

On the other hand, when Brian Garfield told me a book idea of his some time ago I had an overwhelming urge to knock him over the head, lock him in a closet, and not let him out until I'd stolen his idea and written the book. But I suppressed the urge, and Brian wrote the book and decided he'd call it *Death Wish*.

I should have locked him in that closet. Where did he ever get that idea, anyway?

The Poetry of Concrete

Judson Jerome

October 1976

B e concrete! Cut out abstractions!" I am continually telling poets (and I'm not referring to the mid-sixties "school" of concrete poetry). But recently these words of advice blew back in my face—for good reason. They were too abstract. I wasn't communicating. The woman to whom I was writing obviously didn't know what the terms meant—and though I had told her, I hadn't shown her. "Show, don't tell" is the first rule for any writer—but that advice itself is an instance of telling rather than showing.

"I know which part of the poem you won't like," she said in a letter sent with the poem on which she wanted my opinion. "You will think the line about the 'gravel of unease' is too abstract." But that was the best line in the poem—because it was the most concrete! At least it contained an image—gravel. "Unease," true enough, is an abstraction, but it is grounded in that gravel. One can sense it—that is, experience it with one's senses. That's what concreteness means.

At the bottom end of the scale of language, where poets work most effectively, are the words which are most specific, closest to direct experience. Look for a moment at your hand. The very word *hand* is a generalization, an abstraction, in no way capturing the immediacy and individuality of the appendage before your eyes. It doesn't know it is a hand: It is specific corpuscles, veins, nerves, tendons, bones, a specific and ultimately indescribable patch of skin, nails, delicate hair. Most concretely it is beyond language. We may give labels to its chemical ingredients, to its atoms and their components, to the various waves of energy it contains, but we must finally fall wordless before the infinity of characteristics, the inexpressible individuality, the peculiarity, of this thing before our eyes.

If a poet wants to communicate the experience of a hand, he may resort to metaphor. "Her hands lay in her lap like tired lovers. . . ."

The metaphor takes the relatively abstract word, *hands*, and makes it more specific, more individual: It helps a reader *experience* those hands. This is the primary function of imagery in poetry (though not the only one): to specify, to make language more exact, in this case to distinguish one pair of hands from all other pairs of hands in the world.

Yet the word *hand* is itself relatively concrete. I used the word *appendage* above, a more general, more abstract term: It includes feet. *Organ* would be still a more abstract term for a hand, as it includes many more things than hands and feet. *Flesh* is equally or perhaps even more abstract. Let's jump up the abstraction ladder to *thing*, which might include *hand* but includes, as well, washtubs and even thoughts. A word is more concrete if it is more specific, more abstract if it includes more. If your name is Orintha Q. Snugglebut, that name is likely to be fairly concrete. There aren't many who bear it. If you are a *widow*, the term is more concrete than *woman*, another term which includes you, or than *human being*, or *living creature*, all steps further up the ladder of abstraction.

When I complain about a poem's being abstract, I mean it tends to use language that is too general in its application. *Happiness* is very abstract; *giggly* is much more concrete. One can see and hear giggliness; it is experiential. *Happiness* summarizes rather than specifies. It tells rather than shows.

Let me show you. I get up, go to the shelf, to the stack of unread volumes various poets have sent me in the past few weeks, take the top one, open it at random—and here are the first two stanzas of the poem I find there:

> Smog surrounds,
> a curtain change
> on all I know and feel.
> Destroying senses
> of time and season
> direction and space.

She told me in the accompanying letter that she is having very little success with her poetry—and at least one reason is immediately evident. She is too abstract. That second stanza is dead loss in a poem, just prose; and the third line of the first stanza is just as bad.

Yet I can see in those lines, too, evidence of poetic instinct. It may not be very original to call smog a curtain, but it is at least an image: It begins to communicate with some exactness how that particular smog affected that particular person. When she writes "all I know and feel," though, she is throwing up her hands, giving up the effort to find language for her experience, hoping to cover the lack with a generalization. I am reminded of someone who says something was "indescribable" or "beyond words." Experience is, indeed, indescribable and beyond words, but it is the poet's business, nonetheless, to describe and to find words. There is no way you are going to get "all I know and feel" into a poem, but if you are going to write a poem, you have to try. Maybe it changes her like Sure-Jell changes plum juice. Maybe it changes her like a violin changes a jug band. I don't know how it changes her. She has to tell me how—not just tell me it changes her, or changes all she knows and feels.

And her instinct told her she had to specify—and, indeed, that seems to be what she is struggling with in the second stanza. She tries to *explain*. But, no, as a poet, you can't explain. It is like a comedian trying to explain why a joke is funny. If it wasn't funny, explanation won't make it so. If your images haven't caught and transmitted your feelings, abstractions will only make things worse. We may end up understanding her all right, but we won't have felt anything.

It is very difficult for me to imagine any poet making words such as *destroying, senses, time, season, direction, space* work in a poem, especially if they are packed together this way in one dangling phrase. There are exceptions, of course, in great poetry—and I'm sure busy readers will send me examples using all of the above words. There are times when brilliant poetry rises to grand abstractions. Most often, though, if it uses abstractions at all, it follows them with concrete instances.

SHOW ME WHERE IT HURTS

Much poetry exploring delicate states of feeling derives from Keats. But look how he does it, in "Ode to a Nightingale":

> My heart aches, and a drowsy numbness
>   pains
> My sense, as though of hemlock I had
>   drunk,
> Or emptied some dull opiate to the
>   drains
> One minute past, and Lethe-wards had
>   sunk:

It is mighty hard to get away with a phrase such as "heart aches" in a poem (though it is fairly concrete), but having emitted that cliché, he goes on to nail down the feeling he is trying to describe as precisely as possible. "Drowsy numbness" is still too abstract (though much more concrete than anything in the language from the poet quoted above). It was, he goes on, as though I had drunk not *poison*, but the specific, *hemlock*. Or as though I had taken a drug. Not the abstract word *drug*, though, but some "dull opiate." When? "One minute past." All the pressure in the language of the poem is to be specific, exact, experiential. When abstractions are used they call immediately for illustrations, examples, images.

Some people complain that they can't understand poetry because it is too abstract. What they mean is, it is too concrete. If you listen to ordinary conversation, or read ordinary prose, such as this column, you find that nine-tenths of the words are devoid of experiential content—as devoid of it as is the word *devoid* or *experiential* or *content*. If I were to put that thought more poetically I would say the words are like clouds of vapor or blueprints of buildings or stacks of empty cartons. You might not find those similes as easy to understand as you do the abstract, general, prosaic terms I first used. Indeed, you might find them obscure. But if you let the images happen to your senses, you can understand: You not only know what I mean but how I feel about language devoid of experiential content.

When we "interpret" a poem, we translate the concrete language into abstractions more intelligible to our prosaic, everyday minds. For instance, we might say that in the lines quoted from Keats, the poet "means" that he feels a pang of sadness on the verge of being overwhelmed by oblivion. Actually, he didn't "mean" any such thing: He meant what he said. But we can hardly talk about poetry at all without expanding it with the gas of abstraction. It comes to us too condensed, too concrete, too immediate for rational discourse.

But those learning to write poetry often confuse the "meaning" or "interpretation" with poetry itself. They write, then, in lines that look like poetry on the page, scraps of prose explanation of what they felt, perceived, of the experience they meant to convey.

That is what I mean when I tell them their poetry is too abstract, when I say, "Show, don't tell." Make it happen on the page. Cut out all the talk and give us the stuff itself, the experience itself. You can't, of course, for language by its very nature is abstraction, and there is no way you can make words become the equivalent of direct, concrete experience. But that is what you have to try for. Bear down. For every word you start to use, see if you cannot find another that is more concrete.

EXCEPT FOR EXCEPTIONS

I will close by confusing you. In a sense all I have said above is dead wrong. What the poet seeks in his language is resonance, reverberation, suggestiveness: He wants to communicate a specific experience in such a way that it implies, evokes, the widest possible range of meaning, the deepest, most far-reaching significance. If the abstract level of prose is, as I have said, composed mostly of vague and general terms, there is also a level of everyday fact that equally misses the feeling sought in poetry.

Suppose that in "Nightingale" Keats had instead written, "Wednesday I was sitting on the bank of the Thames about five in the evening—dusk these fall days—when I heard a nightingale and felt a palpitation of my ventricle and a dull headache that was so intense I was on the verge of unconsciousness . . . ." In a way that is too concrete to be interesting: We get so preoccupied with exactly what happened to John Keats the man (perhaps worried about his TB) that we miss the general significance of his experience. He was not interested in conveying the mere facts of his experience, as in a diary entry. Indeed, the experience reported in the poem of hearing a nightingale and experiencing certain feelings and thinking certain thoughts might have been wholly fictional—and that makes not the slightest difference. It was the symbolic meaning of such an experience that motivated the poem. He wanted it to be vivid enough that a reader would feel it—yet vague enough that the reader's mind would be released to apply it to many experiences in his own life.

Finally, the job of the poet is not to be concrete or abstract, but to find exactly the right level of concreteness and abstractness to make the poem work as art. But since most beginners err on the side of being too abstract, the advice I have given is usually that which they most need. Worry about getting the experience down in all its immediacy. Let the overtones, the philosophy, the moralizing, the generalization take care of itself.

1980s

To Make a Short Story Long . . .

Orson Scott Card

September 1980

I n the Munich Olympics in 1936, the Germans were very clever. They didn't let the equestrians from other nations see the course the horses would have to race. At one point in the course, after the normal obstacles that all the horses easily coped with, there was a fence. And beyond the fence was a strip of water dozens of yards across, far too wide for any horse to jump.

When the non-German equestrians reached that obstacle, they all tried to jump, of course, and floundered. But the German rider, knowing all about it, had his horse daintily step over the fence and walk gently through the water with perfect form.

It was cheating. But it's the kind of thing many of us face when we try to switch from writing short stories to writing novels. We're used to coping with 3,000 or even 10,000 words. But suddenly there yawns before us a huge expanse of words—a hundred thousand or more. And when we try to leap over it as we would with a story, we end up with a soaking, as often as not.

Six months after I got my first check for a short story sale, I took stock of my earnings. I had sold a total of four stories in that time, for which I had been paid a total of $980. This was still twenty dollars less than my monthly salary at my magazine editing job.

It didn't look like I would be able to go freelance very soon, not on short story sales alone. If I wanted to be a full-time writer, I was going to have to write a novel.

So I sat down at the typewriter and began writing. I was confident. After all, what was a novel, if not a short story that had more things happen before the end? So, page by page, my first novel flowed from my typewriter. It was a science fiction epic that spanned a thousand years and dealt with the lives of twenty characters.

And it only lasted for 120 pages.

I began to suspect there was more to writing a novel than just "having more things happen."

LONGER IS SHORTER

More of us who write fiction begin with short stories. There are several practical reasons for this: Short stories look easier to write. If you write a bad one that never sells, you have lost only twenty pages' work, not three hundred. And—perhaps the most common reason of all—short stories are what your college creative writing teacher wanted to see, and now you're in the habit.

How do you make the leap from short stories to novels? That intimidating stack of blank pages you have to fill is enough to frighten off most would-be novelists. But if you're one of the rare ones who is determined to go ahead, there are some things you can do to help yourself over the hurdle.

How do I know the arcana of switching to the novel form? I learned from experience. I wrote some bad novels. And each one's flaws taught me how to write the next one better.

That first novel—that 120-page thousand-year epic. I knew something was terribly wrong with it. So I took it to a friend, a fine editor who had been criticizing my short stories for me. He read it; he returned it to me silently.

"Well?" I asked.

"Um," he said. "Sure is long."

Long? A hundred and twenty pages? "The problem is it's too short."

"No," he insisted. "The problem is it's too long. It's absolutely boring. From page 3 on, I could hardly get through it."

The novel began like any of my short stories. I jumped into the main character's problem with both feet, and tried to make him personally interesting. It worked fine.

But on page 3, I started really getting into the plot. I introduced two more characters and moved my protagonist into a life-and-death struggle. By page 5, he had resolved that problem and was off on another adventure. By page 10, he had saved the world. By page 30, he had saved another world.

I wasn't writing a novel at all. I was writing a plot outline. I was so keenly aware of how much story line I had to cover that I had raced ahead and not paused to give the reader time to absorb anything.

Short stories are designed to deliver their impact in as few pages as possible. A tremendous amount is left out, and a good short story writer learns to include only the most essential information—only what he needs to create mood, get the facts across, and prepare the reader for the climax.

But novels have more space, more time. When a reader sits down with a book he is committing several hours of his life to reading it. He will stay with you for much more peripheral material; he expects, in return, that you will provide him with a fuller experience than he could possibly get from a short story.

In my first draft of my first novel, I had written *history*—a bare retelling of events.

When I set out to write the second draft, I knew I had to write biography—a detailed exposition of what my characters thought and said and did, and what in their past made them act that way.

My second draft was more than 300 pages long, and included only half the plot of the first draft. But it was a much better book. That is it could be read by a person who actually stayed awake without liberal doses of No Doz.

My friend read it again, and came back much happier. "It still isn't very good, but at least it's *shorter* this time."

Card's Law of Novel-Writing: Longer is shorter.

DON'T GET BURIED IN PLOT

One of the things that fooled me on that first draft was the idea that if a novel is ten times the length of a short story, it must have ten times the plot. But that is rarely the case.

Think of John Fowles's novel *Daniel Martin*—629 pages of always excellent, often brilliant prose. Yet the plot, the actual, essential plot, could have been expressed in a forty-page novelette. I suspect it would be a mediocre story at best, but it could easily be done, because not that much happens on the direct plot line. Reduced to its absurd minimum, *Daniel Martin* is the story of a financially successful screenwriter who returns to England at the request of a dying friend with whom he feuded years ago. The friend's wife was the woman the screenwriter really loved and wanted to marry back in their days at Oxford; the dying friend reveals that he knew his wife had an affair with the screenwriter, and wants the two of them to get together after his death. Having delivered his message, the friend kills himself, and the screenwriter and the woman he once loved do indeed fall in love again, much to their own surprise.

Sounds like a melodramatic little story, doesn't it? And it might have turned out that way — except that stories and novels are not just devices for recounting plot.

When I first plotted that first novel of mine, I was thinking of a short story as a sort of thread through time, a few events long; I thought of a novel as simply a longer thread to fill up the pages. My metaphor was all wrong, however. Writing is not just one-dimensional.

So when you sit down to plot your novel, don't try to come up with ten times the number of events you usually put in a story. You will usually want more events than in a story, of course, but you should still leave yourself plenty of leisure to explore from character to character, from thought to thought, from detail to detail. A novel need not cover a thousand years or forty-eight characters or the Renaissance in Italy; you have the freedom to use the novel form to write about a single life or a single year or a single incident. Despite the deceptively simple plot of *Daniel Martin*, or perhaps because of it, Fowles was able to take his readers by surprise, bringing us to love the seemingly jaded and shallow narrator as he reluctantly showed us his true self a layer at a time.

GULPS AND SWALLOWS

My first novel went through several more drafts, and I thought I had finally found a system for coping with its length. I was a short story writer, wasn't I? So why not cut up the plot into five or six novelettes? They would all lead to a climax at the end, and yet I would be on familiar ground, writing thirty or forty pages in each section, just like a story.

Well, it worked — and it didn't. I sold the novel, and people even bought copies of it and read it, and some liked it. But the critics didn't, and much as it pains me to say, they are fundamentally right. Because that little trick of cutting the novel up into short stories simply doesn't work.

A novel isn't a half-dozen short stories with the same characters. The seams invariably show. Why? Because a novel must have integrity. The novel, no matter how dense and wide-ranging it might be, must have a single cumulative effect to please the reader. Every minor climax must point toward the book's final climax, must promise still better things to come.

But in my first novel (all right, I'll name it: *Hot Sleep*), instead of a series of minor climaxes leading toward the final climax of the book, I had six completely unrelated climaxes. In the first short story, my protagonist, as a child, faces a terrible dilemma that shapes his whole future. But when I start the second story, years have passed and those earlier events are not very important anymore — it's hard to see any real effect they might have on the events of the rest of the novel. And at the end of the second story, all but one of the major characters lose their memories in a disaster in space, and to all intents and purposes the third part of the book is another entirely new beginning. All the reader's emotional investment is gone, and he has to begin all over again. No wonder some readers got impatient!

In a way, however, my instinct was correct. You can't write a novel all at once any more than you can swallow a whale in one gulp. You do have to break it up into smaller chunks. But those small chunks aren't good old familiar short stories. Novels aren't built out of short stories.

They're built out of scenes.

LIGHTS! CAMERA! ACTION! CUT!

Think of the way a movie works. A new setting is almost always introduced with an establishing shot, showing the audience what characters are present and where they are. Almost every time the film skips from one place to another without actually following the characters there, the audience is given some time to get its bearings.

Then, as the film progresses, the camera cuts from one point of view to another, or follows as the characters travel from one place to another. The camera is able to focus on a particular thing that a character is looking at — or that the character is unaware of. But all through a single action, the camera keeps our attention tightly focused on the important matters. Then, when that scene ends, there is another establishing shot; another line of action begins.

As you see the story unwind on the screen, you aren't really aware that between each new setting there are really *many* scenes, small bits of action leading to a single, small climax or revelation. After all, neither novelists nor filmmakers show *everything* that happens. Tremendous amounts of detail are skipped over, left out — hinted at, perhaps, but never shown. All of the action is compressed into the events that *are* shown. While a filmmaker must compress everything into two hours or so, a novelist has a great deal more freedom. Within reasonable limits, you can include all the pertinent information, and the reader will be right there with you.

Like a filmmaker, however, you must present that information carefully. You can't just list the events and motives and speeches of the characters — that's history. Bad history, in fact. Instead, you present the information dramatically, through characters who have understandable desires and who are carrying out understandable actions, and with a structure that helps the reader notice and understand and feel what you want him to.

And the structure you use is composed of hundreds of different scenes, of varying lengths and varying degrees of importance, each one a single continuing action.

A single, continuing action may be, for instance, a sword fight that begins with an insult at a party and continues all over the palace until one man finally gasps with a sword in his chest and the hero, panting, watches his enemy die.

A single, continuing action may be a man standing at the window of an apartment in a tall building, looking out over a city watching a helicopter land, regretting his decision not to be aboard it.

A single, continuing action may be a journey across the United States, summarized by telling, in two paragraphs, the routine of a single day of travel; that summary is extended to cover all the days of travel.

Each such scene is a unit, designed to have its own effect on the reader; when the scene ends, the reader knows something more — and feels something more.

How is that different from writing a short story? Ideally, a short story is an indivisible unit — every sentence in it points toward the single climax that fulfills the entire work. One moment in the story controls all the rest. But in a novel, that single climax is replaced by many smaller climaxes, by many side trips or pauses to explore. If you keep shaping everything to point to that one climax, your reader will get sick of it after a hundred pages or so. It will feel monotonous. To keep the reader entertained (i.e., to keep him reading) you must give him many small moments of fulfillment along the way, brief rewards that promise something bigger later.

How does this work in a particular novel? Let's go through chapter twenty-seven of a recent best-seller, Stephen King's *The Stand*. After each scene number, the number of paragraphs in the scene appears in parentheses, followed by a synopsis of the scene:

1. (4) Protagonists Larry and Rita have noticed that the electricity is beginning to go off, and the smell of the decaying bodies is terrible; Larry is afraid New York will soon be unlivable.

2. (2) Flashback: They found the body of a man they had been aware of, murdered. It affected Rita deeply.

3. (20) Dialogue: Larry and Rita eat breakfast, and Larry makes the decision to leave.

4. (8) Rita suddenly rushes to the bathroom, vomits. She is fast becoming unable to cope with the disaster.

5. (3) Flashback: Rita is not as strong as Larry had thought at first.

6. (1) Larry wonders if he can take care of her.

7. (13) Dialogue: She decides to go with him, even as he comes to resent her more because of her weakness.

At this point, King takes a larger break. There is a line space, and suddenly we are with Larry and Rita as they walk along the streets of New York. In those first seven scenes, there is a definite sense of building toward a single climax, the moment in scene 7 where Larry catches himself hating her. King writes: "Then he felt the familiar surge of self-contempt and wondered what the hell could be the matter with him.

" 'I'm sorry,' he said. 'I'm an insensitive bastard.' "

It is a pivotal moment for Larry; it is the reason why he takes responsibility for her even though he hates the thought of taking her along. It explains his motive. It also sets us up for later tension in later scenes, and finally, in a small way, it leads us to the climax of the novel.

Yet each of the small scenes leading to that climax had a closure of its own. Scene 1 closes with Larry's dark dream of a black thing that wants him. Scene 2 closes with the observation that seeing the dead man had made a powerful change in Rita. Scene 3 ends with a startling change — after a peaceful conversation, Rita suddenly has an expression on her face that scares Larry. Scene 8 ends with the startling revelation that Rita is pathetically eager to do whatever she thinks Larry wants her to do. And so on.

Every scene advances the reader toward the minor climax in the seventh scene. Each scene conveys the necessary information and then closes in a way that increases the tension, the reader's expectation of a climax. And the scenes vary — first bare exposition in the author's voice, then a flashback in Larry's mind, then dialogue between Larry and Rita, then physical action as Rita rushes to the bathroom to vomit, then flashback, then reflection and then dialogue again.

It is as if King had cut from camera to camera, showing us the continuing action from different points of view, revealing bits of information that together built to a whole — the superscene that ends with the line space. And the chapter is composed of five superscenes of varying length that, together, tell a complete episode. The chapter as a whole cements

Larry and Rita together in our minds, despite the tension between them. We end up understanding and liking both. They have managed to get out of New York alive, but we know their adventures are just beginning.

CLIFFHANGERS

These are the gulps you can use to down a whole novel. You never sit down to write 300 or 500 or 1,000 pages. You sit down to write a series of scenes that create a superscene with its own minor climax; you then add the superscenes together to create the climax that completes the chapter.

Yet, while each closure, each minor climax, each chapter climax is fulfilling to the reader, none of them is *completely* fulfilling. Inherent in every climax is the promise of more tension and greater fulfillment later. In its crudest form, this is the cliffhanger technique — putting the protagonist into an awkward dilemma and then leaving him hanging there while the reader waits to buy the next day's installment. Such obvious tricks irritate most readers; but the technique, in more subtle form, is essential to creating a novel as a whole. After all, what is a novel if not the writer's attempt to involve the reader emotionally in a dilemma and keep him involved until its resolution? In your short stories, you could hold off until your single climax because the reader would stay with you for such a brief time; but in a novel, the reader's patience is not infinite.

Of course, I seriously doubt that Stephen King sat down and planned out each of those seven scenes. I wonder if he even outlined chapter by chapter. The selection of what scenes to present is art; it is felt, not intellectualized. For me, most of those decisions are unconscious. It feels right to include this scene; it feels right to interrupt the action here for a flashback that reveals important information; it feels right to describe this particular setting in loving detail.

You *can* consciously plan, however, to keep yourself aware of the possibilities open to you, so that you use all your tools. You can concentrate on the scenes and superscenes at hand, instead of letting the climax of the novel, hundreds of pages away, distract you from what you are creating now.

And, while you aren't writing short stories anymore, you *have* cut that whale of a novel into pieces small enough that you, like the reader, can forget about the hundreds of pages ahead and concentrate on only the few pages needed to reach the climax of this particular scene.

As a friend of mine once said, "I'd a lot rather fight two tons of tiny lizards than a two-ton fire-breathing dragon."

THE SECOND WILL BE BETTER THAN THE FIRST

Novels and short stories are different art forms. They have a lot more in common than do, say, novels and paintings, or even short stories and poems. Yet you are crippling yourself if you try to write a novel under the impression that it's just more of the same thing you have been doing with short stories.

Even if you keep in mind all the things I have pointed out, you will probably find new mistakes or problems I haven't mentioned. After all, there were some things I did *right* in my first novels that you might do wrong. And undoubtedly there are some things I'm *still* doing wrong that I haven't caught yet—and therefore can't warn you about.

Each novel you write, however, will make the next one easier. I'm not talking about mere confidence, either, though finishing one novel will certainly make the next one seem less intimidating. Whether or not you notice what you're learning, you *are* learning. When I was an eight-year-old, first throwing a ball at a basketball hoop, I missed time and time again. But gradually I began to be able to hit the backboard every time, and eventually I got good enough to have the ball come somewhere near the basket on every shot. Though I'm still a miserable basketball player, I did unconsciously learn and improve. In writing novels, of course, each shot takes a long time, and you aren't able to see so easily whether you missed or not. But your brain is still plugging along, learning to become comfortable with the form.

Too comfortable, sometimes. I studied Spanish for eight years and was pretty good in it—but then I lived in Brazil for two years, and spoke Portuguese the whole time. Those languages are so similar that by the end of those two years, I literally could not speak Spanish at all—Portuguese had taken over.

I find a similar thing happening to me now. With four novels under my belt, I find it increasingly hard to use that similar but still different "language" of short stories. I keep forgetting that I don't have hundreds of pages to work with; and my most recent thirty-page story finally ended at 130 pages, and even at that I felt that I had left out two-thirds of what should have been in it. In other words, my short story came out as a novel whether I wanted it or not.

Anybody have any advice on how a novelist can learn to write short stories?

The Seven Beacons of Excellent Writing

Gary Provost

March 1984

D id you ever sit down to write, and get the feeling that things would go fine if you could just keep in mind 543 principles of good writing?

I did. A lot.

It seemed that the writing waters were pretty treacherous, and often while I kept busy watching for rocks I forgot to sail forth. I needed some lighthouses, a few beacons to lead me safely into port. I needed to reduce all that I knew about good writing to a handful of concepts, few enough that I could see them all at once. So I made a list. I came up with . . . or perhaps down to . . . seven. I call them my seven beacons of good writing. They are Brevity, Clarity, Precision, Harmony, Humanity, Honesty and Poetry, and they are posted over my desk. I suggest that you post them over your desk too, and when the seas get rough and the sky grows dark look ahead at them and steer a steady course.

The seven beacons guide me through everything I write. They once led me through an article, called "Apple Harvest," that I wrote for *The Boston Phoenix*. My home area has many apple orchards and the magazine wanted an article about who picks apples and why. I decided the best way to write about the pickers was to be one.

And to use the seven beacons of good writing:

1. BREVITY

Brevity, we know, is the soul of wit. It is also the soul of good writing. When you write and rewrite, don't think about what you can put in. Think about what you can leave out.

Editors want tight writing. They want it short. They want every word to be doing some work. Columns rarely run longer than 750 words, and more and more there is a demand for articles in the 1,000- to 2,000-word range.

To the uninitiated it might seem that writing it shorter is easier. But it's not. Someone (the quote has been attributed to people ranging from Mark Twain to Abe Lincoln to Pascal) once wrote to a friend, "I would have written you a shorter letter, but I didn't have time." Writing shorter doesn't mean saying less. It means saying as much, but with fewer words.

Here are a few tips for keeping your good writing in a small package.

Find a slant, a specific aspect of your subject, and include only information that is appropriate for the slant. If you're writing "Ten Tips for the Bike Buyer," direct at least 90 percent of your words toward those ten tips, and spend relatively few words on generalized information such as the rising interest in bicycling, the health benefits of bicycling, and the number of bicycles sold last year.

Begin at the beginning. Many writers work their way into a story as if they're feeling their way into a dark house. It's not unusual for editors to cut the first five paragraphs from a story without anybody noticing. Save them the work. Look at your first sentence. Is it doing any work? Is it part of your story or is it merely *about* your story, which you haven't yet begun? Cut every sentence until you come to the one that must be there.

The original opening paragraph of my apple-picking article was a typical unnecessary opening paragraph. It began, "I had decided to spend a day picking apples for a day's pay. I wanted to find out what it felt like." The paragraph goes on with a long explanation of why I had decided to spend a day picking apples. It was unnecessary. The article would eventually show all of that. I got rid of the paragraph. Instead of beginning with a paragraph about my decision to do something, I began with the something itself:

> *I reached the apple orchard at nine on a brisk Wednesday morning. No form of logic had influenced my choice of orchard. I'd simply opened a phone book and picked out an orchard in Harvard. I knew that all the orchards were looking for pickers.*

Eliminate unnecessary words. One of the most painful lessons we learn as writers is that a word, a sentence or a paragraph, no matter how beautifully crafted or carefully chosen, is not a good word, sentence or paragraph if it is not necessary. One way to eliminate unnecessary words is to keep your eye on that beacon called Precision, which we'll discuss soon. Remember that a word is unnecessary if it does no work, if it does work that doesn't have to be done, or if it does work that's being done by another word or phrase nearby. For example, "Tuesday is Ms. Coronoa's day off, and she always goes to the video game arcade. Every Tuesday she scoops up a fistful of quarters from her jar and drives over to the video arcade in Elgin. She doesn't have to work on her arcade days so sometimes she stays until supper time."

Also, look out for unnecessary words that you write habitually. Many of my students use *proceed* a lot. Don't write, "Daniel proceeded to open his letters." Write "Daniel opened his letters." Write "I think" instead of "it is my opinion that." Also avoid "I would like to say" (just say it) and "It has come to my attention." (Obviously it has come to your attention, or you couldn't bring it to our attention.) There are dozens of these. Find them and eliminate them.

So write short. Fewer trees will have to be slaughtered, less ink will be used, and more checks will be sent to your address.

2. CLARITY

I don't know where we acquire our early ideas of what constitutes good writing. But there must be some common fountain of misinformation because most of my students make the same mistakes that I made when I was a few years younger. One of the most common and erroneous ideas is that the clever writer hides his meaning. In fact, the good writer makes his meaning as clear as possible. He leaves no room for doubt about what is being read and he is not vague except when he has a good reason.

I have read hundreds of unpublished stories that begin something like this: "The package arrived at 2 A.M. Sammy opened it in a frenzy. He stared at its contents and smiled." The story goes on and we hear a lot about "it" or "the contents of the package" and so forth. If we stick around long enough we discover in the last paragraph that the package contained an adorable little beagle puppy. This is the way children write, not professionals.

A similar common mistake is the use of a mysterious pronoun long before the noun has been introduced. The writer begins, "He hobbled into the church, his heart full of shame. He looked about, saw no one, and moved slowly toward the altar." Then "he" lights a candle, "he" prays. After a while "he" starts to feel better. Then around the seventh paragraph, "Thomas trembled at the thought of seeing Anna again," and the first questions that go through the reader's mind are "Who the hell is Thomas and where did he come from?" After a few more sentences we begin to realize that Thomas is the mysterious "he" whose identity has been withheld from us for no good reason. Be clear. Begin with "Thomas hobbled into the church, his heart full of shame."

Though you should never repeat information unnecessarily, it is better to be repetitive than unclear. If you wrote, "Jefferson and Mitchell met in Troy, New York. He was working as a waiter in a pancake house," the reader could become confused about which "he" was delivering pancakes. Write, "Mitchell was working as a waiter in a pancake house." Also, in dialogue, if you're not positive that you've made it clear who is speaking, write "Diane said," or "Vandenburg said," as often as you must.

Your writing is often robbed of clarity when you get lazy. You're tired, perhaps distracted, you don't know quite what to say, so your writing becomes vague, wishy-washy and you create paragraphs like this:

> *Soon I was apple-picking. Despite the normal problems, I found there was a certain joy and calmness about it, though of course there were some discomforting aspects of it, but nothing much to be really concerned about.*

That's all very vague. What exactly is the narrator doing? What problems? What is he talking about? Go back through your story and get rid of these vague sentences that seem to bounce around looking for somewhere to land. Clear it up. What are you trying to say? In my apple-picking piece what I really wrote was:

> *I crawled in under the tree, found a place for my knees in the deep grass, and began quite merrily to pick apples. Now and then I'd grab an apple and from the quivering branch would come a cloud of tiny white bugs. They didn't buzz, sting, or deposit larvae on my shirt, so I didn't worry about them.*

To be clear usually means to be direct. Get right to the point in simple, unambiguous language. One useful tool is pyramid style; tell the reader immediately what you're writing about, who's involved, when it happens, where and how.

John Bierman began a *Boston Globe* story on termite chemicals with this clear and direct pyramid-style sentence:

> *Jeffrey Lever had his split-level ranch house in East Islip, Long Island, bulldozed to the ground with all its contents last week after it was discovered the house's interior had been sprayed with a potentially lethal chemical.*

One more tip for clarity. Keep related words together. If you write "The streets of London had been very crowded and Jason found that his wallet had been stolen in Paris," a Frenchman is going to get blamed for something an Englishman did. If the theft occured in London, then put it near London. For example, "When he got to Paris, Jason discovered that his wallet had been stolen on the crowded streets of London."

3. PRECISION

Precision and Clarity are closely related. To be clear is to say what you mean. To be precise is to say *exactly* what you mean. Precision is also related to brevity. A precise word often replaces a few words that are not so precise. A precise word etches a sharper picture on the reader's brain and eliminates the possibility of misunderstanding.

Try to make your writing more precise without making it wordier. Don't make a sentence more precise by hooking up a freight train of details to it. Make it more precise by whittling all the possible word combinations to those few that say exactly what you want to say. Go through your manuscript and change the general word or phrase to the precise word or phrase. Change "They won by a large margin" to "They won by forty-two points." If you've written "Various ethnic groups have settled in Newark," change it to "Greeks, Italians and Puerto Ricans have settled in Newark."

You'll find that precision in writing increases believability. If I tell you that some people are out to get me, you're skeptical. If I tell you that three Turks have threatened to garotte me, you begin to think maybe there's something to it.

Also, use a thesaurus to help you find the word that means precisely what you want to say.

In the following example from my apple-picking article, I have made a job, an age, an appearance, a machine and a motion all more precise. In some cases I saved a few words. In others I spent a few more. But in every case I improved the writing.

I changed:

> *"I'm looking for work picking apples," I called to the guy in charge. He was a large, balding older man, rough-hewn and no pleasure to look at. He looked down at me from his noisy machine which he was driving around the apple trees.*

To:

"I'm looking for work picking apples," I called to the foreman. He was a husky, balding man of about sixty, every bit as weathered as the trees he tended. He had a fist for a face and it studied me from atop a yammering forklift which he jockeyed around the apple trees.

4. HARMONY

Writing a story is not a visual art, any more than composing music is a visual art.

When you write, you create music, and when you write well, you create music that is pleasant to the ear. It is harmonious. It doesn't matter whether your writing sounds like Tchaikovsky's *Piano Concerto No. 1* or Elton John's "Crocodile Rock," but it shouldn't sound like both. The music should flow, not leap. There should be no electric guitars shrieking amid the whispers of the flutes and violins. So read aloud everything that you write. Listen to the sound it makes. Listen for dissonance. Listen for sour notes.

A sour note in writing can be an obscure and pretentious word set down in a paragraph that is otherwise simply written. A sour note can be a humorous phrase in a somber story, or a grave comment in a story which is written in a frivolous style. A sour note could be an unintended change in tense or person, or a sudden switch in viewpoint. A sour note can even be a change in the way you punctuate certain phrases. Generally you create harmony in your writing by maintaining consistency in mood, reading level, style, paragraph size and punctuation.

Here are a few tips for creating harmonious music with your words:

Use a variety of sentence lengths. Mix short, medium and long sentences. Too many sentences of similar length create a drone; they bore the reader.

Use a variety of sentence constructions. Don't always use the subject-predicate-object form (Dick and Jane saw the dog). However, don't vary from that form at the expense of clarity.

Here is an example of a paragraph which is boring because the sentences are of similar length and similar construction.

An apple is very real. It is very colorful. It has a reassuring heft, like a baseball. It smells sweet and fresh. It is not easily forgotten. An apple tree is shady. It is also bountiful. It puts dozens of apples in easy reach. It makes you feel secure.

That, of course, is not what I wrote in my apple-picking article. I wrote:

There is something very real about an apple. It is a colorful little item that has the reassuring heft of your first spring baseball, and the aroma that rises from its flesh is a nectar not soon forgotten. And when you can sit serenely under a shady tree and know that fifty or sixty of those sparkling red beauties are just within your reach, it makes you feel as if Mother Nature is going to take care of things, after all.

Also, write complete sentences most of the time. There's nothing wrong with an occasional partial sentence. Like this. But partial sentences get their strength and their meaning from the complete sentences that surround them, so use partial sentences sparingly.

And, finally, listen for the word that "just doesn't sound right," and even if you don't know why it doesn't sound right, get rid of it.

5. HUMANITY

Don't write about crop failures. Write about farmers in crisis. Don't write about romance. Write about people in love.

Put humanity into everything you write. Write about people. Even a how-to article like this one should be largely about a person called "you." Every short story, novel and dramatic script ever written (including the ones that appear to be about talking bunnies or grumdocles from the planet Zoop) is about people. The endless interest that each human being has for all the others is reason enough for you to populate your nonfiction also with living, breathing people.

If you are writing about the state's welfare crisis, begin with an anecdote about one family that lives in a car because they cannot pay rent. If you are writing a brochure to attract new members to your church, don't write about the beautiful steeple and venerable organ. Write about the people who come to church suppers, the people who volunteer for committees, and the people the reader will meet if he shows up on Sunday morning. Humanity.

In my apple-picking piece I did not write:

There are a lot of spiritual reasons for spending a day picking apples and it is, as Bonnie said, "a way to get in touch with things." But the tough economic times and the high rate of unemployment accounted for the presence of most apple pickers.

I wrote:

I ate lunch in a clearing with Bonnie, Roy, and two black guys

*who had come up from Boston. The guys from Boston were unem-
ployed. They had kids. They weren't picking apples for religious reasons. One of them, Sam, told me the forty-five dollars a day he was
making would help to stretch his unemployment check. He ate lunch
quickly so he could get back to picking and "put some bread on the
table."*

One human being who will appear in much that you write is you.
Putting yourself into your writing is neither good nor bad. It depends
on the nature of the work. But nothing should be put into any story for
no good reason, and that includes you. Ask yourself what you gain by
putting you into the story. If you have a good answer, put yourself in.

But if you don't put yourself into a story, put *somebody* into it. Don't
write: "The glow from the fire could be seen against the night sky and
the sound of sirens could be heard for miles. Smoke could be smelled
from across the river, and a tremor in the Earth was felt every time
another building toppled."

Who saw? Who heard? Who smelled? Who felt? Human beings, that's
who! Get them in there.

6. HONESTY

The easiest way to achieve honesty in your writing is just to be yourself.
Don't glut your prose with literary references that are new to you, so
that you'll appear learned when you are not. Don't try to write as if you
are hip, when you are square. Don't try to bulldoze your way into a
personal writing style that simply is not you. Don't try to write like
Hunter Thompson or Erma Bombeck if such styles don't come easily
to you. Try to write like you. Don't use the thesaurus to find words you
never saw before; use it to find words that you already know. That's
honesty.

Don't write damaging opinions without taking title to them. Don't
write, for example, "Mayor Randolph is widely regarded as incompetent." Write, "I think Mayor Randolph is incompetent," or "City Coun-
cilman Ray Turi says, 'Mayor Randolph is incompetent.' " But never
hide behind "It is widely believed . . . " or "Most people think . . . . "

There's nothing wrong with being opinionated, but make it clear that
you are. There's nothing wrong with reducing a forty-two-word unintel-
ligible quote to eight words that make sense, but be certain you are true
to the spirit of what was said, if not the form. There's nothing wrong

with using fiction techniques to improve the telling of nonfiction as long as you don't tamper with significant truths.

However, honesty in writing cannot be measured by some outside yardstick. Ultimately the only measuring tool of honesty in writing is your own conscience. Read each sentence and ask of it, "Is this me?" and "Is this true?" and finally, "Is this fair?"

My apple-picking piece might have been more positive, uplifting and idealistic if I had written: "There is nothing quite so perfect as a day in an apple tree, picking your way to heaven," and gone on to describe a wholly invigorating and untarnished apple-picking experience. But that would have been dishonest and anybody who has spent much time in an apple orchard would spot it. So I wrote, honestly:

> *I had picked 6,000 apples. My hands were as dry as blotters. My trapezius muscles had been stretched like taffy. My shoulders throbbed. The straps had been damn near grafted into my skin. My legs ached and my knees felt like a pair of bricks. I felt pretty good. But it was time for me to split.*

I tell you to be honest in your writing not because I want to improve your morals, but because I want to improve your writing. It feels soft, weak and unconvincing, and if you are dishonest it will usually take a good editor about twenty-three seconds to spot it. And if he doesn't, your readers certainly will.

7. POETRY

Writing should be, first of all, clear. A good word is not a good word if it clouds your meaning. And, of course, it should be brief, precise, harmonious, human and honest. Writing should be functional. Beautiful prose is not beautiful prose if it sabotages the job you are trying to do. Good writing entertains, informs, advises, illuminates. It cannot simply be. It must do.

Often, after we have done the job by writing clearly, there is little room left for what is commonly called art, though writing simply and clearly is itself an art.

But in much that you write there *is* the opportunity to do more than tell the reader what will happen or when or how or even why. There is the chance for you to lift him a few feet off the ground, to slip between him and the earth a layer of wonder and imagination. There is the chance for you to pull him beyond the content of your story and lead him with your words into a realm of thought that is alive with energy and inspiration. This is poetry, and it can happen in a sentence or it can happen in a word. It can happen when you neither expect it nor intend it. It can happen that you bring beauty into the reader's day.

Is there a figure of speech that will enhance your meaning, as well as etch across the reader's mind a vision that will endure beyond the last page? Write it. Can you choose words with such care and arrange them in such a way that reveals not just your point, but also a point about life? Do it. Can you tell an anecdote that will peel away one more layer of falseness and bring the reader an inch closer to the truth? Tell it. If you can turn an essay into a prayer, do it. If you can use words to crown a newspaper article with nobility, use them. And if you can bring your own deepest emotions to bear on a story in a way that is important not just to the story, but also to the reader, do that.

I attempted to put poetry into my apple-picking article by measuring the experience against a traditional fantasy of young men. Early in the article I planted the idea. I described the unfulfilled fantasy that my friend Cliffy and I had in 1962 when we got out of high school. I wrote:

> *We wanted to cut cane in Louisiana, harvest lettuce in California, pick apples in New England. Move. Just like Tod Stiles and Buzz Murdock on* Route 66, *tooling down the highway, rubbing our way into people's lives between odd jobs.*

In my final paragraph I didn't want to simply end with something like, "I left the apple orchard and went home." I wanted to lift the piece into the poetic realm if I could do so legitimately. I wanted to make it something more than just a piece about a day of apple picking. I wrote:

> *My wife picked me up at the end of the day. Wisely, she parked the car across the highway from the orchard. She knows a thing or two about me and she gave me some time to walk, some space to think. For there is something about the feel of gravel underfoot and the taste of sweet air seeping out of the cool green orchard that lets a guy think for a moment that he is Tod Stiles. And if the world is gentle for a minute, he can be almost certain that Buzz is waiting in the Corvette around that next bend in the road.*
>
> *And that if the two of you can just peel off another three hundred miles from the nearest highway, you will most certainly get in touch with things.*

It made me feel good to write that. And it made the piece better. If you imbue your writing with humanity and poetry and love, you will enrich both the reader and yourself.

Your Future as a Writer

Isaac Asimov

May 1986

You may have heard the statement: "One picture is worth a thousand words."

Don't you believe it. It may be true on occasion—as when someone is illiterate, or when you are trying to describe the physical appearance of a complex object. In other cases, the statement is nonsense.

Consider, for instance, Hamlet's great soliloquy that begins with "To be or not to be," the poetic consideration of the pros and cons of suicide. It is 260 words long. Can you get across the essence of Hamlet's thought in a quarter of a picture—or, for that matter, in 260 pictures? Of course not. The pictures may be dramatic illustrations of the soliloquy if you already know the words. The pictures by themselves, to someone who has never read or heard *Hamlet*, will mean nothing.

As soon as it becomes necessary to deal with emotions, ideas, fancies—abstractions in general—only words will suit. The modulation of sound, in countless different ways, is the only device ever invented by human beings that can even begin to express the enormous complexity and versatility of human thought.

Nor is this likely to change in the future. You have heard that we live in an "age of communication," and you may assume, quite rightly, that amazing and fundamental changes are taking place in that connection. These changes, however, involve the *transmission* of information, and not its nature. The information itself remains in the form it was in prehistoric times: speech, and the frozen symbology of speech that we call writing.

We can transmit information in sign language, by semaphore, by blinking lights, by Morse code, by telephone, by electronic devices, by laser beams, or by techniques yet unborn—and in every case, we are transmitting words.

Pictures will not do; they will never do. Television is fun to watch, but it is utterly and entirely dependent on the spoken and written word. The proof is this: Darken the image into invisibility but leave the sound on, and you will still have a crude sense of what is going on. Turn off the sound, however, and exclude the appearance of written words, and though you leave the image as bright as ever, you will find you understand nothing of what is going on unless you are watching the most mindless slapstick. To put it even more simply: Radio had no images at all and managed, but the silent movies found subtitles essential.

There is the fundamental rule, then. In the beginning was the word (as the Gospel of St. John says in a different connection), and in the end will be the word. The word is immortal. And it follows from this that just as we had the writer as soon as writing was invented five thousand years ago, so we will have the writer, of necessity, for as long as civilization continues to exist. He may write with other tools and in different forms, but he will *write*.

Having come to the conclusion that writers have a future, we might fairly ask next: What will the role of the writer be in the future? Will writers grow less important, play a smaller role in society, or will they hold their own?

Neither.

It is quite certain that writers' skills will become steadily more important as the future progresses — providing, that is, that we do not destroy ourselves, and that there *is* a future of significance, one in which social structures continue to gain in complexity and in technological advance.

The reasons are not difficult to state.

To begin with, technological advance has existed as long as human beings have. Our hominid ancestors began to make and use tools of increasing complexity before the present-day hominid we call *Homo sapiens* had yet evolved. Society changed enormously as technology advanced. Think what it meant to human beings when agriculture was invented — herding — pottery — weaving — metallurgy. Then, in historic times, think of the changes introduced by gunpowder — the magnetic compass — printing — the steam engine — the airplane — television.

Technological change feeds on previous technological change, and the rate of change increases steadily. In ancient times, inventions came so infrequently and their spread was so slow that individual human beings could afford to ignore them. In one person's generation, nothing seemed to change as far as social structure and the quality of life were concerned. But as the rate of change increased, that became less true, and after 1800, the Industrial Revolution made it clear that life—everyday life—was changing rapidly from decade to decade and then from year to year and, by the closing portion of the twentieth century, almost from day to day. The gentle zephyr of change that our ancestors knew has become a hurricane.

We know that change is a confusing and unsettling matter. It is difficult for human beings to adjust to change. There is an automatic resistance to change and that resistance diminishes the advantages we can obtain from change. From generation to generation, then, it has become more and more important to explain the essentials of change to the general public, making people aware of the benefits to be derived from change and of the dangers that they must beware of as a result. That has never been more important than it is now; and it will be steadily more important in the future.

Since almost all significant change is the result, directly or indirectly, of advances in science and technology, what we're saying is that one particular type of writing—writing about science—will increase in importance even more quickly than writing in general will.

We live in a time when advances in science and technology can solve the problems that beset us: increasing the food supply, placing reproductive potentialities under control, removing pollution, multiplying efficiency, obtaining new sources of energy and materials, defeating disease, expanding the human range into space and so on.

Advances in science and technology also create problems to bedevil us: producing more dangerous weapons, creating more insidious forms of pollution, destroying the wilderness and disrupting the ecological balance of Earth's living things.

At every moment, the politicians, the businesspeople and, to some extent, every portion of the population, must make decisions on both individual and public policy that will deal with matters of science and technology.

To choose the proper policies, to adopt this and reject that, one must know something about science and technology. This does not mean that everyone must be a scientist, as we can readily see from the analogy of professional sport and its audience. Millions of Americans watch with fascinated intentness games of baseball, football, basketball and so on. Very few of them can play the game with any skill; very few know enough to be able to coach a team; but almost all of them know enough about the game to appreciate what is going on, to cheer and groan at appropriate times, and to feel all the excitement and thrills of the changing tides of fortune. That must be so, for without such understanding, watching a game is merely a matter of watching chaos.

And so it must be that as many people as possible must know enough about science and technology to be members of an intelligent *audience*, at least.

It will be the writer, using words (with the aid of illustrations where that can make the explanation simpler or raise the interest higher, but *primarily* using words), who will endeavor to translate the specialized vocabulary of science and technology into ordinary English.

No one suggests that writing about science will turn the entire world into an intelligent audience, that writers will mold the average person into a model of judgment and creative thought. It will be enough if they spread the knowledge as widely as possible; if some millions, who would otherwise be ignorant (or, worse, swayed by meaningless slogans), would, as a result, gain some understanding; if those whose opinions are most likely to be turned into action, such as the political and economic rulers of the world, are educated.

H.G. Wells said that history was a race between education and catastrophe, and it may be that the writer will add just sufficient impetus to education to enable it to outrace catastrophe. And if education wins by even the narrowest of margins, how much more can we ask for?

Nor is a world that is oriented more in the direction of science and technology needed merely for producing better judgments, decisions and policies. The very existence of science and technology depends on a population that is both understanding and sympathetic.

There was a time when science and technology depended strictly on individual ideas, individual labor and individual financial resources. We are terribly attracted to the outmoded stereotype of the inventor working in his home workshop, of the eccentric scientist working his home laboratory, of the Universe of ignorance being assaulted by devices built of scraps, string and paste.

It is so no longer. The growing complexity of science and technology has outstripped the capacity of the individual. We now have research teams, international conferences, industrial laboratories, large universities. And all this is strained, too.

Increasingly, the only source from which modern science and technology can find sufficient support to carry on its work is from that hugest repository of negotiable wealth — the government. That means the collective pocketbooks of the taxpayers of the nation.

There never has been a popular tax, or an unreluctant taxpayer, but some things will be paid for more readily than others. Taxpayers of any nation are usually ready to pay enormous sums for military expenses, since all governments are very good at rousing hatred and suspicions against foreigners.

But an efficient military machine depends, to a large extent, on advances in science and technology, as do other more constructive and less shameful aspects of society. If writers can be as effective in spreading the word about science and technology as governments are at sowing hatred and suspicion, public support for science is less likely to fail, and science is less likely to wither.

Moreover, science and technology cannot be carried on without a steady supply of scientists and engineers; an increasing supply as the years go on. Where will they come from?

They will come from the general population, of course. There are some people who gain an interest in science and technology in youth and can't be stopped, but they, by themselves, are simply not numerous enough to meet the needs of the present, let alone the future. Many more youngsters would gain such an interest only if they were properly stimulated.

Again, it is the writer who might catch the imagination of young people, and plant a seed that will flower and come to fruition. Thus, I have received a considerable number of letters from scientists and engineers in training who have taken the trouble to tell me that my books were what had turned them toward science and technology. I am quite convinced that other science writers get such letters in equal numbers.

Let me make two points, however.

First, in order to write about science, it is not entirely necessary to be deeply learned in every aspect of science (no one can be, these days) or even in some one aspect—although that helps. To know science well can make you a "science writer," but any intelligent person who has a good layperson's acquaintance with the scientific and technological scene can write a useful article on some subject related to science and technology. He can be a *writer* dealing with science.

Here is an example:

Digital clocks seem to be becoming ever more common these days and the old-fashioned clock dial seems to be fading away. Does that matter? Isn't a digital clock more advanced? Doesn't it give you the time more accurately? Won't children be able to tell time at once as soon as they can read instead of having to decipher the dial?

Yet, there are disadvantages to a possible disappearance of the dial that perhaps we ought to keep in mind.

There are two ways in which anything might turn—a key in a lock, a screw in a piece of wood, a horse going around a race track, Earth spinning on its axis. They are described as "clockwise" and "counterclockwise." The first is the direction in which the hands on a clock move; the second is the opposite direction. We are so accustomed to dials that we understand clockwise and counterclockwise at once and do not make a mistake.

If the dial disappears (and, of course, it may not, for fashion is unpredictable), clockwise and counterclockwise will become meaningless and there is no completely adequate substitute. If you clench your hands and point the thumbs upward, the fingers of the left hand curl clockwise and those of the right hand counterclockwise. You might substitute "left-hand twist" and "right-hand twist," but no one stares at clenched hands as intently and as often as at clock dials, and the new terms will never be as useful.

Again, in looking at the sky, or through a microscope, or at any view that lacks easily recognizable reference marks, it is common to locate something by the clock dial. "Look at that object at eleven o'clock," you may say—or five o'clock, or two o'clock, or whatever. Everyone knows the location of any number from one to twelve on the clock dial and can use such references easily.

If the dial disappears, there will again be no adequate substitute. You can use directions to be sure—northeast, south by west, and so on, but no one knows the compass as well as the clock.

Then, too, digital clocks can be misleading. Time given as 5:50 may seem roughly five o'clock, but anyone looking at a dial will see that it is nearly six o'clock. Besides, digital clocks only go up to 5:59 and then move directly to 6:00 and youngsters may be confused as to what happened to 5:60 through 5:99. Dials give us no such trouble.

One can go on and find other useful qualities in dials versus digits, but I think the point is clear. An article can be written that has meaning as far as technology is concerned and will provoke thought and yet not require a specialist's knowledge. We can't all be science writers, but we can all be writers about science.

The second point to be made is that I do *not* say that writers won't be needed in increasing numbers in other fields.

As computers and robots take over more of the dull labor of humanity and leave human beings to involve themselves in more creative endeavors, education will have to change in such a way as to place increasing emphasis on creativity. No doubt, education by computer will become more and more important, and a new kind of writer—the writer of computer programs for education—will arise and become important.

Again, as leisure time continues to increase the world over, writing to fill that leisure time, in the form of books, plays, television or movie scripts, and so on, will be needed in greater numbers.

In other words, more and more writers of more and more different kinds will be needed as time goes on; but, of them all, it is writers about science for whom the need will grow most quickly.

How to Write Blockbluster Novels

Evan Marshall

October 1986

N ot long ago, an unknown writer's half-finished manuscript threw seven New York publishers into an eight-day bidding frenzy that culminated with an offer of $1,015,000, the highest guarantee ever for a first novel.

What could Sally Beauman have packed into the first 470 pages of her novel *Destiny* to make Bantam Books, the winning bidder, so determined to publish it?

"What she has done," Peter Matson, the agent who conducted the auction, told *Publishers Weekly*, "is make sense of the formula so that *Destiny* will appeal to the Sidney Sheldon and Jackie Collins audience as well as to a more sophisticated readership. She has a sense of history and character and a point of view."

One of the losing bidders, Jim Silberman of Summit Books, told *Manhattan, Inc.*, "I think she feels like a real writer; the book is very vivid. The characters are authentic within the ground rules of this kind of book."

Sounds marvelous — but $1,015,000? Surely the book has more going for it than authentic characters and a sense of history.

Indeed it has: perfect timing. *Destiny* hit those publishers' offices at the height of a phenomenon *Newsweek* has called "the blockbuster craze."

More than ever, readers are buying books by the few authors at the top. For this reason, the big books are their biggest yet: Compare the 200,000 hardcover-copy best-sellers of two years ago to today's million-copy hits such as *Iacocca*, *Texas* and *The Mammoth Hunters*. With the stakes this high, publishers are scrambling for potential blockbusters, especially by authors who show signs of developing into the next Sidney Sheldon or Judith Krantz.

"There aren't enough Micheners and Kings and Krantzes to go

around for all of the publishers," agent Al Zuckerman told *Newsweek*. "So there's an enormous competitiveness for the new boy in town."

What does this mean to you? Chances are better than ever that the new boy — or girl — in town could be you.

What makes a blockbuster?

THINK BIG

First, you need a special kind of plot. A blockbuster plot has good, strong lines; it's clean and easy to grasp. In Hollywood, they call this "high concept" — a story you can sum up in a sentence.

- Three women climb to the summit of success, to find they've lost their souls in the process (*Valley of the Dolls*, by Jacqueline Susann).
- A pampered southern belle fights to save her home from the devastation of the Civil War (*Gone With the Wind*, by Margaret Mitchell).
- A malevolent killer shark terrorizes an island resort (*Jaws*, by Peter Benchley).
- A priest must exorcise the devil from the body of a young girl (*The Exorcist*, by William Peter Blatty).

The blockbuster plot embodies vivid contrasts. Perennially popular, for instance, is the rags-to-riches theme. In Kathleen Winsor's *Forever Amber*, Amber St. Clare escapes the teeming streets of London to become the most sought-after woman in Restoration England, while setting her cap for none other than Charles II. In Barbara Taylor Bradford's *A Woman of Substance*, Emma Harte rises from servant girl to international corporate power and one of the richest women in the world. Jackie Collins's *Chances* is the saga of Gino Santangelo, a tough, hungry street kid who fights his way up to powerful underworld figure. And in Sally Beauman's *Destiny*, Helene Harte, who has "the most famous face, the most famous body, in the world: a living legend," started life in a Mississippi trailer camp.

Blockbusters thrive on extremes like these. Superlatives abound. In *Mistral's Daughter*, Judith Krantz writes of three women in the life of the great French painter Julien Mistral: Maggy, artist's model, toast of Montparnasse, Mistral's first inspiration; Teddy, top photographic model of the 1950s; and Fauve, raised to inherit the world's most powerful modeling agency. In Judith Gould's *Sins* (a novel I bought while an editor at New American Library, and which became a mini-series starring Joan Collins), Hélène Junot claws her way up from penniless orphan to owner of the greatest magazine empire on earth. And in Diana Stainforth's

Bird of Paradise, stubborn, courageous Mara leaves war-torn Germany behind as she gains control of Britain's largest automobile company and eventually becomes the first woman race-car driver.

Inevitably, characters like these live in a state of perpetual high drama. The strongest emotions motivate them: undying love, obsessive hatred, ambition, envy, ecstasy, vengeance, grief. In *Gone With the Wind*, Scarlett O'Hara goes to any lengths to save the land she's been taught matters more than anything else. In *Sins*, Hélène Junot lives to destroy the Nazi who raped her sister and murdered her mother. In Sidney Sheldon's *If Tomorrow Comes*, Tracy Whitney methodically pays back each of the crime lords who framed her into serving a fifteen-year jail sentence.

Emotion rules our lives and creates our drama; it is therefore our key to experiencing the drama of your characters. Moses L. Malevinsky wrote in *The Science of Playwriting*: "Emotion, or the elements in or of an emotion, constitute the basic things in life. Emotion is life. Life is emotion. Therefore emotion is drama. Drama is emotion."

PEOPLE TO LOVE, PEOPLE TO HATE

We never feel ambivalent about the characters in a blockbuster. We may hate them, pity them, envy them or adore them—but we always feel something toward them, and we feel it strongly. We know that Scarlett O'Hara is spoiled and headstrong, but we care about her nevertheless, because we empathize with her determination to save the home she loves. In *Sins*, we root for Hélène even as she commits sin after sin in her quest for revenge, because we share the pain that spawned this quest, as well as Hélène's loathing of the vividly evil Nazi war criminal Karl von Eiderfeld. In *Sophie's Choice*, by William Styron, our hearts go out to Sophie for having to make a choice no mother should ever have to make: Which of my two children shall live? When Sophie kills herself, we see that there was no other way, that no amount of time could have lessened her pain and made life bearable.

Know what drives your characters before creating a story for them, for it is their strong loves, hatreds, goals and ambitions that will dictate the story, almost make it inevitable. Try some character sketches. Where and when was the character born, and into what environment? How did this environment affect his or her outlook on the world? What traits, developed early, are to be carried on into life? Parents, siblings, friends, joys, tragedies—all these shaped the character.

Once you've created these sketches, imagine how any of these people might logically come together. The circumstances you've created for your characters can give you the beginnings of a story; their personalities will then dictate how they'll interact, moving the story further along; characters again interact . . . and so on.

SMALL WORLD

One of the blockbuster's main appeals is that it can give us a glimpse into an industry, milieu, time or place we know little or nothing about, take us behind the scenes of a "world" that holds a mystery or mystique.

Certain authors have made exploring a world their trademark — James A. Michener, for example, whose ambitious novels have told the stories of Hawaii, Spain, Colorado, Poland, the Chesapeake, Texas, even space; and Arthur Hailey, who has shown us what goes on inside international airlines, elegant hotels, sports-car racing, and pharmaceuticals manufacturing.

It's not only fun to read this sort of novel, but we're also learning something in the process. And not the least important, setting your blockbuster in a particular world gives you, your agent, your publisher and your readers a good strong handle (high concept) for your book.

The first way of going about this is to draw on your own experience. Countless authors have spun their lives into best-sellers, proving the truth in "write what you know." Perhaps your profession would make a good blockbuster world. Robin Cook, author of the medical chillers *Coma, Brain, Fever, Godplayer* and *Mindbend*, is a surgeon at the Massachusetts Eye and Ear Institute. Barbara Wood was a surgical technician before she wrote the medical novels *Domina* and *Vital Signs*.

Anne Tolstoi Wallach turned her years as a creative director at Grey Advertising into *Women's Work*, the story of a woman aiming for the top of a large New York ad agency. Fr. Andrew M. Greeley has blown the roof off the church in *Thy Brother's Wife, The Cardinal Sins, Ascent Into Hell, Lord of the Dance, Happy Are the Meek* and *Virgin and Martyr*.

Is there a blockbuster world in your past? English novelist R.F. Delderfield based at least two of his novels, *Mr. Sermon* and *To Serve Them All My Days*, on his experiences as a master at six public schools. Actress Joanna Barnes made a number of films before featuring Hollywood in *Pastora, Silverwood* and *The Deceivers*. As a college student, Gay Courter studied midwifery (the subject of her first novel, *The Midwife*) in Brazil (the setting of her second novel, *River of Dreams*). Judith Krantz mined her years as a magazine editor for *I'll Take Manhattan*, about a woman who transforms a humdrum women's magazine. David Cornwell once served in the British Foreign Service; we know him better as John Le Carré, author of such espionage favorites as *The Spy Who Came in From the Cold*; *Tinker, Tailor, Soldier, Spy*; *Smiley's People*; *The Little Drummer Girl*; and *A Perfect Spy*.

Perhaps a blockbuster world lurks in your family history. M.M. Kaye spent her early years as daughter of the president of the council of an Indian state; she embellished stories she heard to give us *The Far Pavilions* and *Shadow of the Moon*. Morgan Llywelyn pursued an interest in family tales and became an authority on Celtic history, the basis of *The Wind From Hastings, Lion of Ireland, The Horse Goddess* and *Grania*. When China sent Bette Bao Lord's government-official father to the U.S. in 1946, she went with him, leaving a baby sister behind with relatives; it was not until 1962 that the sister was able to leave China. Lord turned the story of her sister's life and her reunion with her family into *Eighth Moon*, and her own visit to China and her reunion with her relatives into *Spring Moon*.

The second way of setting your blockbuster in a world is to research one. You're still writing what you know; you just have to work hard to know it. Jean Auel had certainly never been to prehistoric Europe during the Ice Age, but she researched it until she might just as well have been, and brought forth *The Clan of the Cave Bear, The Valley of Horses* and *The Mammoth Hunters*, with three more to follow in the series. Gary Jennings did the same for *Aztec* and *The Journeyer* (about Marco Polo). Meredith Rich immersed herself in the perfume industry for *Bare Essence*. Tom Clancy was neither intelligence nor naval officer, but an insurance broker who read a newspaper article about a mutiny on a Soviet frigate, researched Soviet-American naval strategies and submarine technology, and wrote *The Hunt for Red October*.

Does a certain industry fascinate you? Does a friend or relative do something you've always wanted to know more about? Once you've done some basic research, ask that friend or relative for help; write to experts or to the public relations directors of organizations. Know the world so well we'll think you've been part of it for years.

TECHNICALLY SPEAKING

A blockbuster is a page-turner, so do everything you can to make yours move like lightning.

Think "movie." Start a scene where it really begins and stop it where it really ends. Better to leave a space and start a new scene than to tell us how John got from one place to another. If it is important for us to know this, slip it in after the new scene has begun: "John felt a fluttering in his chest as he gazed down at the raging falls. He'd taken the train from Marty's house and walked the three miles from the station."

Don't let your writing bog down with unnecessary description or detail. Tell us about it only if it pertains directly to your story, then do so in as few vivid words as possible. The idea is always to let solid, engrossing story be the real substance of your book.

Jacqueline Susann, mistress of the blockbuster (her *Valley of the Dolls* is the best-selling novel of all time, with nearly 27,000,000 copies in print since publication in 1966), had so much story to tell that she couldn't afford to waste any time on unnecessary description or detail. Instead, she'd let a few well-chosen details trigger the rest in our imagination. Here's all she says about the apartment that Anne, Neely and Jennifer take together.

> *She couldn't get over the luxury of the apartment. . . . Just before she left, Anne had run into [Adele] and gotten her scrumptious apartment. Neely kept touching everything—the bedspreads, the lamps. . . . She never dreamed she'd live in a living room that had a white rug.*

Here's how Susann takes us from Neely O'Hara's decision to take the "sleep cure" to her arrival at the sanitarium:

> *Neely would have none of it. "Me go and live with kooks? No siree. I want the plus treatment, like Jennifer had. Champagne for starters, a sympathetic nurse, a lovely needle . . . sleep, beautiful sleep."*
>
> *After frantic calls, Kevin finally located a large private sanitarium in upstate New York. Yes, they knew about the sleep cure. They would be delighted to accept Miss O'Hara and administer it to her. Yes, it would be done with the utmost secrecy—the newspapers would never know.*
>
> *On a balmy Sunday in March, Kevin and Anne drove Neely to Haven Manor . . . .*

Susann knew it didn't matter how Kevin went about finding Haven Manor, exactly what was said on the phone, or exactly where the sanitarium was located in upstate New York. She knew her real story picked up once Neely arrived there, and she was eager to get on with it. Make selective use of this summary-transition technique in your own blockbuster to keep *your* real story front and center.

As for the writing itself, strive to keep it "invisible" so it will stay out of the action's way. Forget being a stylist; put your energy into plot and characterization. (One of my most successful clients often chants to herself as she's writing, "Plot and people . . . plot and people. . . .") Then edit and cut, and edit and cut some more.

Reconsider every adjective and adverb; get rid of any that aren't really necessary—you'll be amazed at how many you'll find. Avoid the passive tense and the gerundive, which lessen immediacy. For dialogue, use *said, asked, replied* and other simple verbs whenever possible; better yet, use nothing at all. Remember that *said* is an invisible word and that you won't seem unimaginative if you use it repeatedly. Rather, you'll seem amateurish if you overuse *stated, breathed, ventured, rasped, queried* and other signs of terminal thesaurus abuse. Use these words sparingly to heighten their effect; the same goes for adverbs after *said, asked,* etc., which aren't necessary if your dialogue suggests its own adverbs.

Analyze blockbusters by writers you admire. In addition to Jacqueline Susann, two of my favorite technicians are Harold Robbins and Sidney Sheldon, who pare their writing down to its most essential lines to give us hard-hitting, fast-moving books.

YOUR OWN UNIQUE TWIST

I once asked a respected editor to whom I'd sold a number of novels, "Is there anything you'd say a writer should never do in a novel? Are there any rules that should never be broken?"

She thought for a moment, then replied: "A writer can break any and all of the rules, so long as he or she does it well. Is there anything a writer should never do? Certainly. A writer should never bore us."

I like to think of the successful novelist as a trick tightrope walker. Only when he's mastered the basics and knows all the rules can he begin to break them and perform mesmerizing tricks. If he tries to perform these tricks before this point, he falls to his doom.

So, once you've learned and mastered the rules—and only then—break them. Here's where your own unique twist comes in, the touch that makes your blockbuster one that only you could have written.

How about a way-out plot?

In Jacqueline Susann's posthumously published *Yargo*, a woman finds true love in outer space. Sound crazy? Perhaps, but the book worked (and so did the equally way-out movie *Starman* years later). In his 3-million-plus best-seller *Thinner*, Stephen King (writing under the pseudonym Richard Bachman) tells the story of a man who wastes away almost to nothing under a gypsy's dying curse. Rule broken in both cases: Don't mix genres.

Dream up a bizarre premise, or give a familiar device a fresh slant.

Judith Michael's bestselling *Deceptions* is the story of twin sisters, both married, who trade places — and then one of the sisters dies. Rule broken: Don't use the twins-trading-places device; it's a stale idea that reminds us of an old Bette Davis movie.

Shirley Conran opened her blockbusting *Lace* with the line "All right which one of you bitches is my mother?" Rule broken: Don't base your novel on so far-fetched an idea.

John Le Carré's *A Perfect Spy* is about a double agent who serves — and loves — two masters. Rule broken: The double-agent thing has been done to death.

How about giving your blockbuster an "unorthodox" structure or format?

Elizabeth Forsythe Hailey told the story of *Joanna's Husband and David's Wife* in alternating diary entries and wound up on the best-seller list. Rule broken: Don't write a novel in letter or diary format. (Years ago, Bel Kaufman broke this same rule by ingeniously "compiling" high school memos, student assignments, graffiti and the like to come up with the now-classic *Up the Down Staircase*.)

Discover a "world" that's never been used before and show us why it's fascinating.

In his upcoming novel *Spangle*, Gary Jennings chronicles the picaresque adventures of a motley nineteenth-century circus as it travels from the post-Civil War South to the turbulent courts of Europe. Speaking of obscurity, who would have predicted that Umberto Eco's *The Name of the Rose*, the literary novel about the investigation of a murder in a medieval monastery, would rocket to the top of the list? Eco had a passion for this world and wanted to pass it along to us. Rule broken: Stay away from settings that are too esoteric or obscure.

Attempt something altogether new, as Richard Adams did with the unexpected best-seller about a community of rabbits in crisis, *Watership Down* (rule broken: Anthropomorphic animal stories don't break out) and *Shardik* (rule broken: Fantasy stories don't break out).

I imagine that in one out of every two blockbusters, we could find a rule that was broken. The key, again, is to know what those rules are, and to break them like a master.

Do so, and there's no reason on earth why your blockbuster shouldn't be the next one publishers fight for.

Writing About Science

Ben Bova

January 1989

Pick up any newspaper or national magazine and you'll likely see articles about science and high technology: Break-throughs in superconductivity. Genetic engineering. AIDS research. Rocket launches. Computers. Exploding stars. Drought in the farm belt. Satellites that spot hurricanes. Ointments that remove wrinkles.

Science-related stories pervade the news. There is not a single aspect of life today that is not affected by scientific research and new technology, which means that every newspaper and magazine is a potential market for articles about science or engineering.

The good news is that more magazines and newspapers are indeed seeking articles about various scientific subjects than ever before.

The bad news is that the market for science articles is tough to break into.

But it can be done. You can become a contributor to the growing number of popular science magazines and newspaper science sections, if you have:

1. Knowledge of science or engineering
2. The ability to write clearly and interestingly
3. Reliable sources of information
4. A fresh idea
5. Perseverance

• *Knowledge of science or engineering.* It's not necessary to have a technical degree, or even to be a working scientist or engineer. For example, my degrees are in journalism and communications. But since my first childhood trip to a planetarium, I have been vitally interested in science. I have read widely in many scientific fields. I have worked with scientists most of my life — as a writer, editor and even as a marketing executive. My interests started with astronomy, then branched into rocketry, chemistry, physics, anthropology and so on.

Of course, if you *are* trained in science or engineering, so much the better. Maybe. Sometimes, unhappily, professional scientists and engineers find it difficult or even impossible to write for an audience of general, nonprofessional readers. When I was running *Omni* magazine, I found that most scientists were trained to write in a style that the "lay" reader found impenetrable. Worse, still, many scientists are terrified of putting anything on paper that their professional colleagues can criticize. Rather than make their writing readable, they tend to clutter it with technical jargon or qualify everything to the point of ludicrous unreadability. You can count on the fingers of one hand the number of scientists who, like Carl Sagan, can write for the masses.

The other side of the coin, of course, is that those tongue-tied scientists *need* competent writers to communicate with the general public. At *Omni*, we frequently paired a scientist and a writer to produce our major articles. We found that technical writers, journalists, and men and women interested in science for their own enjoyment often make better science writers than the scientists themselves. They are less self-conscious about their prose, and more willing to write in a style that the lay reader can understand and enjoy.

In fact, some editors believe that a writer who knows too much about science is apt to lose touch with the general, nonscientific reader. The ability to see linkages between *this* and *that*, the ability to ask penetrating questions, and—most of all—the willingness to keep asking questions until the subject is clear to you, those traits are often more important than a detailed knowledge of the scientific subject matter.

How much science do you have to know?

It is vital to understand the basics, to have a feeling for science, to be favorably inclined toward scientific research. If you believe that science is dehumanizing and scientists are basically amoral, if not downright evil, steer clear of science articles. Writing them would be like trying to write a cookbook when you have never even boiled water successfully, and your idea of gourmet dining is a Big Mac.

• *The ability to write clearly and interestingly.* Writing about science or technology is no different from writing about pet care or gardening. The subject matter *is* more technical, more hedged with specialized jargon, so it's crucially important that you handle the subject with clear, simple, understandable prose.

Jargon can be deadly, not merely because no one except a specialist can understand it, but also because a scientist often will hide behind his specialized language and insist that if you can't understand the jargon you shouldn't be bothering him. But jargon can be — and must be — translated into English.

For example, a recent scientific paper's abstract reads: "High-density demersal layers of krill have been detected in the submarine canyons off Georges Bank by means of a high-frequency, dual-beam bioacoustical technique. Krill densities in these demersal layers were observed to be two to three orders of magnitude greater than the highest densities observed in water-column scattering layers."

The editors of *Science* magazine translated that statement into: "Georges Bank, located off the northeastern North American coast, is one of the world's most productive fisheries. Its productivity may reflect the availability of a ready supply of krill (small crustaceans) in surrounding waters. . . . The density of krill (measured in the water column with acoustic equipment aboard a research [submarine]) varied throughout the daily twenty-four-hour cycle. . . . The canyons along Georges Bank may affect the concentration of krill by funneling them [into the fishery area]."

Where the scientific abstract used jargon to report on the scientists' methods and findings, the editors' "translation" shows the reader a mental picture of what happens in the water of Georges Bank.

Explain technical terms in words anyone can understand. An article about some aspect of science or engineering usually deals with a new idea, a new invention. Why is it so important that I should want to read about it? What does it mean to me? How will it affect my life? Those are the questions the reader brings to the article. Those are the questions you must answer, clearly, specifically, entertainingly.

Let me tell you my personal philosophy about science writing. Most editors, and therefore most magazines and newspapers, tend to think of science as if it were spinach: "I know this doesn't taste very good, but it's good for you and you ought to eat it." My approach, and the policy we followed when I was at *Omni*, was to treat science as if it's lemon meringue pie: "This is delicious! It's fun! Enjoy it!"

To cite a personal example: I was challenged a few years ago to write a popular book about how and why space explorers will one day return to the moon and build permanent communities there. Instead of writing a book that began with the Apollo program of the 1960s and showed what scientists and engineers have learned about the moon, I wrote

Welcome to Moonbase (Ballantine Books) as an employee's manual.

The basic idea of the book is that you are on your way to Moonbase, to work there for a year. This tells you about your job, living conditions, career opportunities — and what it's like to live on a very different world. Instead of a dry, factual account of the scientific and economic advantages of constructing a base on the moon, I presented a picture of what it's like to actually be there, living and working at a thriving, growing lunar community.

We found at *Omni* that millions of readers in the U.S. (and more overseas) enjoy reading about science. These readers find that the intellectual pursuit of ideas can be fun. In most cases, though, they are less interested in science *per se* than in thinking about the future, speculating about tomorrow, imagining and picturing the kind of world that might come about as a result of today's scientific research.

I try to slant the science stories I write toward the future. It's not enough to tell the reader what a research scientist is doing today; I try to show the reader what this work can mean for all of us tomorrow. Everybody is interested in the future. Science and technology literally create the future.

• *Reliable sources of information.* Unless you are *the* expert in the particular field you are writing about, the editor will insist that you base your article on impeccable sources of information. Generally you will start by interviewing a scientist or engineer. Often you will have to double-check your original source against other specialists in the field, because sometimes even scientists say things that are controversial or just plain wrong. Certainly you will have to provide a list of references to back up your article.

The Scientists' Institute for Public Information (355 Lexington Ave., New York City 10017, tel. 800/223-1730) is a treasure house of source information for writers. SIPI's very reason for existence is providing reliable sources for science writers. Write or call to ask for background material that describes what the organization can do for you. SIPI will be happy to put you on its mailing list, and will connect you with scientists who can provide you with the latest information on the specific subject of your article.

• *A fresh idea.* Nothing frustrates an editor as much as receiving an article proposal on an old-hat subject. But in this field you have a great advantage, because science is always coming up with new ideas, and fresh material is being created before your eyes by the world's scientists and engineers every day.

It is vital, therefore, that you stay abreast of scientific progress. If you work with scientists or engineers, so much the better. But even if you don't, there are several fine (and quite readable) journals you can peruse. Among them are:

Science News (1719 N St. NW, Washington, D.C. 20036), a weekly newsletter that does an excellent job of keeping its readers up to date on the broad spectrum of scientific research.

Science (1333 H St. NW, Washington, D.C. 20005), the weekly journal of the American Association for the Advancement of Science. Although most of its technical reports are written for specialists, the news section in the front of the magazine deals with the politics of American (and world) science in a timely and informative manner.

Natural History (Central Park West at 79th St., New York City 10024), published monthly by the American Museum of Natural History in New York.

Sky & Telescope (P.O. Box 9111, Belmont, Massachusetts 02178), the monthly bible of the amateur astronomer.

Scientific American (415 Madison Ave., New York City 10017), which is sort of like a monthly addendum to an encyclopedia of science.

American Scientist (P.O. Box 13975, Research Triangle Park, North Carolina 27709), published quarterly by Sigma Xi, the scientific research society.

The Sciences (2 East 63rd St., New York City 10021), the bimonthly journal of the New York Academy of Sciences.

High Technology Business (9990 Lee Hwy., No. 301, Fairfax, Virginia 22030), a monthly magazine that deals with exciting new technologies such as electronics, computers, biogenetics, etc.

There are, of course, hundreds of other more specialized magazines and thousands of scientific journals. Most state and university library systems carry these magazines and journals.

Every issue of such magazines is stocked with new ideas for articles. Even if you have no speaking acquaintances with scientists or engineers, these pages will give you the information you need to begin working.

• *Perseverance.* Any kind of writing is 10 percent inspiration, 90 percent perspiration. To do a science article, you need perseverance particularly in two areas: the sources and the markets.

While it is possible to write science articles based on nothing more than library research, your articles will be better (and more salable) when one or more real scientists or engineers serve as your main sources. Scientists and engineers are not always the easiest people to interview. Especially if you have no personal relationship or instantly recognizable credentials ("I'm with *The New York Times*, sir!"), the average scientist or engineer may even try to avoid you.

Remember, these specialists often fear having their work garbled and distorted in the mass media. To the average scientist, no news is good news. He or she is more afraid of false sensationalism or outright attack (which could lead to a loss of funding) than of obscurity. You must convince your prospective interviewee that you: (1) Know his or her work; (2) Respect it; and (3) want to get absolutely accurate first-hand information.

If the prospective subject gets the idea that you are out to do a "Dr. Frankenstein strikes again" piece, he or she will flee to the hills. On the other hand, if the subject feels that you are interested in nothing more than a spectacular headline ("Local Researcher Finds Cure for Cancer"), you will get a cryogenically cold shoulder.

You also need perseverance to get the level of understanding you require. Scientists often hide behind the jargon of their field, and you may feel somewhat stupid because you don't understand what the scientist or engineer is saying to you. You are not stupid; the subject is using terms that only specialists understand. Patiently, but unswervingly, you must ask the subject to explain things in normal English. At some point the subject may insist that this is impossible. Don't believe it. I have found myself confronted with plasma physicists, rocket engineers, sociologists and many other specialists. Each had a specialized, obscure vocabulary. Each could speak plain English—eventually.

Remember, there are no dumb questions. It is dumb not to ask, if you don't understand.

You will need a different kind of perseverance in dealing with science editors.

I was with *Omni* magazine when it started, and for several years was editorial director. For the past half-dozen years I have been writing occasional science articles for national magazines. As a writer, I am appalled at the way science editors behave. To be entirely frank, most magazine editors have their own little coterie of favored writers and tend to stick with their trusted and reliable producers. Particularly in science writing, where the demands of getting the science correct are added to all the other demands of writing, the editors are wary of dealing with newcomers or writers they don't know.

How to get around this road block?

Prove that *you* can become a trusted and reliable producer.

Begin with a query letter. It should be short and to the point. In the letter, suggest a specific article about a specific idea. State your background, especially if you have a technical background or some writing credentials. Spell out who and what your sources are. And allow the letter to serve as a good example of your writing skills.

Send your query letter to a specific editor. A human being, with a name. Look at the magazines and newspaper science sections and pick out the market you want to hit. Then do enough research to get a specific editor's name. Most magazines have several editors on their staffs, each responsible for certain sections of the magazine. If the masthead doesn't give you enough information, telephone the editorial office and ask pertinent questions. If all else fails, address your letter to the top editor on the masthead.

The hardest thing is to get an editor who knows neither you nor your work to pay attention to you. Once an editor responds to you, even if the response is negative, you can at least begin a dialogue. What kinds of articles is the editor looking for? What does the magazine need?

At *Omni*, for example, we were in constant need of very short pieces for our Continuum column. It was much easier for a writer to do a 200-word piece for Continuum than to break into the magazine with a full-length feature article or interview. But after a few short Continuum takes, the writer established his or her credentials with the editors, who were then much more likely to listen to a proposal for a bigger assignment.

Kenneth Jon Rose wrote dozens of Continuum pieces for *Omni*, and then went on to do feature articles for several science magazines. A biologist at New York University, he has now published several science books, including *The Body in Time* (John Wiley & Sons), an excellent example of writing about science in language that anyone can understand and enjoy.

Now then, what are the actual markets for articles about science and technology?

To begin with, dozens of daily newspapers around the nation carry regular science sections each week. While much of the material they publish is written by staff reporters, most of these science sections are open to freelance writers as well.

Look up the newspapers published in your region and see which of them have regular science sections. Check their Sunday editions, too, to see if they publish their own magazine sections. The Sunday magazines are often a good place for science articles, particularly if they have a local angle to them.

Then there are the science-oriented magazines. *Omni*, of course, is the most successful in terms of circulation and audience. Started in 1978, *Omni* proved to a skeptical publishing industry that a major national magazine based on science (and science fiction) could become a phenomenal success. More than 5 million people read *Omni* every month.

Once *Omni* showed the way, a spate of science magazines sprang up in the early 1980s. Many of them floundered, failed altogether, or changed publishers. *Discover*, for example, was started by Time, Inc., with great fanfare, but in 1987 Time sold the magazine to Family Media, Inc. I believe that the Time approach to *Discover* was too much like spinach; Family Media appears to understand the lemon meringue tactic.

Most of the other science-oriented magazines are either very specialized or mainly staff written. However, you should look for science magazines on your newsstands and in your libraries. Check out the ones you enjoy reading, and then see if you can write for them. I have never been able to write for a magazine I did not enjoy reading, and I think that if you do not understand a magazine well enough to enjoy its editorial material, you will probably not be able to find the right wavelength for them in anything you write.

Aside from the specifically science-oriented magazines, however, virtually *any* publication can be open to articles dealing with science or technology. And medicine. From *Reader's Digest* to your local weekly newspaper, articles on medicine are always welcome.

Women's magazines are particularly interested in pieces on nutrition and health. Men's magazines look for articles on gadgetry, particularly electronic and automotive gadgets.

Again, it is important to know the market you are trying to reach. It makes no sense to send an article about Supernova 1987 to *Cosmopolitan*. No matter how wonderful the piece is, it is of no interest to *Cosmo*'s editors and audience. Yes, there may be millions of women who find astronomy fascinating, but they do not buy *Cosmo* to catch up on astrophysics.

Similarly, don't bother to send an article debunking flying saucers to *The National Enquirer*. They just won't be interested.

Marketing science articles is just about the same as marketing any kind of nonfiction. You must match your subject matter to the market. But if you examine the magazines on newsstands carefully, you will find that almost all of them are potential markets for science articles.

And remember the lemon meringue pie.

Eight Ingredients of Powerful Nonfiction

Linton Weeks

September 1989

We as nonfiction writers must constantly ask ourselves how we can make our stories more provocative, more challenging, more delightful, more—dare we say it?—readable.

Much has been written about using fiction techniques—plot, points of view, character development, irony—to make for better, more readable nonfiction. Beyond those techniques, how can we make our nonfiction more powerful, able to get at universal truths and change the world and all that stuff? Here are eight things that just might help:

ATTITUDE

There are eight things that will make your nonfiction story more powerful. That's my opinion, my attitude. And an attitude is a good thing to begin with when you sit down to write a piece of nonfiction. Don't just write a story about air pollution in a metro area; tell us "Why Tacoma Stinks"—and in doing so, teach us about the city's ecological dilemma. Rather than give a bland description of a new bed-and-breakfast in Kentucky, tell us that the B&B has the best bed, the worst breakfast or the crummiest management of any you've ever seen.

When Robert Sam Anson signed on with *Manhattan inc.* to profile New Jersey Senatorial candidate Pete Dawkins, he approached the story with a certain amount of naïveté. Anson had always idolized Dawkins, who has been a football star, a military bigshot, and a successful Wall Street businessman. "There was so much public-relations-fed hype," wrote *Manhattan inc.* editor Clay Felker, "that Anson began to wonder about the real man behind the myth." Anson said of Dawkins: "I read the press clips back to 1957, and there was never a discouraging word. He has brought problems on himself, but he was also victimized by the press and senior officers who needed a positive public image for the army at a time when things were going against it. By now he has become the image itself, with very few flashes of the man underneath."

Anson continued: "I would wake up in the middle of the night agonizing about this story, over the effect it would have on him and the effect on an American hero. God knows, the country needs them. I knew I would have to give this story my best shot. That's why I interviewed so many sources, but I kept hearing the same opinions, over and over." And by the time he sat down to write the story, Anson was of the same opinion held by many of those he had interviewed: Dawkins is more style than substance. Anson's opinion of Dawkins fell considerably; the piece reflects this attitude. Here's an excerpt:

> *Dawkins's supporters wrote off most of the barbs to jealousy, and clearly, there was a lot of it. But even among his backers, there was acknowledgment that Dawkins, with his seemingly unslakable thirst for attention combined with his insistence that talents like him ought not to be compelled to traverse the usual army hoops, was making his own life difficult. "Pete is clearly ambitious," says a senior officer who knows him well. "The question has always been, Ambitious for what? Himself or to make things better? With Pete, it's hard to know. You always have the feeling that he is putting on an act. It is a very good act, a very competent act that touches all the bases, but you still don't know what is behind it."*

Anson's attitude is obviously skeptical, and by his presentation of the facts, his skepticism is passed on to the reader, who begins to question Dawkins's character. Apparently *Manhattan inc.* readers were not the only ones to look askance at Pete Dawkins, because Dawkins was defeated in his Senatorial bid in November 1988. Some say Anson's piece, and his attitude, turned the tide.

SCENERY

An attitude, however, isn't worth a tinker's damn if the reader doesn't believe you know your subject. To secure the trust of your reader, you must show—not tell—that you know what you're talking about. That you've been there. That the subject's eyes are dark blue, her hair is the color of straw, her legs are lanky, and her movements are like those of a ballerina.

According to Tom Wolfe, this "recording of everyday gestures, habits, manners, customs, styles of furniture, clothing, decoration, styles of traveling, eating, keeping house, modes of behaving toward children, servants, superiors, inferiors, peers, plus the various looks, glances, poses, styles of walking and other symbolic details that might exist within a scene . . . is not mere embroidery in prose. It lies as close to the center of the power of realism as any other device in literature." And that *power of realism* is found in the best nonfiction. But rather than lapsing into list-making, hoping that the accretion of detail will strengthen his portrait, the most forceful nonfiction writer looks for the significant details that best illustrate the essence, the spirit of his subject.

Here is a telling paragraph from Lynn Hirschberg's *Esquire* article "The Office," about office dynamics:

> *Noble Hook is very tall, has blond hair that clears his shoulders, and rarely wears anything other than black jeans, tennis shoes, and a thriftstore bowling shirt. He is twenty-five, has worked at Dancer [Dancer, Fitzgerald, Sample — a Manhattan advertising agency] nearly three years, and makes $50,000 a year as a writer and art director for ads. His office is full of plastic blow-up toys — beach balls and robots and seals. Noble's office is a great source of talk around Dancer. Clients curl into their chairs during meetings there so as not to disturb a blow-up mermaid or an inflated rat.*

The scene is set, and when Noble's immaturity affects his rise on the corporate ladder, no one, including the reader, is surprised.

REPORTAGE

Gathering great scenes takes time and patience. When Lynn Hirschberg wrote "The Office," she spent three days a week at Dancer, Fitzgerald, Sample for almost three months. "I followed people around, interviewed anyone I got hold of," she told editor Lee Eisenberg. "I wasn't given a desk, which was fine. I wanted to be as invisible as possible. But I was given nearly total access, which enabled my reporting to be as exhaustive — and exhausting — as any I've ever attempted." Through her relentless reportage, Hirschberg was able to give the reader a glimpse into how an ad agency operates — both its creative genius and its backbiting pettiness. She was able to explore a world that for most of us is as alien as Pluto. Hirschberg, for instance, delved into the backbiting and petty politics of the office in scenes such as this one:

> *Stephen Dolleck is at the office, on the phone with Julie Picard. "OK," he says. "Let's talk it out. You wanna do it? OK — come on*

back." He hangs up the phone. "She's pissed," he says.

This meeting, Stephen explains as he nervously paces the width of his office, is really a confrontation. He has been angry with Julie lately. "She has such a sucky attitude," Stephen says, sprinkling a few drops of Binaca on his tongue. She is also angry with him, which Stephen attributes to jealousy over Terry's promotion and a lingering crush he is certain Julie has on him. "I mean, what the hell is wrong?" he says. "If you're unhappy, then look for a new job." Stephen plops onto his couch, resting briefly before she gets there. "I'm very aware of politics," he says. "You know—having her on my territory versus going into hers, standing up or sitting down. I always sit on something in Dallas's office so I'm taller. You know what I'm saying?"

Most of us have neither the luxury nor the expense money to spend time immemorial working on a story such as "The Office." Nor are we paid enough. We're usually lucky to make enough on a piece to buy a long weekend. But we can use our time wisely—interview as many people and investigate as many scenes as possible—to make our reportage more authentic . . . and our story more powerful.

FACTS

Paul Hoffman's "The Man Who Loves Only Numbers" (published in *The Atlantic Monthly*) is a powerful piece of nonfiction. It's a profile of Paul Erdos (pronounced "air-dish"), a brilliant and eccentric mathematician. Hoffman tells us that Erdos "has structured his life to maximize the amount of time he has for mathematics. He has no wife or children, no job, no hobbies, not even a home to tie him down. He lives out of a shabby suitcase and a drab orange plastic bag from . . . a large department store in Budapest. In a never-ending search for good mathematical problems and fresh mathematical talent, Erdos crisscrosses four continents at a frenzied pace, moving from one university or research center to the next. His modus operandi is to show up on the doorstep of an esteemed mathematician, declare 'My brain is open,' work with his host for a day or two, until he's bored or his host is run down, and then move on to another home."

Hoffman does a wonderful job of letting us, the readers, spend time with Erdos. We see him ordering fried squid balls at a restaurant and then drawing cryptic sketches of rockets and hula hoops on the back of the place mat; we learn of his undiagnosed skin condition that compels him to wear only silk underwear and to wash his hands dozens of times a day; we look on as his friends wash his underwear and section his grapefruit for him.

But the most astonishing thing is that, while we read of Erdos's singular behavior, we learn about the history of mathematics — about Euclid and Pythagoras, about prime and twin prime numbers, about integers, perfect numbers, friendly numbers, the Ramsey theory, and a host of mathematical information. If this data had been presented as straight-on facts, they would have been impossible to swallow, but in the context of learning about Erdos's personality, the facts become fascinating. And conversely, because Hoffman teaches us about math as we read, the portrait of Erdos becomes more intriguing. Here's an example from the piece:

> *The prime numbers are Erdos's intimate friends. He understands them better than anyone else does. "When I was ten," he says, "my father told me about Euclid's proof, and I was hooked." Seven years later, as a college freshman, he caused a stir in Hungarian mathematics circles with a simple proof that a prime can always be found between any integer (greater than 1) and its double. This result had been proved in about 1850 by one of the fathers of Russian mathematics, Pafnuty Lvovitch Chebyshev. But Chebyshev's proof was too heavy-handed to be in the Book. He had used a steam shovel to transplant a rosebush, whereas Erdos managed with a silver spoon. News of Erdos's youthful triumph was spread by the ditty "Chebyshev said it, and I say it again/There is always a prime between n and 2n."*

We read nonfiction to learn something about the world. Hoffman's masterpiece of nonfiction, which won a 1988 National Magazine Award, does exactly what Samuel Johnson said good literature must: It teaches and delights.

FICTION

How can fiction make for better nonfiction? According to Gay Talese, "Since my earliest days in journalism, I was far less interested in the exact words that came out of people's mouths than in the essence of their meaning." In other words, Talese is not telling the nonfiction writer to make things up. He is, however, urging the reporter not to let facts get in the way of the truth. Reconstructing scenes, getting at the essence of what people are saying, divining people's thoughts — these activities are no longer solely the domain of the fiction writer. The nonfiction writer can also use these devices to his advantage. Granted, it's risky business to speak of tampering with the straightforward facts in a reporting piece, but it's essential to understanding what makes for powerful nonfiction.

Let's take a moment to examine the apparent contradiction here. How can a nonfiction piece be strengthened by a fictional approach? Suppose you spend two weeks researching a piece on prostitution, and you and your editor decide that the best way to present the story is as "A Day in the Life of a Prostitute." To merely recapitulate a routine day in the hooker's life might not get at the essence of your subject. But, taking a hint from the novelist, if you were to telescope your two weeks into one day—an intriguing, but not necessarily atypical, day—the story might be much more compelling—if, as we'll see in a moment, the reader knows you are compressing time.

A journalism critic once observed that Hunter S. Thompson is "the most factual and least accurate reporter we have." His point was that Thompson might not have put quotes down verbatim or rendered scenes exactly as they happened, but he accurately portrayed what his subject meant to say and the spirit in which his subject acted.

In *Sports Illustrated*, Frank Deford wrote a nonfiction piece about University of Arkansas basketball coach Nolan Richardson as a one-act stage play.

Early in the play, Richardson's grandmother rises from her rocking chair on stage and says, "Nolan and his sisters lived with me ever since his poor momma died when he was only three. And his daddy died when Nolan was twelve. We lived here in this old shotgun house—just this room and the two more, straight back. But we got ourselves an indoor toilet this time. And usually there's enough to eat. I work at a place makes fried chicken, and sometimes I can bring these leftovers home." Richardson's grandmother may indeed have said those words at one time, but there's no way Deford could have heard them. Richardson's grandmother has been dead for years.

Writing about Deford's unusual nonfiction techniques, publisher Donald J. Barr explained that "incidental events were telescoped in time, composite scenes formed, transitional and narrative dialogue created. Deford also fashioned some of the speeches made by dead people. . . ." Deford said: "I chose to do it this way simply because Coach Richardson's life has been so expressive and dramatic. I felt that the travails and tragedy—and the triumphs—would be more vivid in this form." The piece is vivid and artful and powerful. Used wisely, a certain amount of fictional truth can improve a piece or ordinary nonfiction.

SUBSTANTIATION

Of course, there are levels of fact. And it is imperative that the nonfiction writer know when to stick to the actual, no matter how mundane it may be. The nonfiction reporter should not make up quotes, or situations, or descriptions that lead the reader away from the truth of the story.

For instance, *Washington Post* reporter Janet Cooke won a Pulitzer Prize in 1982 for her nonfiction exposé of a young heroin addict. Upon investigation, however, it was discovered that no such person existed— and the Pulitzer was taken away from her. The subject of Cooke's story was a composite of addicts. Now, why was Cooke's creating a composite wrong, while my previous example of compressing two weeks in the life of a prostitute into a single typical day would be OK? Because Cooke led readers to believe that the composite person was a real person, that such an unfortunate was living on the streets. If she had told the truth about the people she met, chances are her piece would have been just as strong. For that matter, if she had simply told readers that she had created a composite, no one would have questioned her. In any case, had Cooke been writing her article for a good magazine, her sins would have been uncovered by a fact-checker.

Just to be sure that the magazine writer adheres to the truth, many magazines have research departments—fact checking departments. Be prepared to face the fact-checkers. Get the facts right in the first place, and keep records of how you obtained the facts—interview transcripts, photocopies of printed materials, and so on—in the second.

Don't look at a fact-checker's queries as an annoyance, or as a signal that you aren't being trusted. Understand that the researcher's job is to double-check the facts of the story—to protect the magazine, yes, but also to protect the writer, who in most cases is legally liable for what he writes, and in all cases does not want to look sloppy or silly.

Nonfiction master John McPhee is a meticulous documentarian of fact. According to William L. Howarth, editor of *The John McPhee Reader*, "McPhee strives for total accuracy, hoping the checkers will not catch a flat-footed error."

UNDERSTATEMENT

Writing emotionally is risky. *Trying* to evoke emotions in your writing is deadly. Perhaps the best way to write emotionally is to not write emotionally at all, but to find something extraordinarily emotional and write about it with understatement. As a device, understatement can be used to drive home tragedy, poignance, sadness, terror and humor.

Here's an example of the latter from Donald Katz's masterpiece, "The King of the Ferret Leggers," which appeared in *Outside*:

> *Basically, the contest [ferret legging] involves the tying of the competitor's trousers at the ankles and the subsequent insertion into those trousers of a couple of peculiarly vicious fur-coated, foot-long carnivores called ferrets. The brave contestant's belt is then pulled tight, and he proceeds to stand there in front of the judges as long as he can, while animals with claws like hypodermic needles and teeth like number 16 carpet tacks try their damnedest to get out.*

The entire fantastic ferret-legging story is rife with understatement and from this subdued approach emerges a powerfully funny — and terrifying — piece about the weirdest, most masochistic sport on earth.

CONFLICT

The best nonfiction writers know the difference between a topic and a story. Nobody wants to read fifty words, much less two thousand, on a topic. But if you can tell a good story, the reader will stay with you as long as it takes.

What makes a good story? We've talked about some of the things: attitude, good reporting, engaging the senses. And how could you *not* read on about ferret legging? But every great story, every story that is compelling to read, contains conflict. Good versus evil. How someone overcame obstacles to endure and prevail.

None of us enjoys stories that are all goodness and light, because we know that life is not all goodness and light. Conversely, none of us revels in a story that is all malevolence and malfeasance. In such tales, we look for hope and redemption. The conflict between the way things are, and the way things ought to be, makes for the most compelling, and most powerful nonfiction.

In the examples I've given in this article, we see conflict between Pete Dawkins the man and Pete Dawkins the myth; between creative people at Dancer, Fitzgerald, Sample; between extraordinary Paul Erdos and the ordinary world around him; between some odd competitors and the ferrets whose only wish is to escape.

For many of us, however, the real conflict is between the way we write and the way we'd *like* to write. But maybe if we can keep some of these eight things in mind the next time we sit down to face a blank page of paper, we'll be able to write a piece of nonfiction that pierces the heart of the reader in a most provocative and entertaining way.

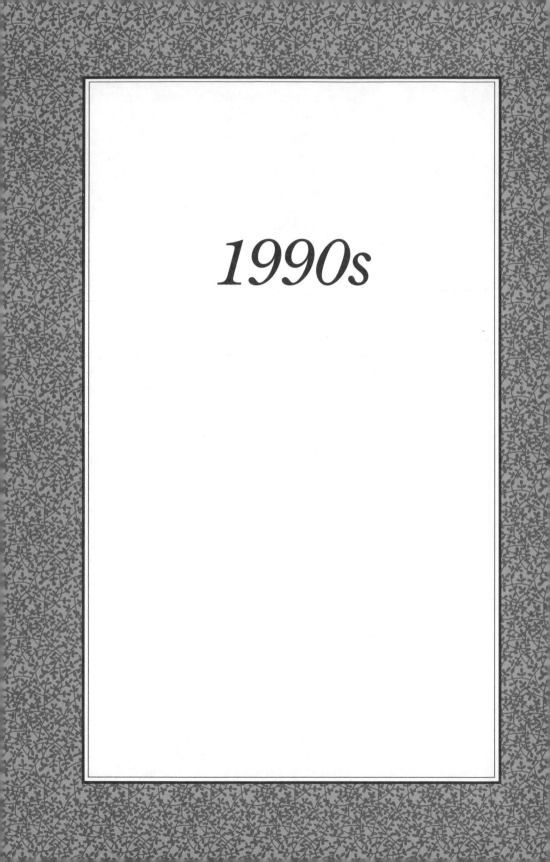

1990s

Romantic Encounters

Jude Deveraux

October 1991

I n the twelve years since I was first published, I've read a number of romances that were beautifully written, exhaustingly researched, but which ultimately, when published, didn't sell. Since I'm the type of person who analyzes everything, I've tried to figure out just what it is about these books that made them fail to capture the imagination of the readers.

There are hard and fast rules to writing a romance, rules that cannot be broken and boundaries that must not be crossed. For instance, you can put a mystery in your romance, but if you put in even a bit too much mystery, you have a book that won't be bought by either mystery readers or romance readers.

Here are nine other common problems I have seen both in unpublished manuscripts and in published books that didn't find an audience.

DON'T GIVE YOUR CHARACTERS TOO MANY PERSONALITY TRAITS.

It's natural to want to put everything admirable into your hero or heroine. Since your heroine is usually your main character, you will probably want her to be all the good things that a person can be. You'll want her to be noble and brave, a lover of children and animals, well educated, a bit persecuted by others (so readers will feel a tug at their heartstrings); you'll want her to be spunky, desired by the best of the men and so on.

Unfortunately, when you assign this whole list of attributes to one person you don't end up with a noble, bigger-than-life character, you create a mess no one can identify with.

For example, let's say you open your book with a scene in which the heroine is being unfairly accused of something by the villainess, then follow with a scene in which the heroine sees a child crying, then show the heroine finding out that the child is crying because her kitten is stuck up in a tree, then have your heroine risking her life to rescue the kitten, then falling out of the tree into the hero's arms, then lashing out at him for daring to look at her in "that way." What you have is a hodge-podge of personality traits. Readers are going to have no idea what the character you've created is really like. Pick out one or two personality traits and stick with them throughout the novel. You can, for example, write a whole book on a heroine who is, first and foremost, a lover of children.

DON'T MISTAKE CLICHÉS FOR PLOT.

By clichés I mean plot lines that have been used over and over in fiction. For example, years ago I read a romance that was absolutely cliché-ridden. When I bought that author's next book, I looked at the back cover just enough to see that it was set on a riverboat. I made a list of all the clichés about riverboat romances I could think of: Either the villain or the hero was going to be a riverboat gambler and wear a gold brocade vest. There was going to be a fire or a riverboat race. Samuel Clemens was going to be the pilot of the boat and they'd dock in New Orleans. There'd be some hanky-panky in the brothels of New Orleans. I wrote an entire page of clichés.

After I'd made my list, I read the book. *All* of the clichés on my list were in there (in fact, *both* the hero and the villain were gamblers wearing gold brocade vests). Today this author cannot find a publisher for her books.

Sometimes as I write I come up with scenes just by thinking of what one would predict a character in a romance might do, and then writing something that is as close to the cliché's opposite as I can make it.

AVOID ADORED/PERSECUTED HEROINES.

This is the most difficult problem to explain to new romance writers. In some manuscripts, every character in the book either loves the heroine or hates her, and by the end of the book, the people who have not fallen in love with her (and this includes servants) are killed off by the author in proportionately vicious ways. In some books this is carried so far that everyone—main characters, minor characters all—are able to put themselves in the heroine's lovely little mind and sense whatever she's feeling.

Instead of having your heroine be the center of *everyone's* universe, make her liked by some, disliked by others and ignored by the rest.

DON'T OVERDO THE SEX.

Romance novels are not sex novels. They are books about people learning about each other and falling in love. Sex is a tiny part of love, but too often the whole "story" of a beginner's romance novel is nothing but a never-ending sex scene. If the heroine leaves her house, some man is going to try to rape her. If the heroine climbs a ladder, she is going to fall on top of the hero, her skirt is going to fly over her head, and of course his hands are going to land you-know-where.

Don't make every bit of dialogue, every bit of action a lead-in to a sex scene. When readers finish the book, they should feel that these two people have more going for them than just a super-normal sex life. How do they settle arguments outside of bed?

WRITE A NOVEL, NOT A LECTURE.

New romance writers often have stars in their eyes, hoping and expecting to receive reviews that say that their books "transcend the genre." But, in their attempts to "transcend the genre," beginners quite often produce not novels but long lectures on some issue such as AIDS or battered wives or drugs (usually drugs), interspersing information about the issue with sex scenes. The result is a cross between a free government pamphlet and pornography. Whatever it is, it isn't a romance novel, and it doesn't sell.

DON'T WRITE DINOSAURS.

When I was first published it was much easier to sell a romance novel than it is today. All a writer needed then was an angry hero, a feisty, big-busted heroine and a lot of sex.

But the world back then was virginal compared to what it is today. Twelve years ago you had to have proof of age to buy a photo of a nude woman. Today perfume ads feature nude women in them. Even though the world has changed so much, too often a reader can pick up a romance novel written in 1991 and find very little difference from a romance written in 1975. In far too many instances, the heroes are still mocking, arrogant and sardonic, and the heroines are still so beautiful that they drive men wild with lust; the plots are about a heroine who stamps her foot a great deal, a hero who desires the heroine, a villain who must have her, and enough sex scenes to fill 85 percent of the pages. The days when such romances were not only published but also sold millions of copies are dead. Today's readers want characters with complex personalities, not simply hormones that put a teenager's to shame. Readers want a plot that has meat.

STAY WITHIN THE CONFINES OF THE GENRE.

When new writers want desperately to sell, they often try to write a "different" romance. This usually means they plan to write a romance with a hero who is a voodoo priest and rather frequently bites the heads off chickens. I've had letters from women who suggest I write a book with a hero who is a wife-beater and reforms; these letters frighten me.

Remember, too, that it's harder to write a good, solid story of love between two people who are rather ordinary than it is to write about characters who are so beautiful that men go insane with lust, or so masculine that women kill just to go to bed with them. Such characters simply aren't believable, and therefore are of less interest to readers.

DON'T PUT ANYTHING INTO YOUR STORY THAT DOESN'T RELATE TO THE STORY.

Quite often a new writer will create a long study of the major characters, including physical aspects, personality traits and whatever else they know about the character. Then, as each of these characteristics is inserted into the story, the writer marks them off the list. In other words, everything she knows about the character is included in the story. Unfortunately, quite a bit of this information isn't needed and just bores the reader while interrupting the story.

Let me give you an example. Often in the first chapter of a romance will be a long paragraph telling the history of the heroine's education, something like, back on the plantation, her father didn't believe in education for women (this goes back to the ol' persecuted heroine plot) so a tutor was hired for her brother. But the brother was only interested in horses so the tutor spent his time with the heroine. Because of this, the author informs us, the heroine can read and write two dead languages and six live languages. After this paragraph the author never again mentions this splendid education, thereby making this bit of information superfluous.

Only information necessary to the story should be included. For example: Say the hero and heroine were tramping about the jungles of South America searching for a lost treasure and they came upon a stone tablet that had the next clue on it. The hero could brush away the dirt, see that the stone was written in Latin, and say, "Great, now all we have to do is travel six hundred miles back through the jungle to the nearest museum and find someone to translate this." At that time the heroine could translate the tablet and the hero could ask her how she knows how to read Latin, and the author could have the heroine tell the story of her education.

An author should always know more about her characters than she tells the readers. Just because the author knows the hero's favorite food, his favorite color, how he got the scar on his wrist, and so on, is no reason to bombard the reader with these facts. If there *is* a reason, the story will point it out.

START THE BOOK IN THE MIDDLE OF THE ACTION.

Books today must compete with television, movies and video games, so they must be almost as fast and as fascinating.

Stories that start with whole chapters of explanation about the characters are neither fast nor fascinating. When I try to talk to new writers about this, I'm often told that this is "setting the stage" or "developing character." What the writers are really doing is giving away all their secrets at the outset of the book.

Let me illustrate. Say your best friend calls and asks you out to a movie, but she won't tell you what you're going to see. You're game for this, so you go to the theater, the lights go down and on the screen comes a man and he begins talking. He tells you all about the heroine's life, about her childhood, her relationship to her father, that she was upset about her mother's death and on and on. After he gets through with the heroine he starts telling you about the hero. I think this boring, lecturing man will clear the theater. People today are used to seeing movies in which three people are killed in violent ways in the first four minutes — and that's in a romantic movie.

What if you went to the movie theater, the lights dimmed and you saw a plain with a hill in the background and as the camera moved closer you saw a single tombstone in front of the hill? Sitting on the tombstone is a young woman reading a book. What the viewer can see and the woman cannot is that coming toward her, over the hill, is a man on horseback riding hell-bent-for-leather, who is being chased by four other men on horseback. Just as the man in front reaches the edge of the hill, he looks down, sees the woman and the only thing he can do is try to jump over her. The woman looks up, sees the belly of the horse going over and falls backward over the tombstone.

This opening, as opposed to the one made up of lectures telling everything that the reader hasn't yet wanted to know, asks a lot of questions.

What is this woman doing out here alone? Is the man on the lead horse a good guy, or a bad guy being chased by a posse? (And my personal question: What in the world is she reading that is so fascinating that she doesn't even hear galloping horses?)

Sometimes a writer will use any excuse to insert her thirty-five or so pages of character study. For example, if the hero and heroine, in order to escape the bad guys, need to hide in a small dark place and the hero would rather be shot at than climb into this enclosed space, the heroine can later say something to the effect of, "You want to tell me about what happened?" Too often the writer will then have the hero sit down on a log and tell twenty-six pages about his rotten childhood, just as though he's had ten or so years of therapy and can analyze it. It is much more effective to have the hero say "no." No. That's all. This simple *no* suggests lots of questions. It makes readers want to find out what caused the hero to be afraid of small places. By doling out the information in small doses, you keep the reader interested and excited.

When you create such questions, you allow readers to discover your characters and live your story as they read it — the hallmarks of all good fiction. And as you create the characters who invite such questions, you'll find you won't need to turn to plots filled with clichés and steamy bedroom scenes.

There are hard and fast rules to writing a romance. And the most important is that you must not fail to capture the imagination of readers.

The Big Finish

Don McKinney

February 1992

N obody ever writes about endings," Bill Zinsser told me once, and while that statement is not strictly true, it comes close. Zinsser did include a chapter called "The Ending" in *On Writing Well*, one of the best books ever written on the craft of magazine article writing, but it's one of the shortest chapters in his book. The fact is that few people have thought much about the best ways to wind up an article. Long-time freelancer Max Gunther once asked a number of editors what kind of endings they liked, and got a lot of blank stares. "I know a good ending when I read one," was the almost univeral response, but there were few useful suggestions.

One thought did predominate: A good ending is satisfying. It leaves the reader feeling that the subject has been covered, the main points have been made, and nothing more remains to be said.

Just as in a play or movie, the ending is what you leave the reader with; his final judgment about the success of the article may well be formed by the last paragraph or so. John McPhee, who many think is the best magazine writer of our time, places such importance on the ending that he claims to "always know the last line of a story before I've written the first one." I once asked freelancer Barbara Raymond how she was doing on an assignment and she said cheerfully, "I've got the lead and the ending, and all I have to do is fill in the rest."

And while Jerome Stern, who directs the writing program at Florida State University, was not talking about magazine articles in his book *Making Shapely Fiction*, his point about endings works for nonfiction as well. "The closer and closer you get to the ending," he writes, "the more weight each word has, so that by the time you get to the last several words each one carries an enormous meaning. A single gesture or image at the end can outweigh all that has gone before."

During my years as an editor, whenever I picked up an article from a new writer I would usually read the lead and then skip over to the end; if the writer had started well and finished up strongly, I would know I was in good hands and would settle down to read with some real sense of anticipation.

Having said all that, what is a good ending? What are the different methods you can use to bring your piece to a satisfying conclusion? "I always try to end sooner than the reader expects me to," Zinsser says. "The perfect ending should take the reader slightly by surprise."

While I agree that pieces should never be allowed to overstay their welcomes, I'm not sure that surprise is always necessary (although it can be wonderful when it works). But there are a great many ways to finish strongly, and I've made up an arbitrary list of ten of them. The catalog may contain a certain amount of overlapping, but whoever said magazine writing was a science?

THE CIRCLE TECHNIQUE

This is probably the most popular, because nothing is more effective in giving the reader a sense that he has covered the subject than a return to a theme introduced in the lead. As Peter Jacobi, a long-time teacher, columnist and writing consultant, puts it, "The reader should be left satisfied, feel that he's read something finished, something with a point clearly made, something with a unity that has moved him from start to finish almost in a circular manner."

Dave Anderson, an award-winning sportswriter for *The New York Times*, has been using this technique for years. In a column written just prior to Nolan Ryan's first start after a recent no-hitter, Dave begins with a quote from former Baltimore shortstop Mark Belanger. It was 1973, and Ryan had pitched a no-hitter in his previous game; he was six outs away from another when Belanger slapped a ball between short and second for a single. "They told me that when I got to first base, Nolan looked at me," Belanger remembered. "Nolan tilts that head and gives you that look." And Anderson's ending: "Now the forty-four-year old phenom has another chance. . . . But if one of the Blue Jays gets a hit, Nolan Ryan will tilt that head and give him that look."

In a profile of Cybill Shepherd in *Memphis* magazine, Ed Weathers began with Shepherd on the deck of her Memphis apartment overlooking the Mississippi, "wearing a 'Memphis Country Club Member – guest' 1982' visor, aviator sunglasses and a black bikini. . . . " Several thousand words later Weathers is back on the deck, but this time it is late in the day: "The sky turns a deeper purple, and Shepherd turns contemplative.

'You know,' she says, 'I regret every sunset I miss here.' As she gazes across the Mississippi, the Memphis sun disappears, headed toward L.A." Weathers has closed the circle, returning to where he began, and the reader feels a sense of completion.

THE SUMMARY

If the word *summary* brings up phrases like "as I have been saying" or "as we have seen," forget them. A good summary ending can take many forms, none of which begins with "in conclusion." Reading through a recent issue of *Reader's Digest*, I found several examples of summary endings in the form of quotes. At the end of an article on people who have been swindled in phony land deals, author Trevor Armbrister quotes an official of the federal Department of Housing and Urban Development: "If it sounds too good to be true, it probably is." This advice has been given a good many times, but it still makes a very apt ending.

Another *Digest* article, this one on the value of helmets for cyclists, concluded:

> *"So many things are totally out of control in a motorcycle or bicycle accident," says Dr. Donald Leslie, a head-injury specialist. "A helmet is one thing you can control."*

A splendid example of the summary ending that does not sound like a summary was used by Saul Pett in his Pulitzer Prize-winning article on the federal bureaucracy and how it got to be so big.

> *The parts multiply like the denizens of a rabbit warren on New Year's Eve. Everybody, it seems, wants something or opposes something and, in the melee, bureaucracy grows larger and more shapeless and threatens to become, in itself, a government of too many people, by too many people, for too many people.*

THE QUOTE

The straight quote ending does not necessarily summarize the point of the piece, but it should reiterate its theme and tone. It's a good idea to look for an appropriate quote when you're typing up your notes; some comment that seems to sum things up in a snappy way. One I particularly like comes from a piece Richard Gehman wrote for us at *True* magazine many years ago. It was about the Dalton family, for many generations (even back to the time of Queen Victoria) the preeminent rat catchers of London. After what amounted to a short course in the history of the rat and how to catch him, Gehman concluded with a quote from Bill Dalton, elder statesman of the clan:

> *He has grown so fond of rats over the years that sometimes, as he is sitting a lonely vigil in a dark room in the depths of this ancient city, he begins to speculate uneasily over the future. "What I wonder," he says, "is this—suppose I'm a rat in the next world? What am I going to do to keep away from the bloody Daltons?"*

THE ANECDOTE

Just as you looked through your notes for a good quote to wind up your story, you might also look for a good anecdote, perhaps the second best if you plan to lead off with your best one.

A fine example of an anecdote ending, which also combines elements of the surprise and the ironic, was written by Joseph R. Judge in an article on early explorations of the New World that appeared in *National Geographic*. After reporting that the first European settlements were Spanish, predating the English colonization by almost a century, he wound up this way:

> *Thus it was when a Spanish caravel came into the Chesapeake in 1611, under pretext of searching for a lost ship, and captured a young English pilot named John Clark. Three from the caravel were stranded ashore and were jailed. One died of starvation; another, found to be English, was later hanged for treason. The third, Don Diego de Molina, survived four years imprisonment in Virginia, railing in letters smuggled home against English designs in a land to which Spain had such an ancient and honorable claim, and calling Jamestown "a new Algiers in America."*
>
> *Clark had been taken to Spain and interrogated, and in due course of time each man was returned to his native land. Clark returned to the sea and found work to his liking as first mate on a ship bound for America.*
>
> *Her name was Mayflower.*

THE END OF ACTION

This is sometimes appropriate for a narrative, but not always. It, like the summary, gives a feeling that the last act has taken place and the events about which the article was written are over. In Joan Didion's classic collection of articles, *Slouching Toward Bethlehem*, she includes a wonderful memoir of coming of age in New York called "Goodbye to

All That." After remembering what it was like for a young girl to come to the big city from California and try and make her fortune there, she ends:

> *The last time I was in New York was in a cold January and everyone was ill and tired. Many of the people I used to know there had moved to Dallas or gone on Antabuse or had bought a farm in New Hampshire. We stayed ten days, and then we took an afternoon flight back to Los Angeles, and on the way home from the airport that night I could see the moon on the Pacific and smell jasmine all around, and we both knew that there was no longer any point in keeping the apartment we still kept in New York. There were years when I called Los Angeles "the Coast," but they seem a long time ago.*

And is there any more perfect end of action than the closing lines of Melville's *Moby Dick*? (True, this isn't a magazine ending, but it's one I've never forgotten.) The whale has destroyed the ship, and it is about to sink. "Now small fowls flew screaming over the yet yawning gulf; a sullen white surf beat against its steep sides; then all collapsed, and the great shroud of the sea rolled on as it rolled five thousand years ago."

THE IRONIC ENDING

In a marvelous essay called "Journalese, or Why English Is the Second Language of the Fourth Estate," John Leo crams in many of the worst examples of newspaper writing in one nifty closing paragraph, even including the cliché of the summary ending.

> *In sum, journalese is a truly vital language, the last bulwark against libel, candor and fresh utterance. Its prestigious, groundbreaking, state-of-the-art lingo makes it arguably the most useful of tongues, and its untimely demise would have a chilling effect, especially on us award-winning journalists.*

Irony should be used sparingly, but when the subject matter is appropriate, it can really drive the point home.

A combination of the anecdotal, the ironic and the quote comes in Rex Reed's splendid profile of Ava Gardner, taken from his book *Do You Sleep in the Nude?* It had been a long afternoon of talking and drinking, and they are all going out to dinner.

> *Ava is in the middle of Park Avenue, the scarf falling around her neck and her hair blowing wildly around the Ava eyes. Lady Brett in*

the traffic, with a downtown bus as the bull. Three cars stop on a green light and every taxi driver on Park Avenue begins to honk. The autograph hunters leap through the polished doors of the Regency and begin to scream. . . . They [Ava and her entourage] are already turning the corner into Fifty-seventh Street, fading into the kind of night, the color of tomato juice in the headlights, that only exists in New York when it rains.

"Who was it?" asks a woman walking a poodle.

"Jackie Kennedy," answers a man from his bus window.

THE SURPRISE

Surprise endings are hard to find, and most articles, particularly long ones, don't lend themselves to this sort of treatment. Truman Capote pulled it off effectively in a piece called "Mr. Jones," which appears in his collection *Music for Chameleons*. Although Capote may have been best known as a novelist, he was an excellent reporter and matchless storyteller. Jones was a neighbor of Capote's in a small Brooklyn rooming house. He was both crippled and blind, with few friends and no known occupation, but no one thought him remarkable until the day he disappeared.

Then, ten years later, Capote was riding on a Moscow subway when he looked up and saw his former neighbor. "I was about to cross the aisle and speak to him when the train pulled into a station, and Mr. Jones, on a pair of fine sturdy legs, stood up and strode out of the car. Swiftly, the train door closed behind him."

What had seemed a simple sketch of a casual acquaintance suddenly turned into a spy story—and a memorable one.

THE POETIC ENDING

In this case, the writer is allowed to indulge in some flowery writing, perhaps even a bit of philosophy. It can be self-indulgent (be wary of this), but it can also leave an echo in the mind that the reader will not soon forget. One of the best I know is from E.B. White's classic essay on New York, originally written for *Holiday* magazine back in 1948 but reprinted dozens of times since. The New York he wrote about is gone, as is the great Mr. White, but his final image has stayed with me.

A block or two west of the new City of Man in Turtle Bay there is an old willow tree that presides over an interior garden. It is a battered tree, long-suffering and much climbed, held together by strands of wire but beloved of those who know it. In a way it symbolizes the city: life under difficulties, growth against odds, sap-rise in the midst of concrete, and the steady reaching for the sun. Whenever I look at it nowadays, and feel the cold shadow of the planes, I think: "This must be saved, this particular thing, this very tree." If it were to go, all would go — this city, this mischievous and marvelous monument which not to look upon would be like death.

THE ECHO ENDING

This carries the circle technique to its ultimate extent by repeating a word or phrase frequently throughout the piece, so that it becomes almost a theme in itself. In Max Gunther's *Writing the Modern Magazine Article*, a truly excellent guide which is unfortunately out of print, he recalls an article he once wrote on the history and legends of gold. He dropped the word in frequently, in the form of one-word paragraphs, after many of his anecdotes, and closed with "It's the bloodstained metal. The metal that can make you rich. Or dead.

"Gold."

THE STRAIGHT STATEMENT

While this sort of ending does summarize the point of the article, beware of the simplistic "as we have seen" approach. Remember that your conclusion is the final thought you want to leave with the reader, the one that reemphasizes the point and answers the question: "Why did I read this piece?" I like to close with a thought that drives home the essence of what I have written. An example I'm fond of is from an article Sen. Eugene McCarthy wrote for *Geo* magazine. His subject was political campaigning, and he concluded:

Defeat in politics, even relative failure, is not easy to accept. Dismissing the troops, as both Napoleon and Robert E. Lee learned, is not easy. Soldiers do not want to take their horses and mules and go back to the spring plowing. It is better to win.

IN CONCLUSION . . .

This list obviously does not include every possibility, but it should give you some ideas. The point to remember is that the ending is probably the second most important part of your article, after the lead, and you should be pointing toward it all the way through. A weak ending leaves a soft, squishy feeling about the article; a strong one will cover for a multitude of sins. When you've finished writing, and waited the requisite day or two before reading your work again, see if you haven't gone on longer than you really need to. The best ending may well be a few paragraphs back—maybe even a few pages!

I've quoted the estimable Mr. Zinsser frequently, so I think I'll let him have the last word: "When you've finished telling what you want to tell, just stop."

Truth and the Writer
(Young and Old)

Harlan Ellison

The Writer's 1961 Yearbook

The Writer's 1990 Yearbook

When I wrote the following essay in 1960 — it was published in 1961 — I was twenty-six years old, and had been a professional at my craft for only four years. Now, almost three decades later, with forty-five books written, more than 1,400 stories, essays, articles and columns published, a dozen movies and three dozen teleplays turned out, and an embarrassing number of awards listed after my name in *Who's Who*, I am called upon to face that bombastic tot who careered across the pages of *The Writer's 1961 Yearbook*, shooting off his mouth with such *obiter dicta* about the holy chore of writing. I reread that essay, and I wince. How filled with hot air and looniness that kid was. Like a banjo player who had a big breakfast. And close on thirty years later, I must reflect on what he wrote, what he believed, and how it looks to that kid's descendant self.

It looks ... well ... different. How could it not? The world in which I sit, as my fifty-fifth birthday looms just a month away, is not nearly as salutary a place as it was back in 1960. There were certainly parallels in 1960 to all the awful things I see today — Sen. Joseph McCarthy then, and the Ayatollah's death threat against Rushdie now; censorship from the Far Right then, and the demented devil-screeching of the Fundamentalist Right today; low pay and slow pay then, and the destruction of the midlist in publishing today — just to name a few — but it was a simpler time, a more hopeful time as the sixties came charging in. Or perhaps it's just that I was a kid and didn't know any better.

So I find the bravado and hip-shooting of that twenty-six-year-old Ellison a matter for to blush. But, astonishingly to me, I find that what he had to say, flensed of all the rodomontade, quite a testament to the nobility of spending one's life at the writing rigor. I'd say it less flamboyantly now, perhaps, but I'd very likely say the same things. Nonetheless, it's not to justify where I was nearly thirty years ago that I write this update.

Here are a few things I learned later. They may help.

First is the big secret. The one no one ever tells you. And it is this: Anyone can *become* a writer. (If you doubt it, consider some of the current occupants of the best-seller list. If people who write that badly can become writers, then even the dippiest of us can become a writer, chacma baboons can become writers, sludge and amoeba can become writers.) The trick is not in *becoming* a writer, it is in *staying* a writer. Day after week after story after year. Staying in there for the long haul. Because, at final moments, when they plant us, and Posterity takes a scrinch-eyed look at what we've done before deciding to remember us or forget us, it is not a single book or story or play that wins or loses the day, it is the *totality* of what has been produced. Not a single hill, but a mountain range that stretches and rises and dips, and has sweep that can be judged. Through all the fads and successes and times when the critics ignore a writer, it is the work that goes on unabated. And finally, it is all that sustains us.

Second, success is a killer. It twists you, and bends you, and lies to you. When you are in the public eye, you are treated like Athena sprung full-blown from the forehead of Zeus, and you get used to the praise. When the vogue passes, and all that remains is the quality of the work, you must put the cheap pleasures of celebrity behind you, and keep producing. Eventually, if you live long enough and keep working well long enough, they find their way back to you, and new generations of readers find you, and it's better, warmer, much better indeed. Trust me on this one.

And last, and most important, if you want to be the writer that you confront thirty years later without shame, learn to ignore your readers. They mean well, and for the most part they are terrific people. But they *know* what they like from you, and if they have their way they'll demand it again and again — as reflected in the demands of the market and the editors and the reviews — and thirty years down the pike you'll find you've written the same book eleven times. So thank your readers and the critics who praise you, and then ignore them. Write for the most intelligent, wittiest, wisest audience in the universe: Write to please yourself.

And *never* let mere money be an influence. A good writer can always make money, even if he has to drive a truck or lay brick or work in the steno pool. Money is never a reason to sell out the holy chore.

As John Steinbeck said: "The writer must believe that what he is doing is the most important thing in the world. And he must hold to this illusion even when he knows it is not true."

That ought to sustain you. Ibsen said to live is to war with trolls, and I promise you that if you write well, and your words become popular, there will be trolls aplenty trying to give you an enema with a thermite bomb. Be tough, be contained, be very good at the keyboard and perhaps, thirty years down the line, you can face yourself and grin at the kid. . . .

[1989]

Toulouse-Lautrec once said (or so Jose Ferrer leads us to believe), "One should never meet an artist whose work one admires. The work is always so much better than the man." This is as true of me as it was of him (Toulouse-Lautrec, not Ferrer), though I hasten to explain I am in no way comparing myself with Henri de Toulouse-Lautrec.

It's just that I find rapport in what he is alleged to have said, because though my stories often reflect goodness and truth and subtlety and courage, I'm incapable of being good and honest and subtle when writing about my writing. (You notice I said *my* writing, not just Writing in General or The Art of Writing, because as far as I'm concerned, when it comes to Harlan Ellison's Writing, I'm a hell of an authority—and I think I'm good. I admire Malraux and Saint Exupéry and Hemingway and Schulberg and Hardy and Conrad and Ed McBain and William Goldman, but they're authorities on themselves [and don't believe any of that flapdoodle about a writer being unable to estimate his own work; if he's anywhere near talented, he knows better than anyone else] so all I can speak, for or about, is what *I* write, what I am. And since I've got to believe I'm something, I've got to believe I'm good. I'm not as lean and hard as Hemingway, and I'm not as bittersweet punch-in-the-belly as Goldman, because I'm me and they're they, and I'd never want the twain to meet. When I was seventeen, I wanted to be another James Joyce. I wised up. I settled for being the first Me. Not only is it less strain, but it stays within the limits of possibility.) But, I digress.

Stick with me, I've got a point.

Writing isn't a game with me. Neither is it "a job" as it is with many of my friends in "the trade" who work from 10 to 4 with an hour off for Beaujolais and biscuits. It is my life. Now snicker all you wish, that happens to be the plain and simple of it. And it not only offends me, it disgusts, short tempers, and enrages me to see people *playing* at being writers.

I'm not saying anybody doesn't have the right to tinker with the greatest gift in the world; I'm not saying you can't go out and have your swill put between hardcovers by an ego press, or donate your stories free of charge to a little magazine that can't afford to pay but *can* afford to steal; I'm not saying you can't write three hundred novelettes and hide them in your trunk because you're too frightened to show them to anyone, under the pretext that you "write only for yourself"; I'm not even saying you can't sell a few pieces to a reputable magazine, and settle down to calling yourself a writer.

I'm not saying you can't do it.

I'm just saying you can't stop me from looking on you with contempt.

In short, this article is a statement of purpose . . . a declaration of my place in the Universe and my thoughts about what I set down and what it's worth. To me. So if you are a fat little old lady in Mashed Potato Falls, Wyoming, with an antimacassar hat and a penchant for astrological poetry, if you are a dewy-eyed college student who accepts everything they tell you in creative writing courses without compunction or cerebration, if you are (in other words) a phony, a dilettante, an imitator, a hack or a humbug, pass on the articles that tell you what words to put into your characters' mouths or how to lick the mailing label, because this thing I'm writing will offend you.

And that would be just what I'd want to do; and you wouldn't want to give me any satisfaction, now would you?

But if you *know* you can write, if you *have* to write, if you spell like an aborigine and phrase like a longshoreman but have *something to say*, please, for God's sake! stay with me, because you aren't alone . . . there are many like you. I'm like you . . . we think alike, we suffer alike, and we want to go — where? —*there*, alike! This is for you.

You're a writer.

Credentials, first. Why listen to a guy if you don't think he's been where he's sending you?

I'm twenty-six, I've sold eleven books and three hundred-odd stories published all over the lot. I've never sold to The *New Yorker, Saturday Evening Post* or *Ladies' Home Journal*, and I don't have to downgrade their editorial practices because they wouldn't buy *my* kind of stories, and I won't write *their* kind, so we have a nodding acquaintance — I say nodding and they say nodding. I started writing when I was old enough to spell kat, and I haven't stopped. I've got a big mouth.

I sold my first story to Larry Shaw in 1955 when he was editing *Infinity Science Fiction*, and it was a very bad story by my standards today. That was my first and it tasted good, Lord how good it tasted! It was like jumping with all my clothes on into the ocean and catching that first, freezing crash right in the face. It was like loving all the best-looking girls in the world at once. It was like making a muscle and finding one! Hard and smooth and just right because it was all mine nobody else's just mine. And I ran through the streets of New York, so help me, I ran and waved the check like it was the standard at the front of a B-movie cavalry charge. And I cried. Because now somebody else believed. Now somebody else said, "OK, kid you can stop screaming, I believe you can write. And I'm willing to give you a penny a word to back up my faith."

You're chuckling at that penny a word?

Don't bother, because I'll bust you right in the jaw. That was the sweetest penny a word I'd ever known. Before or since. It was the birth and the puberty and the having it all, wrapped up in one check. So don't laugh; that's a warning.

If you're wondering when I'm going to get down to it—the point—then turn on, because you aren't a writer. You may be an author, but you certainly aren't a writer. If you understand what I've been saying, that I have *been* saying it since I started, about what it is to be a writer, and how it's got to be—at least for me—then you, too, are a writer.

That's the difference. There are writers, and there are authors. *Any*body can be an author. With the demand for material as great as it is today, any poor slob who can write without bumbling over his syntax can sell. But it's one thing to get your name under a title and get it set in type, and quite another to be a writer. Many of the latter never see print. That's a crime, but it's the way the world is run, unfortunately. Some guys write because they have found a relaxing, nonstrenuous way to beat the hard work system. Others do it because it's cathartic; these are the gut-spillers. Others do it because they like to keep eating . . . regularly or gluttonously, it doesn't matter which. Then there are the poor, damned souls who *must* write, who haven't any more choice in the matter than whether or not they breathe.

That's me. I *have* to write. When I was younger (last week) I was wont to say, rather melodramatically, that I wrote from the gut. This led to all manner of clever ripostes from my contemporaries who compared my effusions with the more advanced stages of gorge-buoyancy. Since then I've tempered my semantics and relocated the source of my

work. It comes from the heart and the soul and the head and the index
fingers of my right and left hands which are the only ones (poor slobs)
that ever learned to type.

But that's the gut, too.

When you start out, and you don't quite know how or what to write,
and all you know is that you *must*, it's easy to get led astray. So you
write penny-a-word blood-and-gore mystery stories, you write science
fiction novelettes at 30,000 words around a bad cover idea, you write
anything and everything, because it's all pouring out of you and the heat
is so great that if you stop it up you'll split wide open like a pumpkin
out of a tenth-story window.

So you write.

And you write.

It's training. It's learning the basics of plot structure and characterization and dialogue in the only vineyard that counts: before the editors
and the professional critics and your fellow writers who know the roots
and background of the field — not the nice folks you've let read your
story in hopes they'll bolster your ego. Now you aren't a chipmunk on
a treadmill, running after a sprig of parsley. Now you're out in the open
where they can belt you . . . or applaud you. The pulps were a great
training ground for many of the valuable writers of today; you've heard
that before. Don't pay attention to the snobs who tell you it's "commercial" and art it ain't. Guys like F. Van Wyck Mason, Marquand, C.S.
Forester, Dashiell Hammett and too many others to go into here, got
their starts and their basic training in the commercial pulp markets.

Though the pulps are with us only shadowedly these days, and fiction
outside hardcovers is divided nastily into warring camps of bland *Cosmopolitan* fiction with its "average boy and girl" stick figures, and of "pas-
tiche" fiction without destination in the arty periodicals, the writer of
fiction can still find markets for his work. If it's good. That's all it has
to be. Guys who beg off for their bounce notes with comments about
how they're ahead of their time, or how the editors buy only from their
relatives, or how they write only to purge themselves . . . these are not
writers, these are the Mollusks. They aren't hungry enough. They don't
want it as badly as you or I.

Writing for the detective magazines, the science fiction magazines,
the sophisticated men's field, these are all reputable backgrounds for a
conscientious writer; they may be sneered at by the sybarites, but I'll
take one solid Charlie Beaumont to the three dozen pudding-gutted

one-story wonders in the "little" magazines. The former is a man capable of writing octagons around the herd of the latter.

But there are dangers in the pulps, too. You have to know when your apprenticeship is at an end. You have to recognize when you're writing for the buck and not because you have to write and you don't care what it is as long as it broadens and deepens you.

And then one day you find you aren't saying anything. You're running the backside off your hero and getting him sapped over the head at regular intervals to meet the word requirements, and you stop. Just like that. You freeze. And then you know for sure you're a writer. You're a writer who has flown up his own tail like the *sakahachi* bird, but you are, sure as God made little green apples, a writer. Abruptly you realize that you are tired of conning your readers and, worse, conning yourself. You find you've got things to say about the nature of life and the inevitability of loneliness for the sensitive person in our times and the stench of prejudice and the transitory nature of success . . . and you curse yourself.

You are a liar.

You are a cheat and a thief. You've cheated yourself and stolen from your talent. You've deprived them of what you have and what you could tell them. They need it, you need to give it to them, you've got to make your stand. Because all you are, all I am, is what I write. Away from the typewriter I'm a man, but behind it I'm something else entirely.

I'm something more than a man. I can say what I believe, what I truly believe, and it will be read and understood by *someone, somewhere*, and I'll have communicated. Do you understand what I'm saying? Do you realize what a feeling that is? It's creating the Heaven and the Earth in less than seven, and being God to yourself. That's what it is.

Laugh at Kerouac all you like for his trickery and his self-deceit, but *he* feels it. All you have to do is *read* the man, let him talk to you in his own voice, and you'll know he feels it. Not when he's tinkering for a buck, but when he's joyful and true and completely with it. Then he is only slightly less than immortal, and I've been that way, and if you understand what I'm saying, you have been, too.

You're a writer. And that's better than being a millionaire. Because it's something holy.

Over my typewriter I've got a few Words to Work By. They work for me. They might not work for you. I'll give them to you, with the understanding that I'm not trying to be lit'ry or pushy. They just help me, and what the hell . . . maybe you, too. Like so:

There is no use writing anything that has been written before unless you can beat it. What a writer in our time has to do is write what hasn't been written before or beat dead men at what they have done.

That was Hemingway in 1936. He's right, too, you know. And if for a moment I had to believe it's all been done, I think I'd shrivel like a spider web in a flame. Then Matthew Arnold said it all just right about what it takes to write. He said:

Produce, produce, produce . . . for I tell you the night is coming.

Which is the whole story. Guys who give me the old line about how they're "thinking it out" or "living it up" before they can get to the pen or the typer, give me the coolie-jams, because the only way to write is simply . . . to write. And the last thing I write by (though I've found it's the hardest of the three to live up to) is something Flaubert said, as translated by Budd Schulberg in "The Disenchanted":

Art is a luxury. It needs clean hands and composure. If you make one little concession, then two, then five . . .

I've also got up a quote from Brendan Behan, but what that old tosspot has to say is more in the nature of an antisocial way of *living* for a writer and doesn't really have anything to do with the practice of same, so I'll just taunt you with its obscure reference.

Yet no amount of quoting or philosophizing can say it for you. I was motivationally researched the other day by a gentle little woman who came to my door asking me to look at a presentation folder of ads and then tell her why I didn't flip my nut when I saw a photo of a Hammond organ, and when it was all done, she asked me — rather timidly, as most nonwriters who consider Writers something supernatural are wont to speak — whether writing courses would make a person a writer.

I had to answer honestly, because I have neither the patience nor good sense to lie, that as far as I was concerned, if you're a writer, you know it when they drag you squawking out of the womb. You may be able to fake it by attending writing classes, but you haven't got it *here*. I know a couple of writers who make close to thirty grand a year doing nothing but pounding a machine, but they aren't *writers* by my definition. They are nice, sweet guys and wonderfully competent authors who can write in any style you designate, at any length you set, for any market and with whatever viewpoint you require. I despise their writing. I try to get them to lose money by writing what they feel, not what they reason out for story value.

They ignore me.

And a damned good thing. They'd go broke in a week if they tried to be writers. They're authors, the same way some people are bricklayers or die-stamping press operators. There are men with talent and perceptivity and empathy who write commercially, who turn out fiction that doesn't really live within them—Harvey Swados, Herb Gold, Charles Beaumont, R.V. Cassill, to name four that come to mind—but they do it well. They do it on a level few "quality" writers can match, and they do it with the inherent flair for knowing the right thing to say in the right way that makes them writers, not authors, in the manner no amount of articles on how to be a writer can tell you. It's something in the genes. Not the intellect. These men may not *like* writing pure moneystories (though I suspect they derive the same aesthetic pleasure out of a well-turned commercial piece as they get from their more feeling works) but they *can* do it when they feel they must . . . and they know the difference. It makes for a schizoid personality in a manner of speaking, but it also tones up the blood, brings apples to the cheeks and improves the complexion.

If you can do it, you're not expected to be judged on that sort of work, those stories. Every working writer has to learn to do it.

Just know what to do with your emotions once you've learned.

I've done it, and I can't go back to read those pieces.

So I froze. I didn't write for a while. And those who had tagged me as a writer on juvenile delinquency (because of my first novel and book of short stories on the subject), and those who had tagged me as a writer of science fiction (because of my ditto and my ditto) wondered what had happened. They wondered if I'd hit a slump. Which was nonsense. No writer ever hits a slump. As Algis Budrys (who is a helluva writer, and who taught me about half of what I know) once said to me: You don't slump, you just reach a plateau. Then you have to get your wind, and readjust your thinking and your synapses, and get set to write better, with more maturity with greater passion and purpose. He was right.

(An explanatory note: Earlier I said writing could not be taught, and above I said Budrys had taught me about half of what I know. This is not, though on the surface it may seem to be, dichotomous. Budrys— who is, in case you haven't discovered him, one of the few writers of the past ten years in the field of science fiction to demonstrate memorable qualities of true literature in his work—taught me intangibles. How do you estimate the education of a writer in things like *get out of college and start writing* or even *fawning praise can kill you: get yelled at more often, it'll toughen you*? How do you estimate their value? You don't. You just realize years later that the most valuable training you had was watching a writer like Budrys plotting a cover story, or having Budrys turn you on to Cozzens before the mass got hold of *By Love Possessed*, or being shocked and terrified at how much Budrys could blue-pencil out of a 3,000-worder you could have sworn was tight as a Chianti cork. Get taught how to write? Not on your life. But a mentor — even a reluctant one — can often work the embolisms out of your talent. Schools . . . (uh-uh).

I started writing stories that I reread and stared at with astonishment. What the hell are you *writing*, Ellison? I asked myself.

In "Daniel White for the Greater Good," I tried to say Negro prejudice stinks, by making a strong case for the necessity of lynching a Negro.

In "Final Shtick," I psychoanalyzed my own childhood from the focal point of anti-Semitism in an Ohio town.

In "Lady Bug, Lady Bug" I propounded the theory that love can only uplift and cleanse, thus destroying the safety of mediocrity, loneliness and bastardliness.

In "May We Also Speak?" I presented four views of the not-so-beat generation, and discovered to my horror, pleasure and satisfaction that I was talking about a new breed of human being, The Hung-Up People. All my stories were examining the moral, ethical and physical attitudes of the Hungry Ones, who have come into being in the past fifteen years. Who would buy these stories?

No one, that's who.

But I *had* to write them. I didn't have any choice.

Throw myself at the typewriter. Pound away at it for six and eight and even eleven hours straight, with nothing but pack after pack of cigarettes, and my gut started to feel cold and misty the way you feel the next day after waking all night on No Doz and hot, black coffee. And when they were done, exhausted, drained, lying back with no means of expression, an empty thing, all of it there, down, set and right and the way you wanted it. That was the way it had to be.

Then along came Bill Hamling at *Rogue*, and he was another one of the important ones, another of the ones who said, "You write it, and I'll publish it, because you've got it. You're saying things your own way." So he published "May We Also Speak?" and about twenty others, and Knox Burger at Gold Medal will be figuring a way to market a whole book of stories about my hung-up generation I want to call "No Doors, No Windows." (But which will get bounced because Knox has enough sense to know he can't really market the thing to the mass, but what the hell do I care, he's got the novels, and they're good and Knox knows it, and he's about the best goddamn editor I've ever had.)

You see, they're important. The editors. You have to say something to them. You don't have to write for them, "slant" for them — oh, that goddamn odious phrase. All you have to do is write true. And anybody who writes for the fat man with the cigar, behind the big editorial desk, is a cheat and a liar and not worth the type fonts to set him up. He is stealing from the people, and from himself. He's writing other people's stories, other people's ideas. But the editors are important: the real ones, the good ones, the ones who want to buy books and stories, not just material to fill their pages or meet their schedules.

And guys who sell themselves out, who lie and make it to Hollywood or Book-of-the-Month Club or big-time TV, those guys are cannibalizing themselves, and I weep sad and long for them. Because they are killing what they had to offer. And I swear to myself that if I get lucky and somebody bites on one of my stories, and I make a potful in H'wood, I won't let myself get suckered into the solid gold trap. To hell with the swimming pools and balling the starlets and impressing everybody.

Because, you see, I'm nothing. I'm nothing at all without writing. Without truth, my truth, the only truth I know, it's all a gambol in the pasture without rhythm or sense. It's empty. God gave it to me (so help me, Deist or no, I believe that!) and I can't cheat myself or you or them or anyone by not doing it the best way I know how.

That's the heart and head of the writer, to set it all down before they put him down the hole. To get it all out the right way, the best way, the truest way you know how.

Do you feel it?

Do you know what I mean?

Then you and I are family. We can meet at the phony cocktail parties where the buffoons say, "I've led this real wild life, see. It would make a great story. All you got to do is write it and I'll split with you fifty-fifty," so that you want to give them a rap in the mouth, and you and I, we'll go over in the corner and talk, because you and I have a sacred trust. We aren't authors, we're writers and we live off what we do, not where we appear. We see some of it, and we dismiss Isherwood's "Camera" theory because we've got to live it as well as write it. So we'll talk.

You and I.

You and me.

The both of us writers.

I'll talk to you.

You talk to me.

I'll understand you, and you'll understand me.

We're the blessed ones. We're the damned ones. We're the ones who can do one thing in this world but oh God how well we do it! We can write.

Talk to me.   *[1960]*

INDEX

A complete catalog of Writer's Digest books is available FREE by writing to the address shown below, or by calling toll-free 1-800-289-0963. To order additional copies of this book, include $3.00 postage and handling for one book, and $1.00 for each additional book. Ohio residents add 5½% sales tax. Allow 30 days for delivery.

Writer's Digest Books
1507 Dana Avenue
Cincinnati, Ohio 45207